This book has been a while coming as generally my writing has had a point of delivery at magazines, newspapers or journals for the b2b sector. I've written a dozen or so books, annuals, guides and the like, some published when working alongside others but this one is as they say, *all mine*! The hope is that you will find this book helps to understand more about how we grew up in the Essex countryside other than in town. It's an autobiographical slant on the world where I have played, worked and played even more, all of that mixed with the fair reporting and pictures from years of interfacing business, sport and leisure events. I approached my writing of *Burnham Boy* in very much the same way as I would work at the editor's desk for magazines. Some things never change though, to get here I found the research and the work took a bit longer than anticipated. I'll admit this is another time when I have not met the deadline, yet when your journey pans out that way then surely it's because you'll have been having fun. That I most certainly have!

Peter Lumley

In happy lives there is always plenty of sharing, without that way of living we'd end up being poor friends and poor communicators. It was working with bovines and doing agricultural work how my father and his father laboured, living as near a cottar's life as you could get but still be paid a wage. That's a clue to how things could well have gone for me had I not skipped out of full time education and gone into full time learning in a quite different line of business. The twist of fate brought challenges and an equilibrium forged in a job at a newspaper office where stories of the day and plans for tomorrow were readied for printing in the local weekly paper. This connected lives and news from around the community, as with the hatched, matched and dispatched column of the newspaper, which puts in a slightly less than polite context what were the weekly announcements of births, marriages and deaths. Those notices grabbed top space on the first page of the *Burnham-on-Crouch & Dengie Hundred Advertiser.* This column immediately below the masthead was real community news in a community newspaper and probably much more keenly read by people than the stories and results from local football, seasonal cricket matches or sailing club news. This Friday paper would carry my first writing and reporting in print, sixty five years on I am sure it is being a writer that helps to keep my pawls ticking, that and carrying a camera.

The influence of family and friends, then my apprenticeship alongside work colleagues in the Dilliway's publishing, printing and stationery office built the future for Burnham Boy. Me being me, it could hardly have been easy for them, yet by their investing the valuable contributions and lessons for my learning and growing up time, it brought the start of a journey which has been so very rewarding. My writing and photography has always helped generate opportunity for the sharing, the telling of discoveries and reporting so many encounters across the years. Everything I have achieved began to take shape right there in Burnham, *and for sure, I'd not want to change one bit of it!*

Peter Lumley . May, 2018

beingThere . bike . hike . travel . tourism

BURNHAM BOY

Peter Lumley
beingTHEREguru.com

Published in 2018 by FeedARead.com Publishing

Copyright © Peter R. Lumley
in association with beingThereguru.com and KSA
First Edition

        A CIP catalogue record for this title is available from the British Library.

On those times I have been here it is the serenity which grabs you, from the road a second day of walking then across a glacier to pitch beside this calm arctic lake which is about to thunder through a narrow rock gorge. The water is ice-cold but potable, as fresh as when it was melting snow starting to flow to here.

On Foulness Island in Essex where
there was no road to her hamlet
and only the *Doomway* got you
there when it was low tide, that was
where my Nan was born in 1879.
In the school at Churchend her roll
call name was Ethel Linda Boosey.
In London she would marry William
Friederich Gustav Warnecke, after
dancing with the young Prussian at
the Grand Hotel in Brighton. Their
youngest daughter Rosa Ella was
to become my mother. My dad,
Charles Henry Lumley came from
Long Melford in Suffolk. We are
both farmer's sons.

beingThere

The author expresses his sincere thanks to the many people who have helped by contributing to the story illustrated here from press clippings, photograph albums, newsapers and from magazines where they appeared. Much of the researched material is held in the KSA archives or privately.

1   starting out

At just about the time I was getting confident enough to toddle across the road from outside our front door someone thought it would be a good idea to start another World War, it meant soon our town became known as HMS St Mathew. In this case the St Mathew name came with just the one letter *t,* some reckon being it was spelt that way in recognition of centuries old Royal connections. I'd favour it was more a case of linking those two *Royal* yacht clubs which were neighbours along the river front. Rolls of spikey barbed wire which reached half as high as a house and a great deal longer by miles soon appeared all over the place, the river was boomed and no-one but the military or essential workers made it onto much of the seafront of the Quay or promenade at Burnham-on-Crouch. The armed services took sole right of entry there, they built a pier reaching to the deep water channel of the River Crouch, searchlight batteries and gun emplacements took shape. The town simply heaved with soldiers, sailors and Wrens all going about their uniformed business, and military bands sometimes played. Loudly!

All this was as Europe again geared up to be a battleground, which was not exactly music to anyone's ears and even more a distraction to my parents who were to have two very sickly children on their hands. Just three months past my third birthday I was fighting a serious bone disease in hospital wards at the Chelmsford & Essex General Hospital, whilst my sister Jean, born after me, already had been treated for a life threatening health condition in London's Great Ormond Street Hospital. Life was not so good for Charles and Ella Lumley although in fairness they were far from being alone in a world going wrong by the day. For me though, this was as bad as it would get and come a couple more years I was heading in the direction of being lucky, all coming with super destinations on the horizon. A warning for readers though, what follows here isn't written down so much in chronological order, more a beingThere life related tale with connections at the crossroads and side turnings which everyone will themselves encounter on any journey. You may plan the trip, yet once you're on your way then the trick is to be happy, avoid the obstacles even those that are odd, or seemingly intended as a frustration, maybe simply placed there to get in your way. The place where I was born is about as close as you can get to the end of the line, it's the end of the road along a peninsula and midway aside the river that gives Burnham-on-Crouch its name. Pass through the town and then follow the river bank, pretty soon you can overlook the German Ocean, on a wave of a place out there is the North Sea end of the English Channel and the Continent of Europe just over the horizon. Mud and salt water is the area's most common denominator, with a lot of flat, polder-like farming country on the landward side of man-made defensive walls holding back the river, a sea, the Channel, the ocean. An upward fold or two in the countryside to the west and the north helps locals imagine they actually have hills at their doorstep. *Oh yes, but no!* There are ridges and rises but only Danbury has a small cone of a hill. Burnham-on-Crouch sits over a deep bedrock of London clay, and without the dyke building, ditch cleaning and upping of the sea defences it would still remain marshland in every sense of the word, seeing so much of the area is below high water mark twice every day. The Doomsday Book lists Burnham as *Burnheham*, two hundred years later the town's High Street was widened to as it looks today to allow for a market granted to the Fitzwilliam family by Royal Charter in 1253: they owned the manor so why not the street! The unmistakable feature of the town High Street today is the 1897 built Clock Tower, the hours and the quarters it sounds through the day can clearly be heard right where I was born little more than a hundred yards away. When that distinctive clock bell rings people hear the memorial chime paid for by public subscription to Laban Sweeting, an oysterman whose family caught and sold fish and owned a little shop in Shore Road. When I was growing up this was by the yard of the White Harte Hotel, the other side of the street from St Mary's Church of England Endowed School where I was taught by Mr Mills, the headmaster, and the other school teachers. At English lessons my first-ever favourite poem became Robert Burns' *"My Heart's in the Highlands"* - of which the first and last verse say it all, and all the way to now in my later life. The school we attended was eventually converted into homes with people coming to permanently live under a broad roof where once we recited poetry and tried to *count proper* as us wartime Burnham kids would have said!

Fishing had been a mainstay local business along with boatbuilding since before Roman times, the River Crouch being something of a watery highway for travellers and a route for trade that was international in every way. Possibly the name Crouch derives from the word Creek or Crick, whilst some old records show it was once known as the Huolne River. On some maps and navigation charts it also appears as Burnham River. Never much more than a muddy-banked tidal waterway, the inlets and saltings are the playground for flocks of waders and wildfowl. Time was when this was a punt-gunner's paradise, hunters wreaking havoc on flocks of water-settled birds with their long barrelled blunderbuss set at the prow of a canoe they quietly paddled or drifted towards fowl ambush. On a leisure and travel front the River Crouch has always been the place where sailing boats really are at home doing their thing or swinging on their anchor chain to point into the flow of the tide as it switches from ebb to flow then back again. The masses of people arriving in the town to sail those craft has helped sustain the local population, not that everyone has always appreciated the incomers. Burnham-on-Crouch is not the only town in the land to have been reshaped and developed, yet without the through-traffic which usually overwhelms traditional values and features in a place then this Essex town still retains a remarkable amount of its original quaintness.

The outlook south from Burnham-on-Crouch is but a spit of a distance to the next river that-away, the Thames. In between, Foulness Island stands as a lot of sea-water, mudflats and seawalls, some of the island is now breached to allow tides to rampage across former farmlands which had been tilled and reaped after a much earlier in time rescue from the waves. The highest point of all natural ground around here comes at a lowly 6ft above sea level, when someone built there they decided it should be known as Hill House. Around these parts, as well as watching river wildlife it is boats and sailing that makes things work for visitors and locals alike, in Burnham town several yacht clubs have berths for bodies and boats which guarantees a steady influx of visitors. Downriver it is the River Roach as the last tributary before muddy water swishes towards Goodwin Sands way, saluting in passing the stumpy tower at Churchend on Foulness, a lonely hamlet where my Nan was born with the given name of Ethel Linda Boosey. I'm not sure if she tippled so very much but one thing is for certain, Nan didn't just become my grandmother she also took on a full life's task of being my second mother, something that contributed so much to how and why I do things, right through to today.

Nan had come to Burnham from the other side of the river, a little hamlet where the churchyard today holds some family members buried, beside drowned sailors and residents of this remote riverside settlement. At the time she lived there no complete road reached this isolated community of Church End, on the northern tip of the Foulness peninsula of salt marshes between the Thames and the Crouch. The nearest big place was, and is, Southend-on-Sea and to get there then meant a long trip over the flat seaward firm sands called the Broomway. Firm, that is, between the tides, so you definitely needed to get your timing right for the rushing water would quickly become your enemy! Those short miles along the Broomway sit on a ridge of firmer ground edging the Maplin Sands and something like three hundred yards from the main shoreline. In Edwardian times the path was reckoned to be the most perilous byway in England, even being called *"The Doomway"* and my Nan told me about a doctor who had delayed his leaving a patient, or maybe the hostelry at Church End too late, and he had floated off somewhere never to be

I see Burnham's Clock Tower and High Street every day I go to my writing den, the framed colour wash pen drawing is by Charles Grigg Tait who was my father in law. Beside it is a cycling cartoon by Johnny Helms and a photograph of Tony Crickmore in Club racing strip. I married the artist's daughter Barbara, my Maldon Grammar School English tutor Joy Hulett would become his wife.

seen again: they found the horse dead in the shafts of the upturned buggy, but no doctor. Foulness gained its first real access road courtesy of Military might, when after 1911 the MoD purchased much of the land from the Finch brothers. The Island then became a bomb and warfare testing site and years later in Burnham we'd often hear the big bangs, crumps and heavy thumps as ordnance of some sort or other was testily detonated. In 1953 the seas dramatically came ashore on Foulness, around us too in Burnham as a big North Sea salt-water surge so disastrously flooded Holland and put a lot of England's east coast countryside under the torrent. On Foulness two people died in the flood, then after two days rescuers came for around 400 cattle, 14 calves, 28 horses, 72 sheep, 6 lambs, 3 pigs, 670 chickens, 100 ducks, 2 dogs, 10 rabbits, 4 budgerigars and 16 dairy cows. On our side of the river in Burnham we heard stories from rescuers who found wild rabbits and hares sitting together on tree branches above the lapping water, alongside foxes and the odd cat. A lot of cattle and pigs drowned and of the hundred and twenty families that evacuated, some thirty four decided they wouldn't be returning to their island home. The water did plenty of harm in Burnham town, although the only local deaths were a couple of pigs in a smallholding sty near the Royal Corinthian Yacht Club. Much of the boat industry operations sat behind seawall defences which had failed to hold back the sea surge, leaving homes and businesses and workshops alongside the river very damaged. Hulks of timber sloshed around as matchsticks in a kitchen sink, boats found new higher and drier berths as the tide surged and left them stranded. A story circulated that people rowed a dinghy up Coronation Street from the Tucker Brown end, then tied it to a gas lamp standard across the road from Princes Cinema. Salt water stood around for quite some time afterwards, and a lot of seawall defences had to be heightened and rebuilt. The year was 1953, and I was coming seventeen years of age when the flood struck, I ruined a bicycle by riding through it.

There is a good chance that my Nan was even younger when she first came to Burnham, probably along farm tracks across Burnham marshes and past Dammerwick, there almost fifty years later our family would live at the big manor house and father would be head dairyman. At the farm I saw my first canary - Nan spotted it flying around the garden and we put crumbs or seed, something to attract this little Yellow. From the kitchen we took a mesh meat fly-cover, the forerunner of the fridge people tended not to own in those days, propped it on a peg so when we pulled the attached string, securely captured was the canary. That little bird lived for years at Nan's Lime Street house, happily other than one year when the feathers on its head fell out and we put that down to escaping gas from the lantern in the living room. Possibly the truth it was a Gloucester Corona, and the head crest had simply called it a day. To cross from Foulness Island to the peninsula my Nan would have caught the 19th century ferry from there to land at Holver Stage near Holliwell Point on the north bank, close to the Holliwell Farm which is one of the several farmsteads spread across the deep dyked marshes that make up this southern slice of the Dengie Hundred. To travel on from there to places such as Chelmsford people could catch a newly operating horse and coach service connecting Burnham to the Essex County town, around twenty miles away. Travel opportunity broadened when in 1842 a railway link opened for passengers to get from Essex to London or to Suffolk and Norfolk in the opposite direction, then as 1848 came a rail link from the Blackwater River towns of Maldon and Heybridge reached Witham, a station on the London to East Anglia line. Steam driven trains were beginning to compete with the river traffic servicing much of the region and beyond, London's river was the main street that led to all round the world, Burnham was just one of the stops along the seventeen navigable miles of the River Crouch.

For people who wanted trains, more linked-up travel was offered from 1889 with a new branch line built from Wickford to stations at little villages such as North Fambridge, Althorne, Burnham and to the end of the line in Southminster. The London service reaching Wickford could also carry you to Southend on Sea, with the possibility to travel to Foulness and then Church End after crossing the treacherous Broomway sands. In those days a round trip hereabouts, by rail, road or by horse power would have taken almost to eternity, yet in our modern era you still need ages to get places - there have very few new routes opened in this coastal strip other than ones speeding traffic to the next bottleneck of course. Widening the concrete and macadam hasn't done so much good for travel times, whilst those old railway tracks along the Crouch valley still sound quite rickety. This part of the world makes good cycling country, although there is a lot of travelling on the same stretch of each and every way road going not far, a sure sign you are on the Dengie Hundred. As railway building progressed in this corner of Essex to reach further away places it improved the way people could travel to find work in towns, rather than take jobs in their own locality. The bicycle arriving in more the same time-spell also became a fashionable mode of transport to help broaden horizons, or help you get to work even! It was to well over a hundred miles away, on the south coast in Brighton, where Nan took a job and would meet the Prussian she would marry. The way it happened, she told me, was during a Grand Hotel function when the Lady she attended as a personal maid was asked by a smart young man if he might *"dance with your daughter."* They danced, they fell in love and married in London in December 1899. William Friederich Gustav Warnecke was a son of Karl and Christine from Brandenburg, he was born in Hannover so they must have been a family moving around a lot. Ethel Linda Boosey was my Nan's maiden name, the man she married travelled a lot to work at banquets and events in palaces and grand places for special occasions and functions. Of where he went, I recall her little attaché case filled with a collection of letters and postcards her husband had sent from hotels and big houses spread around Britain. The impeccably written messages were in nothing less than perfect English, a skill I have failed to grasp, although I do seem to have inherited his travel genes: it's the pity that I missed out on having conversations with him in German. But then my Mother Rosa Ella was barely two years old when her father died and she wouldn't have shared much of that tongue either! The couple lost their only son who didn't live beyond six months; Nan had four daughters when her husband died in 1911, to become head of a family which was now going to look a tough life full in the face. The truth is she'd continue all her life without re-marrying, happy with being the widow Mrs Ethel Warnecke, someone who did a great deal acting as my second mother.

Burnham-on-Crouch was never easy to reach, poor roads or a steam train that rattled along beside the Crouch was as much as people got unless they arrived by water, to help people reach the place quicker airstrips were built for the new fangled aeroplanes, Burnham's first was organised as a winged fighter base in 1915, pilots flying from a field near Wick Farm. Here I must digress, about spelling that is: I grew up knowing this place as Wycke Farm, and saw it sign-written that way on the farm gate, the Ordnance Survey maps write it the *wick* way, and I reckon they've got it wrong. It's not wrong that military forces operated that first airstrip as a night flight station with biplanes under Royal Navy Air Service command. Then it was taken over by the Royal Flying Corps who flew as the 50th Wing of Squadron 37.

In the 1930s a civil airfield was opened at the bottom of the High Street behind the Victoria pub, a place where our Compass touring caravan has often landed up on the Silver Road caravan and camping ground. The airstrip closed ahead of WWII to ensure it could not be used by enemy invaders, and the same to stop any likelihood of them landing on Burnham Playing Fields between Station Road and the river the flat open space was obstructed by tall vertical baulks of heavy timber sunk into the ground like giant cricket stumps. The authorities acted to ensure it would stop the town turning into a potential Arrivals Hall for the Luftwaffe, similarly eight miles upriver close to where trains on the Maldon branch line from Wickford steamed into Stow St Maries Halt, the Royal Flying Corp had operated from a WWI airstrip to make sure unwanted arrivals received the message they were not welcome. The airstrip here closed in 1919 but a score of buildings survived the rot as part of a farm operation until 2008, since then the site has been developed to become a significant centre for historical aircraft and display flights.

Different sectors of flying interests make up the story of how the British military air power developed, and we know that the Royal Navy Air Service and the Royal Flying Corps merged to become the Royal Air Force. In those formative years Noel Pemberton-Billing was a local man who had lobbied tirelessly as a Member of Parliament both for developing aircraft and using them to do battle. Born in London but living most of his adult life in Burnham-on-Crouch, Noel Pemberton-Billing founded his own aircraft manufacturing company, financed in 1913 with £500 won in a wager with Frederick Handley Page that he could gain his flying licence within 24 hours of first sitting in an aeroplane. He did it of course, and that company later went on to produce the famous Supermarine Spitfire fighter plane. In 1948 when Noel Pemberton-Billing died he was buried at Burnham-on-Crouch, remembered as one of those people who have helped our town take its place in the history books.

Nan Warnecke, so much my second mother really, who taught me so much and cared about me even more. The littl'un hiding his face is first son Antony. Christmas in Marsh Road, Mum and Dad pulling a cracker and to this day I have wondered if my photo caught a reflection from tinsel or was it really the flash of the little bit of gunpowder exploding you can see.

I recall a Burnham-on-Crouch incomer telling me there wasn't anywhere called Lime Street in the town, he was some sort of historian who had found Burnham a better place to live than his west of London haunt. "Well, you can't win them all Sir," I retorted, "but please do check into the Census returns and tell me what you find." I didn't hear from him again . . .

You are looking along Lime Street, on the right behind trees in the foreground was 3 Pear Tree Cottage where my mother grew up then lived with my father. I was born there in Nan's home and would often stay with her to my mid-teens.

The street is a bit narrow, the left side wall is the shop I knew as Carter's Yachting Stores, on the opposite side the bakery that produced Dilliway dough and through that first window on the right I'd see their work being done late at night.

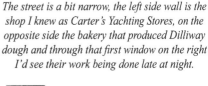

On the right, four doors or so up the street past the black gable end of the two storey houses is the Providence cottage where we lived for a short time before moving to Dammerwick farm across the fields on Burnham Marshes.

Here's the leafy end of what we always called The Passageway taking us from Nan's house to Chapel Road where we would be living when I was first hospitalised. A big open square here was where authorities built a community brick bomb shelter for wartime. Thick concrete roof, dog-leg entrance doorway and an emergency exit of waist height only, at the building end.

2   Burnham – just one road in

A rail track to London, a sailing town on a corner of the Dengie peninsula, the Crouch tide something of a salty lifeblood bringing and taking people, goods and chattels. A lot of what I remember about Burnham is no longer the case with many of the houses I knew being no more and who nicked the pear tree that stood in the garden at my Lime Street birthplace? If Dr Beeching had done for the Southminster branch railway what he ingloriously did to so many quite undeserving places then this riverside town would have remained even more the cul-de-sac. Burnham does offer a real bonus for those wanting to go about things independently though, I saw that at the five roads junction of what is now known as Five Ways where all these roads converge on the Railway Hotel that's no longer, but nothing to do with Dr Beeching by the way. I watched cyclists come from every direction here, so many riders circulating that you could believe you were in Holland and they were not only youngsters but people going back and forth on shopping trips, basket-fronted bikes with a single or hub gear rather than the ones with hooked bars. These bikes were light roadsters or closely styled to the Raleigh bikes my parents had ridden all those years previously, and perhaps with through traffic not happening for Burnham then this enhances the encouragement to be self propelled around town. Houses I knew as home are no longer there and the years have taken away more than the builders can ever put back, hard as they may try, and that goes for Burnham Ramblers too who moved to the Maldon Road end of town so now the visiting teams and their supporters miss discovering that a town so small can have so many pubs.

That there must be something in the air you have to believe because local families seem to stay and stay, which is about right seeing my Nan never moved more than a mile from the Burnham home she'd shared with her husband. With her girls she had lived in High Street before moving to Pear Tree Cottage, a family remaining together until Mum's sisters married and moved away to other towns. This little house would almost fall about her ears before Nan was re-housed to a new bungalow in Arnheim Road, a place I remember as where her family doctor once arrived a little unceremoniously. Disregarding the locked front door Dr Wilson stepped over the sill of the low front window into her living room, he was a rather special and caring family doctor known to be always hurrying to the next patient, and then one day he hurried off to Australia so becoming a big miss of a man from the lives of locals who loved and trusted him.

After leaving school my mother had taken work as housemaid at a big Georgian house standing near the lower end of High Street and also as a helper in a little shop in Station Road. Teaching me about the value of money she remarked that pennies were a little hard to come by in her childhood, and I should take that as a warning! I was told to always put something aside for another day and saved from her first ever wages she had done just that: a thick but very worn and heavy Victoria penny carrying the bold image of a young Queen Victoria. She regarded it as a very *special* coin because it linked the *then* and the *today* in her life, shiftily it was gathered up and secreted away with other things from amongst this old lady's personal gatherings and memories. Methinks it's still in Burnham, taken when she wasn't looking and by someone my mother thought she could trust in the last few lone years of a long life. Wrong move, Mum.

The home she lived in as a young girl is just off the High Street opposite the Clock Tower where a narrow road separates what was Carter's Yachting Stores and the former Dilliway bakery, so narrow is the gap here that there is no room for a footpath into Providence. Beyond the two buildings the first stretch is Lime Street where opposite an alleyway through and under the terraced houses sat a cottage on the right, gable-end onto the road. This semi-detached pair was the Pear Tree Cottage home where all the letters for my Nan were addressed to Number 3 Lime Street, Providence; the place where I was born. As for the name, a gnarled old pear tree was the clue I guess, both to the name of the cottage and the big next door place called Pear Tree House. A census shows the address here as Lime Street, even though nowadays few people realise this, Nan's home was a small semi-detached two-up, two-down cottage, it had the drinking water for the house drawn from a standpipe tap in the garden by the flush privy, one of a pair shared with the cottager next door. In that four roomed house lit by gas only downstairs, my widowed Nan raised her four daughters and a grand-daughter, heat in just the living room came from an open grate under a small coal fired oven. There was a wide and high fire-place and Nan often told me you could see stars if you peered up the chimney at dusk. You'd see stars alright if you banged your head on the chimney bricks above the oven but luckily it took a few years for me to be that tall enough! This was a home where I'd often come to stay, even when our family lived only a street away or was living a mile uptown past St Mary's Church, and before that in the time when we lived across the fields on Burnham Marshes.

I remember it as a happy home where music from a scratchy old wind-up record player was very often heard, and especially time and again when *'Miss Otis regrets she's unable to lunch today, Madam . .'* was playing. This Cole Porter number from 1931 was probably Ethel Waters singing on a blue labelled Decca shellac 78rpm record as it scratched its musical circlings on the gramophone. At her home Nan was good at cooking and knitting and making clothes rather than spending money she didn't have, her house was very much the nice place to be and even with the haunting thoughts from the tragedy when one of my Nan's brothers deciding he'd slit his own throat whilst staying there. When I was born in Spring 1936 my father and mother were living at No.3 Lime Street and those first couple of years together would have been relatively relaxed as my dad had only a short distance to reach his job with the dairy herd at Wycke Farm. I was just coming to be a few months short of two years old when my sister Jean was born, the beginning of a worrying, tense and tough time which our parents would stressfully endure for at least the next dozen years and more. Jean was taken to Great Ormond Street Hospital in London within a week or so of coming into this world and then with barely the year gone after that I'd be whisked into Chelmsford hospital, our parents needed to spend every spare penny and more on two sickly children needing a lot of looking after and with so much travel to hospitals.

By this time our family home was a couple of streets away in Chapel Road from where on a Sunday morning my dad had left home all decked out in the Essex Territorial Army uniform, he was going away to a military training camp in Kent and a place that was just about as far away from home as he would travel in all of his life. After just three hundred days he was released from service on compassionate discharge, sent home to help cope with a pretty sickly son and just in time for that emergency trip on a Sunday morning when Dr Wilson didn't wait on an ambulance being sent to me. He drove us to the Chelmsford & Essex General Hospital himself where his prognosis was confirmed: it was osteomyelitis. Doctors explained that even when this disease in a child is diagnosed promptly and is treated appropriately, there is still the very big risk it could mean death. Inside a day I had the first of what mother had counted as twenty-six or so surgical operations across the coming ten years or so, then on one visit to hospital she was told that my right arm would need to be amputated to help save my life. What she related later and also wrote about was in this early 40's time the doctors said this was the only thing they could do, yet a mother's care for a son's future kicked in strongly and in a little diary affirmed the words she had said to Mr M. Harris . .*"if you cut off his arm he will never be able to work on the farm, will he. I am going to hold Peter's hand and then you can't cut it off, can you."* We know the surgeon went to others to talk about what could be done and my mother was told they would try a new drug, which she

I recall the names of only a few from amongst these classmates of 1945 at St Mary's Church of England Endowed School, by the Clock Tower in the High Street. It could well be me in the back row behind my cousin Rita Fuller. In the front row, second from the right is Leo Woods, he'd go the the Grammar School and later work in Paris. There are Cardnell kids and Harveys too, it was obviously hair-ribbon time for a lot of the girls and us lads were all in short trousers. Not all socks were staying to attention! From memory, the tall lad at the right is Mick Burnett who lived near us in Green Lane near Eves Corner.

Go to the Pound on the Quay and learn to swim on an incoming tide my mother advised - "that way if you drift off you'll only float upstream so we can find you. If you swim on a dropping tide then you'll likely end up out at sea, and we won't be able to." The name of the lass in the picture I don't recall but I am sure it is Bob Woolard with the curly hair sharing some of the sun that we enjoyed at times on the shingle of the river shore in the Quay Pound.

The trick about swimming is to make sure you don't drown - it had been after a day by the river when George Deacon's mother had become very upset he'd gone swimming when wearing his best Sunday suit. In later years he came clean as to why - "don't you remember me fetching you out of the river, Peter?" He explained how someone had shouted 'a kid has just pitched into the water' and without even a second though he'd dived over the seawall to rescue me from swallowing too many mouthfulls of the of salty sea water stuff. It was certainly a lucky day for some!

named in her little diary and book as *pinklin*. There is a faded little press cutting she saved from a year or two later which tells that in 1943 penicillin was released for administration to the general public, and there on that cutting Mum had added . .*"this is the drug they used to save Peter's life."* I would be nineteen years old or so before we were told the bone disease was reckoned to have been fully stemmed. Some people just get lucky, don't they! It was a Scottish farmer's son named Dr Alexander Fleming and his team discovered penicillin which they realised brought the potential to overcome serious bodily diseases. Knowing that it could do so much to help people around the world beat serious illnesses, rather than profit personally from their invention the patents were transferred to the USA and United Kingdom governments. This unselfish kindness was in time for others to invest into mass producing the drug, and at Chelmsford & Essex General Hospital war casualties were being treated at the very time I was taken to the hospital for surgery, which almost certainly cancelled that probable amputation. It seems I became very lucky that day, all down to the help from Mr Harris and the persistence of my mother. For six or seven years surgeons operated on my arm time and again so there must have been nothing but continual worrying for parents who would get even less respite for in just short years three of their four children needed significant hospital care and attention. There was also the moving house as my dad moved to another farm and a new cow-herding dairy job.

Before leaving school I'd have seven local addresses, add the couple of places when we lived further out in Essex and you will soon realise that as a cottar family then the packing to move was a regular experience for the Lumley family. It meant different schools to attend, several sets of farm fields and localities I'd have to become familiarised with, along with building up friendships and sharing fun with other kids in a new neighbourhood. Across the twelve years of those new home experiences I'd be going back and forward to Chelmsford & Essex General Hospital for surgical treatment and how my parents handled all that I can never imagine, but they did. There is another little twist, writing this at the beginning of 2018 brings another connection to those spells of hospitalisation and penicillin; my son Antony working with British Gas was given a job to do in the Lillian Road home of a nurse, retired to Burnham after working at St Mary's Hospital in London. The picture of the hospital attracted Tony to ask where it was, and the lady said it was the hospital where she was working when Dr Fleming made that monumental discovery. She was quite intrigued with the story of my penicillin treatment at such an early time, and also that she would come to live in our hometown. Such a small world, one where miracles can happen too.

sisters, aunts, cousin

I have gleaned too little of my Mother's experience when she growing up with sisters in a small Essex town, just two years old when her father died young so it would always be something she wasn't going to talk very much about to anyone, so I'd guess that included me. Looking back, as I see it both Nan and my mother were very much alike, suffering the same grief of having their man die too early. Of our forebears and the Prussian grandfather I could never know there was never much conversation on that subject, other than how much her father had travelled around Britain. With the afflictions of two World Wars very much in mind who can blame anyone in the family and probably, at best it was something they never wanted to talk about although I do recall once in a chat about her parents my mother told me that *"he spoke German, didn't he."* I recall the conversation didn't go any further but I was never bold enough to seek amore nswers of how the family grew up, and remembering she was barely school age when that conflict fully erupted in Europe, would it have registered with her? It is known that things-German were very much a public concern at the outbreak of WWI, and in July 1917 when social unrest was for real King George V issued an Order in Council which meant that thee British Royal family now became the House of Windsor: my mother was seven years old when that happened. As to how our family took that on board could have been answered by my Nan, mother or anyone close enough to know those things, but now it's too late to revisit those times so I can only ponder what it was like. I'd imagine that my Nan was a typical of the age, a quietly proud mother and hardly inclined to talk about the reality of her being the head of a one-parent family enduring a very frugal existence with nothing in the way of money but an awful lot in the way of hard times. In reality, a lot of other people had nothing but very hard times about them and especially during the years of the Depression and when the Victorian years were the classic them-and-us era of big houses, lots of riches and a dirt-poor existence for the working class, if they could ever get work! Nothing much changed around the place just because my mother had been born, nor I, it seems times of depression would mostly pop up in the country every two years or so all the way through the lean nineteen-twenties and to a post-War time: it afflicts our 21st century with but only personal perspectives the moderator of misery in existing on nought, having opportunities and life stifled. It pays to see the glass as more than half full, no point in thinking it's a near empty one, anyway.

There were riches around certainly: being a grandson and being seen as Nan's little boy coming into her home where there had been daughters and a grand-daughter she had raised through to womanhood as her very own. My second mother was nearby and helping when the bone disease affliction struck in my third year and her caring ways becoming deeper my mother told me, but Nan didn't say much about that perhaps remembering that her own little son had died so young. The other family grandsons were Ronald Minnel and Maurice Foster, both well older than me, along with Alan and Alex Ross who were born during wartime. Of my aunts I remember each of them for quite different reasons really, one lived in Burnham, another in Surrey and there was an aunt at Dagenham. In my early years these places seemed about as close as the other side of the English Channel, us being all so pre-occupied with hospitals and pretty regularly moving house then leisurely travel was not so much what our family did until I was getting into my teens. Come the Second World War things had changed little for how Nan lived but probably since the trauma of 1914-18 was still in mind she tried a ruse hoping it would help dilute the wider public awareness of her marrying a German: although that had been long ago in the previous century! My Nan vainly set out to be known as plain *"Mrs E.Warner"* although the idea didn't work so well with some unforgiving locals, even to her face. I got to know about Burnham bigotry too, as a back-end of the War pupil attending St Mary's Church of England Endowed School I regularly got a kicking from much older school kids *"you have a German grandfather"* being the reminder! I'd guess it was *their* grandparents rather than school-kids themselves putting the boot in: it didn't ease any of the hurt and fear and it always upset my Nan if I mentioned such happenings when getting home from school. Certainly my own experiences with war-time schoolmates left something of a scarring but others we didn't actually know were also keeping an eye on things, too; I remember the letter arriving . . *"opened by the Official Censor"* appeared boldly on the envelope. My Nan wept uncontrollably that morning, the letter on her blue Basildon Bond writing paper was savaged by scissors and had her words blanked over by officials. The loving notes she'd written to my aunt in Surrey became tear-tinged before they were consumed by flames in the grate, so if only she hadn't thrown the letter into the fire then we'd know just what she'd written to be such a threat to national security. I believe she told my aunt just how busy Burnham had become with army and navy people and how they were building fast boats at Kings Boatyard, along with flat bottomed boats too. It wasn't exactly a local secret as us kids would often rush to see an iconic Motor Torpedo Boat launched down the shipbuilders' slipway into the river. Fluting for the torpedo tubes across the deck reached towards the bows, a craft powered so they could cruise at over 25mph the giveaway that this was a real predator of enemy boats. The MTBs had wooden hulls which meant no limpet mines were going to stick to her hull and these craft were definitely the stealth bombers of the Navy, also used by the Fast Boat Patrols they would pluck airmen from watery wastes after they'd ditched crippled planes into the sea or baled out under the canopy of a parachute.

When they came to visit Burnham from Surrey my aunt Ethel May and her hubby Walter Minnel would take the London Underground to Liverpool Street then the Southend LNER train, before changing at Wickford onto the Southminster branch line. On one occasion it would be a long trip that ended as close to tragedy as you'd want to get. The newspaper would have reported that *"a seven year old boy drowned in the River Crouch on a summer Sunday"* this all beginning with me intending to show off imagined dinghy rowing prowess to my cousin Violet. I'd first need the boat, one attached to an anchor rope tied to wooden steps of the White Harte Hotel jetty. Dinghy owners often anchored their boat to be afloat beyond low water mark, a tide-depth short line ran down to an anchor on the riverbed and from that a longer line reached inshore. Thinking all I needed to do to "borrow" that boat was to pull in the anchor I began tugging, but being a farmer's son from the other side of the tracks it had never occurred what an underwater tangle of rope lines and anchors were all waiting for an idiot like me to put in some heave-ho! Reacting very much in the way of an enraged Roman siege catapult the taut dinghy lines flipped me head over heels straight into the drink, which wasn't a great idea seeing I was in meet-the-family Sunday bests. Worse, I almost certainly shouted for help so swallowed a lot of seawater but luckily a rescuer arrived. Also wearing their Sunday-bests they'd kicked off their shoes and dived into the River Crouch to look for me under the waves. There isn't *anything* that comes better than being rescued from drowning and for years I told people how pleased I was that Peter Warren had saved my life: actually he hadn't! Of an evening probably some fifteen years later at the Orchard Road home of Les and Doris Martin with their son Les and his wife, we were tape-recording silly jokes in true Burnham accents whilst quietly swilling alcohol: things done when cycling club people gather. In broad Burnham-speak George Deacon told us how his mother had been very upset he'd once gone swimming even when wearing his Sunday suit. To me he said *"don't you remember me fetching you out of the river, Peter?* He explained how someone had shouted *'a kid has just pitched into the river'* and hardly without thinking he'd dived over the seawall. Of that near-drowning I still recall the day as once rescued from the water, as well as being very scared I was doing even better at being very sick, and looking a right sight being very wet and bedraggled, Sunday suit or no Sunday suit.

Cousin Violet had done a fast run back to Lime Street and as I staggered around being very ill in Shore Road my very breathless mother arrived on the scene, in some sort of panic and probably thinking that all may not have been so well with her son. If that seems ridiculously silly then remember that up to a few minutes before then everyone was enjoying their Sunday afternoon entertainment, although I'm not too sure how George Deacon explained things to his mother arriving home, equally wet and bedraggled. I hope he was more than very triumphant of his deed, though! I suppose I had a favourite aunt, and my Dagenham living Aunt Minna took the biscuit. Together with hubby Bob Foster they regularly called on my Nan right up to when uncle Bob stopped being a train footplate man on the local LNER and moved into working at a pigfarm, near Hornchurch. The first day he took me there I immediately noticed his animals didn't have the sweet smell of the cows back home and were even vicious enough to take off your fingers if they had the chance. Cows and calves will lick at you to discover who you are, not so the noisy pig, an animal I have never liked; clever animals they may be but they can be nasty with it as I saw when watching two sows corner a frightened fowl. It couldn't and didn't escape so they then chewed the bounty and left nothing but longer wing pinions on the floor of their smelly pen, no blood, no guts were left of the chicken. Dagenham with the Fosters is where I spent my first holiday away from home in a place that was not a hospital ward. There was always music and fun in their house and still I remember hearing over and over again Fred Astaire and July Garland singing the Irving Berlin classic *"we're a couple of swells."* Aunt Min certainly was a swell and I recall her as being a lady needing to check her lipstick just to answer the door to a postman! She laughed a lot and always was saying *"hey boy"* with something of an accent that was neither Essex nor London, a lovely aunt who was quite like my mother in many ways yet had town-life mannerisms which were something quite new to me: this coming ten-year old country boy. In Dagenham I discovered a new world never thought about back home . . joining crowds of people to watch an open air wrestling match at the Merry Fiddlers pub was one, and the bus ride to Barking to buy two white mice as pets another little adventure.

Yet thinking about it . . pet mice to take home to a farm? I also heard stories about the thieving character in the neighbourhood of Stockdale Road in Dagenham, the local patch for a renowned burglar who gained the name Flannel Foot. Aunt Min told me the name came from his habit of nicking tea towels and bathroom laundry to wrap around his shoes so he could creep around unheard but maybe he was bit house-proud and preferred not to leave mud on the carpet? He emptied coppers from the gas slot meter, which must have been a lot of weight to carry if he was hurrying off to do more thieving, and what little *value* had he actually nicked. In pre-decimal money days two hundred and forty made an English pound, with the Romans having added their bit to the number with the letter *d* depicting denarius, once you had twelve d then that became a shilling! The arithmetic of pre-decimal money and how it was counted doesn't figure so much with people today and in truth is a half remembered memory for those who spent cash before 1971. You may struggle with the definition of a shilling in real money or how you only got

IF THERE SHOULD BE A THREAT OF WAR ACT AT ONCE AS FOLLOWS :

1. Fill at least two large buckets with water and *see that they are kept filled.* During an air raid you cannot rely on getting water from the domestic taps, because all the supply may be needed by the fire brigade. Have a bath or tank also kept full of water to refill the buckets in case of need. Put the buckets and other appliances, if you have any, on or near the top floor.

2. Have two more buckets half filled with sand—one to use in controlling the bomb and the other for putting the bomb into when you have scooped it up.

3. Tell the members of your household what they must do and see that they understand their duties. While one person might be able to deal with the situation if it is tackled promptly, two or even three would be better. If a handpump has been provided and three people are available, one should tackle the fire, another should pump, while the third should bring up supplies of water.

4. In a small house the sound of a bomb striking the roof would give adequate warning anywhere. In a large house it may be necessary to have a watcher on or near the top floor. He should if possible have a whistle to summon help. See that all doors which need not be open are kept shut. If the fire cannot be quickly got under, someone must call a fire patrol or report to the air raid warden or a policeman, according to the local fire brigade arrangements.

IT IS NOT POSSIBLE TO GIVE FIXED RULES TO MEET ALL CASES OF FIRE CAUSED BY BOMBS. BUT STUDY THE ADVICE GIVEN ABOVE, DECIDE WHAT YOU WOULD DO AND PRACTISE IT UNTIL EVERYONE IN YOUR HOUSE KNOWS THE PART HE OR SHE HAS TO PLAY. THEN YOU WILL BE PREPARED TO FACE THE SITUATION CALMLY AND WITH CONFIDENCE.

In 1939 digitally driven social media was not about to happen any time soon so literature would arrive through the letterbox to warn people to avoid cuddling any bombs they came across - and please remember that a gas mask is not intended as a party disguise although you should alway take it with you when you went about at socialising times.

Letters between doctors will often take a more serious note, although the message from the Chelmsford Hospital surgeon Mr. M. Harris answering queries about my arm definitely was in the good news category. Luckily that had become the case after he decided I should be treated with the penicillin antibiotic in 1941. My mother had also been right there on the case too!

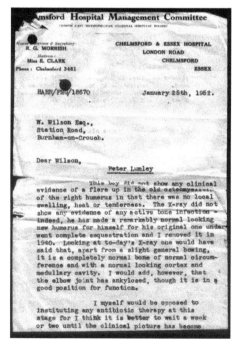

twenty of them with each pound but to Flannelfoot things would have simply got heavy, in those pre-decimal days twelve of the copper alloy round bits made well have made a silver shilling coin but the thief wouldn't be getting any of those! At this point a warning: for Americans the penny is a completely different thing so this conversation wouldn't take place over the pond, you can bet your bottom dollar! People in our country who called out the cost of something they were hoping you would buy may say eighteen pence, and the purchaser knew immediately this meant one shilling and a sixpence - not 6d always but six pennies that came as a sixpence coin which itself was also silver. Or sort of, anyway, because minted coins of any denomination get made with cupro-nickel alloys which is a 25/70 mix of nickel and copper, that gives the coin a silver colouring to make it look worth more than it actually is. Blame that on Henry VIII, he set about saving the silver he didn't have by reducing the amount of it in his coinage, piling in copper instead. Mind you, nothing new there as at Chollerford in the Roman museum you can see their way of hiding the truth: they wrapped thin silver around copper innards, and this was termed inflation coinage. What we carry in a purse now is corrosion resistant copper-nickel coins that won't tarnish, the electrical conductivity brings a specific electronic signature to help prevent fraud in vending and coin-handling machines, but not always in a hand-to-hand deal. Gold, silver and bronze or copper were the coinage metals of the ancient world, which began circulation at some time around 700 BC. All that means when Dagenham's Flannelfoot made off with copper coins of the Crown in the 1940's he was carrying a lot of weight for not a lot of money. In old and real money terms each penny weighed 9.49g, which added up to about five pounds in weight, but still only £1 in money. The same weight in £1 coins today, as used in slot machines, would have raked in about £260 for the thief. aked in about £260 for the thief.

Forget gaining profit by being a burglar, at Dagenham cinema the money I spent went twice as far as it did at home, I could watch films there twice through for the price of the one ticket, whereas at the Burnham Cinema the house closed once the final reel ended. One film I watched several times in Dagenham was a wartime melodrama featuring Pat Roc, Britain's first home-grown star to go to Hollywood. It's said she became romantically associated there with a newcomer actor Ronald Reagan, Pat Roc was reckoned to be incredibly attractive and I thought so too. I managed to get from her Film Studio a photo and her autograph, all at my very first attempt although it was possibly just an automated function from PR people! The film star herself gained a "first" when she acted in the inaugural episode of the tv series called The Saint. Back in Burnham I had an aunt called Dick, who few would call Dorothy, but more interesting to me was her hubby Fred Fuller who served with the Parachute Regiment in WWII. Coming home on leave he'd bring souvenirs, mostly things he'd brought from Germany such as balsa wood models of British bombers and fighter planes used to train Luftwaffe pilots in recognising the other side, they became toys only a lad would appreciate as toys. I remember him telling me his girls wouldn't have appreciated them, and anyway it wouldn't be so long before they'd have a baby sister to play with! Uncle Fred also gave me a Nazi SS dagger with an embossed Swastika on the handle, it had *blut und ehre* engraved on the blade which slipped into a steel scabbard, yet it wasn't up to so much as it broke in half when I was cutting a thin alder tree branch. The Fuller home was a little timber and brick cottage which faced directly up High Street towards the Clock Tower, it backed on to the grounds of The Lawns which during the War was a very "off limits" mansion of a place with military occupants, possibly where they spent time poring over coastal charts and maps in the planning of the D-Day invasion. At this narrowing end of the High Street to the left was Riverside Road, a street having fewer houses than the number of yachts and cruisers stored there on wooden blocks; the corner shop was an Off License and only a short stride down the street was the Victoria Inn, one of nine pubs in the town and with at least five other Club premises for those who couldn't make it to one or wanted to be in members' lounge as in High Street at the Constitutional Club. Next door to here was a big hall, used as a cinema for the sailors and soldiers billeted in the town.

Now living across in Southend way, Pauline was almost the same age as my mum and brought up by Nan as her own daughter, she was actually my cousin although as a kid I always called her Aunty Paul. As an athletically strong lass she had excelled as a strong swimmer and raced in galas held in the river, based around a floating pontoon with different level diving boards that was anchored in the yacht mooring lines in front of the Royal Burnham Yacht Club. Pauline married Alan Ross, his family ran a footwear business in Westcliffe on Sea. Out of all our family here was the proper cyclist, wearing real cycling shoes with an accentuated large tongue that exited the shoe and flapped into place over the laces and stopped them being chafed on steel toe-clips. They are no longer in fashion! Alan encouraged my interest in cycle touring and later helped me select a second-hand Leach Marathon frame to build it into a touring bike. Bill Leach built his frames near the Stratford Railway Station in East London using the hearth brazing technique I have seen just the once, by Bill Betton's squad at Mercian Cycles in Derby. Alan Ross was more than an uncle, he was my cycle mentor who also talked to me about life-in-town businesses where there were more shops than you find Friesians in the dairy herds I had become used to. He was a fit bike rider who'd quite happily take a thirty mile round trip on his bicycle with two sons sitting in the front basket of a heavy, single speed Tradesman's bike. Sometimes when visiting Nan they were on a tandem with a two-seater Swallow sidecar, riding from their house by Belfairs Park. This became our regular tea-stop when visiting Tunbridge Road Cycle Stores shop in Prittlewell or on a trip with Tony Crickmore on the way to watch the Saturday evening racing at Rayleigh Rockets Speedway. Tunbridge Road Cycles wasn't just a bicycle shop, it was an emporium of very exotic bicycling hardware to tease the money out of your pocket. I bought both my Leach Marathon frames from there, with them a pair of the sealed Harden hub wheels and May Bruton also lent me stuff to ride such as a classy Claud Butler track bike. Over a year or so my parents bought three sturdy three speed hub Raleigh Superbe roadster tourers fitted with the Sturmey Archer dyno-hub and the back-up battery system so the bike lights stayed on for when stationary, one was for my sister Pat. On two occasions we rode these bikes back to Burnham from Prittlewell, although no-one was actually on them: Mick Wheeler, Tony Crickmore and myself shared the "towing exercise" with us on fixed wheels, one hand on our bike 'bar and steering the Raleigh bike in the other. It was fun to do a swap without stopping and we almost made it all the way home in one go although getting down the hill in Rayleigh was just a hill too far! Each time May Bruton gave me train ticket money for getting back to Burnham with the bikes. But I am sure she would have been proud of us for riding home instead!

Burnham-on-Crouch became a famous Carnival destination in my teens, with its first processions lit by people carrying flaming pitch torches. Our Crouch Cycling Club entered unto the spirit of things when Harry Rees and I built a dragon onto a trike with a long trailing tail. On another occasion we entered the procession with a Windscale soot emitting Pedal Steamer built on a pair of tandems.

The cottage where my father was born in Long Melford no longer exists, Back Lane was the address, leading to fields the other side of a railway line which Dr Beeching axed. When I called by to check the place there was vinca, otherwise known as periwinkle flowering amongst straggly grass and brambles by the brick ramparts of the bridge where train smoke would have greyed the air as dad played there when a kid. The landscape is flat for sure, Lavenham's St Peter and St Paul church dominates, being known for the eight windows in its nave, the eight bells in the tower of the church in a village with eight letters in the name. Were there once eight streets, even eight pubs?

How about this for a chance meeting and a link across time - when visting Barleylands near Billericay in Essex and photographing the house where our family once lived I met Harry Wade, taking a rest from driving the steam engine at the Farm centre. I told him that when the doodlebug crashed nearby the ceiling of my bedroom in the house across the road smashed the bed where I would normally have been sleeping. His quick response was to tell "I was born there." What a small world! And how lucky can you get.

This is serious stuff, with bell pads on their shins and looking to do great damage with their baton waving here Morris dancers do traditional things at Thaxted. The church here counts itself as one of the grandest in Essex, 183 feet long and 87 feet wide, said to be beautiful enough that it could well claim to be the Cathedral of Essex.

3   Suffolk roots

Dad was a Suffolk man, coming from the other side of the track and I don't just mean the railway line that looped Burnham town. My father was born in Back Lane at Long Melford, today all that remains in that stretch of lane are two new houses coming just before the brick bridge reaching over a long-gone railway line. It's here where the road becomes a track then slims into a footpath leading across fields and beyond, a place where my father would have seen then smelt billowing funnel smoke and heard the huffing of steam engines riding this line. It's another of those arterial routes that Dr Beeching would steal from people some decades later. This act of folly slaughtered opportunity for all the coming generations of tourists and travellers, my recollection of rural railway stations is where you found a metal railed corral as the collecting and holding point for farm beasts on their way by train to a market or the slaughterhouse. The *"packed in like cattle"* comment heard about commuting trains today just about reflects how those holding pens would have been thought of by beasts waiting there to board the wagons. Rail commuters who know that feeling could have been spared the indignity and misery endured today and be travelling on much better rail services if British Prime Minister Harold Macmillan hadn't noticed that in Britain there was increased production in major industries such as steel, coal and motor cars. This was leading to a rise in wages, exports and the like which led this PM to say *"in Britain you see a state of prosperity such as we have never had in my lifetime - nor indeed in the history of this country."* To make good the advantage of that situation the Tory leader put rail travel affairs into the hands of physicist Dr Richard Beeching and that is when the big rail rip-up started. Mrs Thatcher, who never travelled by train, would have liked to have seen even more opportunity taken to remove rail services and cut the transport arterial for carrying coal to market, all of that making it even easier for her to then set about dismantling the coal mining industry and its communities. Good things can happen though, so possibly on a former railway line pretty close to where you live a once obliterated track used by trains is back in life as a traffic free cycling and walking route by courtesy of the sustainable transport visionary John Grimshaw.

The Long Melford where Dad grew up and played is a small town that made good use of East Anglian rail links, moving people and produce to what is reckoned to be the longest High Street of any place in Britain. It is wide verged, well planted with trees and at the top of the town a large expanse of village green triangulates in front of Holy Trinity Church, so big and bold as this place was an important wool town. A church hospital in front was erected centuries back with an almshouse for a dozen old men and during the 50's on the Bury St Edmunds road I remember a local baker having stacks of firewood faggots piled outside ready for heating his ovens. The Kings Head pub has been a haunt of motorsport enthusiasts returning from a Snetterton circuit session, on one weekend ride I spotted half a dozen powerful Bullnose Morris beauties lined up and being fully envied. The local townships around where Dad grew up had for a century or two been at the centre of weaving in wool and horsehair and coconut, as in matting and checking the records shows that in around 1890 a lady from Macron in Ireland brought with her more horsehair weaving skills before marrying into the Lumley family. The weaving was staple for the area around Long Melford with beginnings thought to be back to the Iron Age, in 2010 a long horse bone comb was recovered during excavations at Mildenhall, the working tool thought to have been used in about 300 BC. There is plenty of evidence that such work has continued since then, local tribes were on the ground before the Romans invaded, who then got a bit beaten up when that lady Boudicca, with an Essex group of Trinovantes joining an Iceni revolt that sent shock waves through Camulodunum, later aka Colchester. It may be reckoned that here was the first capital of the Roman province and the oldest town in Britain, but never mind the fame or not it still got burnt to the ground. Being an Essex lad leaves me quite proud of locals who did history-making damage to a settlement of discharged Roman soldiers, perhaps I shouldn't mention that all the defenders were massacred! Around Long Melford it's the straightness of the main road that suggests the Romans were definitely on a mission, building a main street two and a half miles long that's not just the longest High Street in Britain but has got sliced up itself with part of that highway called Hall Road. When Queen Elizabeth the First carriaged along it to stay locally for a few days in 1578 the several visitors with her overwhelmed the town's population: actually the Queen brought along over 2,000 servants and helpers to cope with necessary chores. John Lennon is also known to have hung out here and then, myself on a feature foraging exercise, I once spent a night under the roof at The Bull. It's quite a place with the feel of an ancient inn about it, it is also the pub at the end of the road where my Dad was born in Back Row, possibly he'd have bought bottles of pop there or taken back empties he'd found, to reclaim the deposit. Now that's an idea for someone to try, re-cycling all bottles would help end the throwaway culture and tidy up Britain!

This part of East Anglia carries the age-old strong relationship with the wool trade so you can guess sheep have always done well for people around here, it brought the riches which local landowners and businessmen then turned into fine timber framed houses and stone built buildings that soar over the lightly rolling countryside. In my early cycle touring rides around Suffolk these mansion-like places were often hidden from view by stands of tall Witch Elms, the hedges and flurries of willow but that screening was lost once Dutch Elm Disease felled these giants. That meant now seeing right through Suffolk's tree-shorn horizons almost all the way into Norfolk or south into Essex, although the going has always been a bit more wrinkled and travellers climbing from the River Stour at Sudbury to then crossing the border between the counties have something of an effort to walk or ride a bike, or to plod uphill behind a laden cart along leafy lanes. But the trees died by the hundreds, Dutch Elm Disease has been a real killer and when working as news editor at *Gardeners Chronicle* I got my first sighting of diseased and browning leaves in a hedgerow at Ingatestone in Essex. In the *HTJ* b2b we'd carried news of the disease spreading across the country and my fears were well founded when that lane eventually ended up stunted with stark elms that remained leafless from then on. At Danbury, just after the scourge first hit our part of Essex there was a big tree on the hillside green all hooked up to a drip tube, looking something like a car crash victim in a hospital ward. This was a tree-centric car crash of a disease spread by elm bark beetles and it obliterated elms all over: the fungus Ophiostoma novo-ulmi blocks the water carrying veins so the branches wilt and die. First sign - browning leaves, just as I had noticed in that Ingatestone lane.

As a lad born in 1913, my father Charles Henry Lumley followed brothers and sisters into schooling before taking on the regular work of a country boy: no one has told me he did anything other than become a farm hand then progress to specialising in looking after dairy cattle and things that happened in and around the milking parlour. For the whole of my time from before I went to school and then to married life the job my dad did was to tend and milk cows, I recall around a dozen different milking herds he looked after in no more that number of years and when he milked at Little Heys Farm near Cold Norton to get there he would travel about six up and down miles to work, a bicycle was his transport! The working relationship he had with dairy cows was eventually brought to a close when farm boss Ralph Sadler sacked my father, moaning that the Hall Farm Dairy milk cheque was a bit down and he wanted to save money. Sadler apparently didn't do niceties, saying *"as the two other milk parlour hands are younger than you Charlie, why not pick up your cards next Friday."* Why not, after all no-one hardly needs any experience to manage a herd of milk producing beasts, do they! Yet the truth is you need time earned skill for that job, and I remember how well Dad knew ways to work skitty cattle and bulls, he even survived one near-epic with another bad tempered animal at Hall Farm. A short sighted bull - aren't they all! - didn't recognise the flat-cap topped outline of my father coming into his pen to fork over the straw and check the feed. The bull turned on him. He legged it over the stall door and as we lived just a short distance away in Marsh Road he legged it more quickly to get home and recover his old trilby from the fire grate, almost as the washing copper was lit on this family laundry day. Experience told him the bull was probably un-nerved by seeing the different outline in front of him, and that was just because of the hat mind! Apparently mum had already sprinkled it with a dose of paraffin to set the grate burning, but that trilby went back on his head and between times it stayed on a peg for whenever he needed to be with the bull in that stall. Was there ever any more ill-tempered playfulness than you can get with a bull, but bovines are quite unpredictable and real farmers all know that so tend not to be caught out. In my own world when near animals I carry not a mite of fear with even the oversize ones . . but dogs, that's another matter and only one wee canine has ever come into my life without giving me worries about teeth or temper. Previously I'd never look a dog in the eyes, then came Boots and the dog I'd often have snuggling beside me in a little tent somewhere, we'd cover hundreds of miles beingThere together, and if only he had mastered the trick of taking photographs.

In the Suffolk of my grandfather and others before him the Lumley family had worked in dairy farming, arable agricultural work and the like, which meant they engaged the something of a very lost art in these modern times: hedging and ditching. That's the autumn and winter months job of cutting back and layering hedge growth and clearing mud and silt from ditches. If more of that was done in modern farming then less rainwater would lay on fields or end up running onto roads and flooding into buildings, it's easy to see this style of good farm husbandry has wilted as workers became the dying breed on farmsteads and I am surprised just how much good growing land is allowed to be blighted through not attending to how water will flow and attain its own level. For some reason our branch of the Lumley family moved on from working in Suffolk, what had brought bad grace in Lavenham was never revealed to me but the family certainly would not have been in a happy mood. For starters they trudged up that long hill out of Sudbury towards Essex and it would have been heavy work dragging on forever. Of that necessity I've heard the moving-on was because a local land-owning farmer promised that come hell or high water there was never going to be another job for a Lumley in the County, so *"sod off somewhere else!"* My Father's family weren't exactly escaping from the Black Death that the local area managed to survive in 1349, but possibly in the genes of family forebears and since there is the earnest-ness of locals who had engaged the thick of the peasants' revolt in 1381. You need not ask which side the

Lumleys would have stood and although I have not unravelled so much about the 20th century spat, I do know my Dad was barely out of school when the family put all their belongings into a borrowed bullock cart, sometimes a tumbrel, and set off to begin their new life by walking south into and across Essex. Whatever happened to the family in Lavenham stayed with my Dad because I do remember he'd always want to influence fairness and honesty being shared between people, employer and fellow workers: Charles Henry Lumley was never happy when he heard or saw bosses or workmates forcing the hand of the other, and I know that inclination well. Walking pace transportation took the family towards a new life although there was a lot of stopping and starting as they unloaded then reloaded the carts so beasts and carriages could be returned back along the road to owners. Mostly a third time for that same stretch of road was walked before loading once more onto a borrowed cart and continuing the journey. There isn't a lot of change from the sixty or so miles it takes to get from Lavenham and arrive in Latchingdon to a new home on the ridge where a tall round water tower building stands on its legs beside the Althorne to Fambridge road. You can only guess at how long it took but the family's travelling to and fro across Essex to get there probably meant over 150 miles of struggle and toil to reach that place, and how long would that take you? Latchingdon's Tyle Hall stands across the road from the new home where the Lumleys would live, a moat guards the lawns and the 16th century two storey house. I was always wary about cycling past the place - there was always a lion sitting on the lawn there.

Settled in their new county the job was the familiar toil of farm work and looking after the resident beasts, it brought in the wages for the family through working sons, and the two daughters, then my grandfather died in 1939. Over time I visited my Father's family living in the villages of Althorne, Tillingham, Writtle, Latchingdon and Mayland, which is where both my Father's parents are buried at St Barnabas Church. My parents, living in Burnham town or on the Marshes weren't great travellers and by the time I was almost seven I had visited relatives in places all as far away as a full 22 miles! Sometimes we started out by train or on a bus but often reaching a destination by cycling there, on one trip I remember being taken to a pub at Galleywood, a hilltop of a place near Chelmsford that today is reckoned to have living there the highest percentage of retired folk than anywhere else in the country. The two-legged age stakes have a long connection here as on the Common is the now closed circuit that probably counts as the oldest horse racing course ever in Britain. Someone was painting still-standing track railings white when I last rode past but with the too many road crossings breaching the layout of the track, all horse racing was abandoned here just after the War.

It was pretty well known that my dad didn't suffer fools, and especially where tending beasts was concerned so for sure he thought more of looking after an animal than he would worry about niggardly workmates, or even his bosses. Over the years he related a few of the tales from being a man so obviously comfortable with animals under his care and there were many tender times of helping a newborn calf moved closer to suckle, or my dad working all night helping the cow suffering mastitis after he'd recognised there was a problem, something he'd have seen through the change in the texture of the milk and spotting it in the final stripping out of the udder after the Alfa Laval milker had sucked at the best. Probably that daily routine and close involvement with a dairy herd was the reason my father never became a great traveller and I have always thought mid Kent was as far from his home as he ever went, although his Army Discharge papers of 1939 were signed in Wiltshire. West to Chiswick in London he visited only to get treatment for chronic arthritis but I don't recall he ever travelled back to his home county of Suffolk to stay the night. That tramping south from Lavenham had turned him into being an Essex lad and he was a so-contented country man, happy to smoke hand-rolled Old Holborn ciggies, playing darts on a Saturday night and drinking Gray's beer. He'd bring home for me a copy of the Salvation Army *War-Cry* and supplemented that reading with a treat of Smith's potato crisps, these ones had inside the packet a little blue paper twist holding the salt to shake on to the rustling Crisps. An evening like that happened only at weekends, and after completing his late afternoon milking time at the dairy on other days he happily tended his garden patch before walking out around field hedgerows. He'd possibly be setting snares to catch a rabbit, or bringing one back for the pot and he was also a dab hand at wild-sowing the flowers and vegetables he'd fetch back home later in the season. Proudly honest to a style of country living that no longer seems the case, he retained a work ethic that put him quite happy to rise before 5am year-round, have breakfast only when the first milking session was done and then go back to the cowshed or milking parlour to finish off the jobs for a second round of milking the herd. He'd hope to take a very un-English siesta between milking parlour sessions after the work in the morning that was the routine sloshing out and cleansing of the dirtied cowshed then sorting feed for his band of Bovine Ladies who'd come back from the field for the afternoon milking session. Dad also tended dairy herds that stretched to a three-time milking day, all of it by today's standards strenuously hard work with long hours and a lot of personal responsibility for the living creatures in his care. And, no joking, he was just one of the many farm workers who were a long way under-valued and under paid by the owner-farmers who bossed the scene. But you shouldn't mention that sort of thing to the likes of Ralph Sadler, people who took no care for cowshed workers and sacked them if a milk cheque slipped a bit.

Come later times when I travelled around on bike tours or with the caravan on the road to overseas Trade shows I developed one little un-realised trait which my mother identified, she'd always said how much she liked the picture post cards I would send but then one day came the comment *"have you noticed that nearly all of the pictures have a cow or a farm in them."* My dad would have been pleased, he never complained that dairy milking times stretched from very early morning and went on until after most other working people had got home from work, eaten their tea and were catching up with the Light Programme on radio. Some nights there'd be a cow dropping a calf or a busy spell helping a sickly animal, but that was only for a bit over three hundred or so days in the year. The routine is routine because beasts come with their own body clock and a herd of cows have their day set out for them no matter if it is summer or deep winter. My father never drove a car or a motorcycle, yes he was licensed to take the wheel of a tractor but the only personal transport he ever owned were bicycles. When you consider the life a dairy stockman leads then that could well be the reason why I didn't follow into the family trade of working with beasts and on farms, after all the hours are downright beastly. This lucky Burnham Boy though, happily has indulged and appreciated beingThere all with all the benefits of the bicycle times introduced to me by my father on a little stretch of road beside Dammerwick when we lived on Burnham Marshes.

4   from town to Dammerwick

Being so often in hospital for the beginning of treatment for my arm I have no recall of our family leaving the wood clad terraced house in Chapel Road and moving to Providence, just a bit up the road from where Nan lived. There was a pub just across from us called the Queens Head, unique from others in town as they were either on the Quayside or the main road so possibly this one was more for the locals or was this part of town a centre for commerce? For me this street is a place of memories and some imagining and especially with that mystery of how Lime Street misses the attention of incomer historians and even others born and living close by, it is as though they are somewhat reluctant to accept it was ever there. It was busy for sure, yet almost of enclave stature and I sense the hereabouts in this short thoroughfare was of a somewhat different character to other parts in the town, this meeting point of roads and alleyways leading to where Pear Tree House stands. Lime Street and Providence is above the spur of a crossroads with the wider market place space of the High Street by the Town Clock and opposite the stretch of Shore Road leading to the river. Go up Providence and it leads either in one direction towards the top of town or eastwards out into the close surrounding fields. As for the street name, has it a connection to a sailors' mission which my Nan told me stood to the rear of the Dilliway bakery? Certainly having a baker at each end of the road indicates there was plenty of dough around here and spent not only on bread and cakes for at the side of Pear Tree House was cart wide access to the back of houses and the one next door where the Cardnell family lived there was a broad shop window look to the frontage. Opposite them stood a chapel, beside it The Queens Head alehouse and when we lived across the road from there an open piece of ground faced us: was this the resting point for horses and their carts coming to town on market day?

Perhaps this was the original commercial centre for the town, it certainly has all the hallmarks of being that; Providence with that pubic house where traders and carters could meet so very close to where the Town Market would have been held on the broadened High Street. At the quay cargo boats would tie-up with wares coming out of Shore Road to cross the High Street and only the short distance into Lime Street and to other stretches of houses such as in Granville Square, Witney Terrace and then Chapel Road in the one direction, access towards Ship Road to the other. At each end of Providence were those bakers so traffic from out of town would first be reaching here from the farmsteads on Burnham marshes. Here could have been the hub linking Orchard Road and further out to Station Road, which surely would not have been named that until after 1899 when the railway line was opened. Lime Street and Providence would have made a quiet convenient centre of things so I am musing as to what it could have been like when Nan's little cottage was built beside Pear Tree House. Then each year, just how leafy and fruitful was that pear tree in the garden, it was looking old and gnarled when I was not yet ten years old although it's said that forty years of fruit bearing may not be the end of the tree, but it's usually the end of its pears being picked. The cottage was gable end on to Lime Street, and I wonder . . was there a continuing pathway across the house frontage coming from the alley sideways opposite and then through to Ship Road? The Old Ship Hotel had an open space with an orchard and I suspect that this would have fronted Nan's cottages before the single brick wall surround was erected, it finally crumped loudly and flat when a storm knocked it to the ground one night. So where Nan lived could had been aside a busy hub of living and trade activity, now the cottage has gone and long before that the Seamans' Mission closed, then the chimney of the bakery at the top of Providence stopped smoking. About the only thing I remember opening new around here was where the Catholic priest from St Cuthbert's Church built, by himself a Church hall on open ground between Ship Road and Providence. He led worshippers at St Cuthbert Church on the junction of Chapel road and Western Road, an early 20th century build it became the centre for recuperating clerics from west of London , being designed with interior doors made wide enough to allow bath chairs to pass. Church people had come to Burnham for the fresh salt air and the quiet ambience to recover from illnesses.

We'd hardly settled in to our second house in Providence before new neighbours arrived, their own home ambience having been shattered by the bombs dropping on London Docklands. The father and his son were both called Les and the Martin family became so much closer than any of us could ever have imagined at that time when us two small boys played together in the back yard. It would be something like a dozen years later when Crouch Cycling Club was founded that Young Les would become one of my very best friends and then our lives became even more entwined. Providence was once the first part of the town I'd head back to in Burnham, with half closed eyes standing to sniff the air and waiting for the Town clock to strike, my head spinning a kaleidoscope from a load of memories delivered me since being born in Lime Street. In many ways this was a street of dreams and the reality of my time spent in this short stretch of road contributes so much to my way of growing and doing and travelling. Certainly it had been a good and happy place to start from! From Providence we next moved house to the farm on Burnham Marshes where my father became head cowman at Dammerwick. I remember this as an old manor house type of place with a gravel drive to the main house door with its steps, there was a walled garden beyond which a fig tree grew in the sun-catch stretch beside the pathway that led to a backdoor of the cowshed. The dyke here was close enough to the milking parlour drains to be smelly from the outwash, the Hawthorn bushes, willow and elm shrouded the house from winds out of the east. Dammerwick, loosely known as the manor was built with a basement kitchen and cellars, the rooms upstairs and down all had buttoned pull cords used by earlier occupants to summon servants probably; the spring-loaded bells we often rang just for the hell of it and to annoy mother! It was a big and grand house the likes of which I had never before entered let alone lived in, far more rooms than one family like ours would use so the floors upstairs were empty and echoing. It was a safer than safe playground for a coming five years old lad who could chase after the imagined ghosts from earlier days of the big house. I imagined and imagined . . . possibly there were real ghosts, but after three town addresses we were now living on a farm not in a street and one that was jam packed full of four legged farm stock and lots of machinery. Then across the road was an Army defence and guard post, hidden in the hedge and under trees as part of local defences to secure what was really a coastal fortification: the Dengie Hundred being thought the likely target for enemy invasion. When I stood on a chair in the basement kitchen I could look out through a little ground level window to spy on soldiers at the barricaded gun positions. Barbed wire wasn't being used just to keep the cattle in the fields, it was rolled out in big loops along hedgerows around and across the farmland to the river and towards the town. This was a wartime defence line, placed right where I was growing up!

Living on Burnham Marshes put our home directly under the flight paths home for the enemy planes on their mission of re-arranging London's architecture and to keep people from going about their businesses. In that nasty bit of work there were more people in one street of the Capital coming off very much worse in the one night than all of the twenty or so houses that got wiped out in Burnham town during the war. It was September 21 in 1940 when a Heinkel 111 dumped its unwanted load of a landmine in broad daylight on people below, one who died in Princes Road was five years old Sheila Bigmore; the tally of planes which ditched on the Dengie Hundred was close to eighty or so, with a big number of pilots ending up dead or captured or tended in hospitals as lucky survivors. At Dammerwick we listened more or less every night as *"one of theirs"* droned overhead, we also heard the engine noise from *"one of ours"* adding to the stressed sound of aero engines up there in the dark. One night a downed Dornier was deeply entrenched in soft

Very early one morning after abandoning the tent I was testing through a storm-swept night when river waves raged noisily onto the shingle by my beachside pitch I came into the calm and serenity that is the Chapel of St Peter-on-theWall. It stands at the end of a pathway out of Bradwell on Sea village, where around here the seawall is all that stops surging water returning the land to mud and marsh. St Peter's was erected on a former Roman fort by St Cedd in around 654.AD, then on a day as recent in time as June of 1920 it was re-consecrated. It is reckoned that the tall chapel tower was used as a beacon during the time of Queen Elizabeth 1. Of the man who was founder of the chapel, he travelled many times from his native Northumbria and as well as being on the Essex coast was engaged also on missionaries to places such as Mercia. Travel wasn't that kind to him in the end as he became afflicted by the plague and died at Lastingham in Yorkshire.

Travel was kind to these people, they all had bicycles and were on a mission to spend as much time riding them as they could. This is a 50's time photograph of Crouch Cycling Club members celebrating a year of youth hostelling, cycle touring and riding time trails, the twenty four of them beingThere and doing it, all under their own steam!

ground by the river on the Marshes, laying there undiscovered for fifty years. When the bomber was dug from the ground it uncovered the crewmen still in their seats, an undelivered bomb was racked inside the plane and a landing tyre was still firmly inflated. It was German-made, from the Continental tyre company. The legend in the moulded inscription said *"made with rubber from the British Empire."* The war may well have brought an element of excitement for a growing Burnham lad but it truly was all so much closer to home and nastier than it was realised. My mother scribbled some notes on a page from the *Maldon & Burnham Standard* report of the plane being found. She recalled a night of skies lit with gunfire and aircraft noises yet what was more telling was her remembering that the next morning *"there were so many bits in the trees, the crows were making a great racket as they fed amongst the twigs."* What my mother wrote suggests a lot of *"unknown grave"* or *"missing in battle"* could have been recorded on this particular night. This was happening in the Strutt & Parker country where we lived, a salty-marsh fiefdom of dyke lined watery bleakness mazed into collections of fields with no obvious way out from one to the next. Only waterfowl and other birds wouldn't need to retrace steps to get from this cul-de-sac of fields patterned just like Dutch polder country but with slimmer waterways. The estate manager lived in a big house at Eve's Corner on the Southminster Road and I often saw him striding around the green pasturing, checking fencing and stock and striking at the fluffy crowning blue-headed thistles growing on the fields with his knife-ended walking stick, or perhaps it was a golf club? Whatever, I stayed right out of his way!

The countryside here is panhandle low and flat and with the highest point above sea level being where Marsh Road rises over a man-made hump that crosses over the Southminster to Wickford railway. It's the steepest hill for miles and more of a climb than to rise over the bridge beside the town's railway station. Perhaps when the line was being laid and the men were building bridges then there was rivalry between the work gangs or possibly it was two site managers with one after trying to win a bet. You can only wonder. From the Marsh Road vantage point it's easy to appreciate the flat landscape edges right to the coastline, which stands out as the ridge of a man made seawall. Farm buildings, farmworker houses and clumps of tall elm trees or willows and blackthorn cluster alongside bull-rush bearing dykes. From his man-made vantage point is an all-round vista of a world set under a sky that is twice bigger than all the land at your feet. Sculptured shapely clouds shade bits of the land itself, whilst the bright and glinting ribbons of water reflect from ditches and dykes. Black pitch covered wooden clapboard built barns, feed stores and cattle pens, horse stables and a brick built cart-shed made up part of the Dammerwick farmstead, from the through road you entered a building encircled stockyard for horses and cows, close by was the ubiquitous dung heap. The dairy stood a bit away across the yard from the milking parlour itself, in front of the farm cottage where the Browns lived. Cows, heifers, suckling calves and also a Friesen bull, nose-tethered with his chain out on the field, this made up the collection of animals that were my father's work. This was almost a village of its own, farmstead cart-sheds that were open to the Marsh Road side held a collection of carts and farm tackle such as the wooden flail reaper and binder use dfor the summer harvesting of wheat, barley and oats. Haymaking kit stood with the ploughs, alongside chain harrows and wheeled seed sowing boxes that got aired at different seasons through the farming year. Sparrows clouded all the time, no cloud like murmurings of starlings were ever noticed but a lot of them lived under and around the eaves year round, their chattering was loud and the feathered flurries seemingly uncontrolled yet all in unison as they repeatedly alighted and departed their playground, the farm. In the summer the migrating swifts and swallows hid nests in holes or barely seen places, but house martins preferred building their mud cup nests under the eaves of the cowshed wall by the dairy or on the Brown's cottage. For us, the farm also became an open playground with several haystacks across the road from the buildings, our home-ground here threaded by deep and wide ditches bordered by stinging nettles and brambles interspersed with tall stretches of hedge. There were elms and a long row of horse chestnut, aka conker trees at the roadside, the blackthorn thickets were covered with sloes come autumn, a million sparrows played hide and seek amongst thorny twigs. The farm hostler Mr Duce lived a bit along the road where a row of white cottages faced south, his Suffolk Punch horses pulled a loaded tumbrel to the fields or at harvest time a longer four wheel wagons which had slot in "wings" above the high wagon sides that spread upwards and wider than the wheels. This meant really big loads of corn or hay could be carried back to the yard and stacked, there were no straw baling machines used in the time we lived at Dammerwick.

Mr Duce was one of the farm people who reaped, ploughed, harrowed and seeded the fields behind horses he also took to ploughing matches and the annual Southminster Agricultural Show, he went to vie for winner Rosettes. It was all a rotational lifestyle because after the summer haymaking and the corn cutting time the horses also turned the stack elevator to lift straw and hay for building into tall stacks which would be straw thatched against the weather. The poor horse went round and round in a small circle, deftly stepping over the drive shaft from the central cast iron ratchet that propelled the elevator. It wasn't a quick job and a lot of workers were involved to deftly twitch the cut sheaves with their smooth shafted hayfork. The farm which was very much our Dammerwick home and a farming workplace no longer exists as I knew it. But then farming life has changed, and you shouldn't blame only BBC Countryfile for all of that! One beautiful big beast that did the rounds of farms was the steam traction engine, examples of which we now see only as a pricely-restored exhibit performing at Steam Engine Shows. I remember the flexing steel hawser connecting steam engines stationed at opposite sides of a Dammerwick field, where they were deep ploughing the heavy clay soil. Each engine had a winding loop set beneath its belly, an endless cable pulling the plough blades firmly through the ground. I saw that just the once, yet every year we'd have a steam engine turn up with a thrasher behind and set to turning corn sheaves into straw and grain. Men sweated, the smokestack whispered quieter than the engine clunked, a flappy belt drive oscillated to set up whirrings and a rhythmic clatter whilst the sparrows flocked and tweeted in joy at the easy pickings. This was the farming community at work on essentials of the day, one you don't see it come around anymore: coal is *persona non-grata* and also RIP Fred Dibnah. People today just don't know what they are missing from that hissing world when steam was all the rage and power and movement!

The big black timber framed barn at Dammerwick had a loft, the hatch door in the ceiling sat higher than a wagon loaded with hay. Sparrows played hell there and although it hadn't been built to be our playground we simply took it and used it that way. Ground level was a parking place for farm tackle, animal feed and stuff for the dairy which included those round cardboard bottle tops with the partially perforated centre-piece you popped open to pull the stopper from the milk bottle. Old style that but also an early-age small frizzbee, flicked to annoy teachers in class or used as the base around which to wind wool to make bobbles for hats. The wool was pulled through the centre hole, round and again through it until there was a quite plump mass, scissors cut round the outer circumference and the bobble centre was tied. Bobbles, we made dozens of them to adorn knitted headwear! From the barn came hessian sacks we'd trim to size to make mats, using a clippy tool to thread narrow strips of old blanket or coat material into the hessian weave. It was evening entertainment and anyway there was no tv to distract us, was there! The dairy at Dammerwick sat central in the farmyard back from the road and beside the long brick cowshed, the cows were called into the milking parlour which opened out from the nearly always muddy field entrance leading to year round grazing. They'd know their own place in the parlour and this was shown by some cows shuffling around the one in front of them to then muzzle into the trough at their own stall. The Dammerwick herd was milked twice a day and churns of milk collected from the farm for processing at the creamery. Some bottled milk was taken to the Burnham shops, as well as churns for the house to house deliveries in the town on the Dammerwick Dairy's little two wheeled delivery trap, the milk churns were brimful for ladling into customers' jugs on the delivery round. There was not so very much attention to health and safety matters on the milk round, the different measures used to ladle milk from the churn hung on hooks by the wheels of the little trap. My Nan often mentioned it before I went to buy milk for her . . "*boy, watch out you are not at the head of the queue, let someone else be first getting the dust or if a dog has cocked its leg over the measure can.*" At Dammerwick the farm bull was big and chained for pasturing in a field a bit away from the dairy, sitting there with a distinctive brass nose ring. When pole-walked to be housed in the cattle shed or readied with the heifers, that bull was the handful for sure. My father wrestled that job often and amongst my keepsakes is the rather heavy, spring loaded nose-grip he used additionally to ensure his bull walked all collected and calm. Ouch! Calves came from the heifers served by the bull, their mothers having names such as Ada and after the calf's weaning they would join the milking herd. Cows remembered their own milking stall making it easier for dad when they slotted into place and he'd note the yield to chalk numbers on a slate hung above their stall, later to be added to farm record. It was with one of these slates and using a slate pencil my dad used in the cowshed that my mother taught me to write, and write, and write . . paper was a scarce commodity for those early teachings.

Of people who came to the farm I remember the man who sliced hay-ricks for a living. Burnham's Mr Brasted lived in Crouch Road, he cut hay parcels from the well settled straw thatched stacks that had stood there a year and over a cup of tea at our house he was often talking football with my dad. The hay would be sliced with a specially shaped big bladed guillotine-like knife into brown lumps which resembled big slices of cake, it cut a perfectly straight-lined way through tightly settled-down matted mass of hay to leave standing there a honey coloured wall. The hay went to feeding cows and other stock on the farm, some of it also fed our hutched rabbits during winter, when we no longer could forage sheep's parsley, thistles, dandelions and other greenery for their feed; the rabbits were not pets, we bred them for the plate. Nowadays that skill of Mr Brasted is redundant seeing that haymaking time doesn't lead to people building haystacks. Mown grass dries out to be hay then along comes a baler and fields end up being scattered with what look like huge rolls of hay in shapes resembling elephant toilet rolls. Alternatively there is the silage process, less affected by weather drawbacks always found in farming; with silage the fodder is cut green so no need to fully dry out plant material and 30% of dry content in the mix will make good feed for farm animals. This is cut from varying field types, be it from specialist short-term leys to permanent pastures or ryegrasses that have better quality and the ability to utilise nutrients. Of the man with that razor sharp hay cutting knife I have another happy memory: he was always talking about football with my dad, his son Gordon Brasted became a professional player after being spotted on the field playing for Burnham Ramblers FC, he joined the Arsenal FC team as a striker, then in 1953 transferred to Gillingham FC where he'd scored four goals in five appearances. When I was young the Ramblers played at their Wick Road ground, past Silver Road, which today is a housing estate.

When I was barely five a short stretch of road between Dammerwick house and Pannel's Brook bridge was launch pad to my bicycle riding, a short stretch of tarmac bounded by a broad swathe of stinging nettles on one side: I got well and truly stung when one trial of pedal pushing went wrong and I was just too slow to the brakes. Here where I learned to pedal became the start-out point for my first ever significant long ride, aside my father I passed St Mary's Church, then after Bullfinch Corner we were through Southminster to the hilly bit at Asheldham before getting to Tillingham, and my Uncle Arthur's house. In Asheldham my dad pointed out pockmarks from a Luftwaffe shoot-up of the brick built Water Tower - no longer standing there - which they may have been using as target practice or possibly just beating it up just in case it was a look-out point. The German planes often called hereabouts to jolly up the airstrip at RAF Bradwell Bay, a fighter base that has the distinction of being the only fighter airstrip with FIDO, which is not *F-it and drive on* as some thought, but the acronym for Fog Investigation and Dispersal routine. This burnt a lot of petrol helping planes to land in fog pea-soupers. The former RAF base is near where Bradwell Nuclear Power Station would be built, along the coast is the site of a monastery of the Saxon period where St Cedd founded his Chapel after he had arrived from Holy Island to begin to jolly up the locals to a better life with Bibles and the like. The local landscape has certainly attracted people from other places too, the Romans arrived on this estuary corner of the River Blackwater to erect a fort with walls fourteen feet thick, thought pretty good in defensive terms until the Danes arrived to indulge their particular style of ransacking. What was left was handy for St Cedd to recycle into a Chapel and then at a modern Bradwell the first generation Magno power station was built and commissioned to be the second of Britain's new commercial nuclear generating stations to come on line and supply electricity to the National grid in 1962. Some say they sparked electricity ahead of the nominated winner but building the complex was an employment opportunity which gleaned local workers from traditional businesses, devastating local bosses who faced a workforce with anticipation of better pay than they were getting: farm labourers and lesser skilled boatyard or foundrymen gained in the process!

The influx also required accommodation, with a new part of Southminster became a building plot, for cyclists the road from Latchingdon to Bradwell became a better drag-strip for time trial races when the road was widened and a lot of the bends straightened with a nicely surfaced road laid. Crouch Cycling Club certainly would make good use of it, and it has become something of a test-bed TT course for Alex Dowsett, the multi-champion who first tested himself again the clock on the Steeple road. My first test on a bike had come with that ride to Tillingham with my Dad, where my father's brother Arthur lived by a large village green overlooked by St Nicholas Church, a scene which years later would be the backdrop in a tobacco company's advertising shot with Reg Harris, the track cycling World Champion. He was a rider well recognised as a pipe smoker although I don't recall the tobacco brand he was promoting but as for the bike brand out of Nottingham, the whole world recognised it as a Raleigh. The tobacco advertisement didn't actually have bikes in it, but a dozen or so years later the village pump, the church and bicycles did feature in photos, showing the first ever Tramps Run of Crouch Cycling Club in 1974. This was a Christmas time revel that goes down in the Club's annals as the time when we didn't just cycle past a pub but got to drinking inside! In that age pubs shut at 2pm, but later if there was a Landlord's lock-in of course! The bike riding had to be pretty swift between when beer was chucked down throats before getting back and pedalling to the next pub. Some places may have their Boxing Day football matches, silly swimming or a bit of running but none can, nor could ever, outdo the hilarity that happened when a bunch of scattily dressed cyclists made it on a round of Dengie Hundred bars.

I was a youngster but also old enough during our time at Dammerwick to recognise and remember that around the place we were seeing as lots of barbed wire and searchlights, gun emplacements, Forces in uniform, droning aircraft in the night sky, and sometimes the wreckages of downed planes. As a five and coming six year old I was taken to see several of these on Burnham Marshes and there was once a little huddle of a mound covered by a farm tarpaulin: too late jumping with the parachute, I was told. Soldiers came and went on patrol or manned the sandbagged defences across the road from the house. A mile or so way up past the upriver end of town things were happening which we didn't know very much about at the time. Creeksea was the headquarters for the Naval Motor Torpedo Boat Squadron and the RAF fast rescue ships and launches. Their training was based in the reputedly haunted Creeksea Place, between the railway line and the riverside area we called The Saltings. There the navy built a long concrete ramp and jetty for the military craft to get into the river whatever the state of the tide. Certainly the whole of the country was on close war alert but on the peninsula of the Dengie Hundred life was just that bit more tense for the local people, our own little bit of Britain was a closely controlled area and a lot of attention was paid to even local people moving around as it was expected that if there was an invasion then this locality was a prime target.

Burnham-on-Crouch itself was home to HMS St Mathew, a Combined Operations training base. In the year between April 1944 and April 1945 there were nearly 500 Officers, almost 300 NCOs and 1,900 or so other ranks in training. They had 70 landing craft to work with as they readied towards the D-Day only top brass knew about. Burnham town had undergone a big change with the conversion of empty houses to meet Naval requirements, there was a Royal Marine camp at Creeksea where around 700 Marines were based. Requisitioned homes became the private billets in Burnham for 250 ratings and Wrens. Buildings such as Royal Corinthian Yacht Club and Royal Burnham Yacht Club were militarily commandeered for the Operations use. The Creeksea site had installed its very own cinema with seating for several hundred people, nearby at the river shoreline the Navy built concrete blocked jetties and a causeway so that personnel and craft could access the river or come ashore at any state of the tide. As youngsters, come 1946 peacetime we'd play at these river places the military had now abandoned, we'd picnic and swim on the inlet saltings when the tide was right. I'd always been told and believed the mud saltings at Creeksea was common land, and as much of it flooded on each tide so how can *anyone* own this tidal reach? There was an admiralty built slipway that stretched to low water mark, and for a time some W.Prior & Son built cruisers and yachts were brought by road to be maiden-launched here. Prior had lost the use of their big cast iron jib crane after it had snapped under the load of a new boat being put into the water, luckily no-one was physically hurt but the boat was smashed near in half. That slipway at Creeksea, so often the playground of Burnham people having a picnic there and swimming and to sunbathe, found that in 1957 someone had sneaked in and took title by some process or other to snatch from public use what had definitely been seen as part of the local heritage, in fact the local peoples' own common ground. In my book the incomers stole this chunk of the riverside for private purposes and to house their gin and tonic dens; the *"act of thieving"* even gained a seal of approval from sailor and Prime Minister Ted Heath. We can only hope keels rot or drop into deep water from any of the boats that are hauled up that former Admiralty slipway or berth where we once freely and happily swam on that Creeksea beach. The hope must be that all the halyards and sheets get kinked and knotted, with voracious and poison-fanged shrimp-things attacking the watersport people who robbed town residents and future generations of their rights.

When the church bells pealed on the evening of May 7, 1945 it followed the BBC radio announcement that peace had been declared in Europe. Hey, we would no longer need to pull the blinds closed or darken the windows of our the normally paraffin lamp-lit room. We all went late into the garden where we lived at Mangapps to marvel at what looked almost like ground level searchlights that were playing through the trees and hedges. Actually it was just cars with full headlamps rolling around the bends on the Althorne road, lights were being lit up everywhere again. I was just nine years old and how funny that us kids actually knew so very little of all that military might which had been training on our doorstep and around the place. But later for the town itself new names would appear on the panels at what is the War Memorial, sitting by the river in sight of the Clock Tower and standing right where it can never be missed. Yes, for the families of those 28 people who had left but never returned, there's a different meaning to that word *"missed."* After VE Day Burnham started being itself again even though the Ration Books for food and clothing would be mandatory for a lot longer, my uncle Fred Fuller was de-mobbed then come the summer of 1946 we were beginning to get our town back and the pier the navy had built became a part of the super playground us kids took over for ourselves. We could swim at the end of the pier all day long, although that was not for the faint-hearted as the river rushed past dangerously fast out there. On the jetty by the town pound where it's a tide-washed shingle beach, day clothes were changed for swimming trunks inside stacked empty gun turrets salvaged from war craft. A lot of navy blue-grey paint was seen, the barbed wire tall gates that had barred access to the riverside walk had all been removed. What remained was frugality, thrift, shortages in the shops and coupons for food, coupons for clothes yes, but we all had fun being ourselves, the Chocolate Box tearoom where they had once gladly sold fruity tasting water ice lollies they now were selling real dairy ice cream. Raven's sweet shop had Fox's Glacier mints, and I know that because empty tins left on the shop doorstep were ours to collect, nowadays the term is recycle and containers are cheap plastic rather than tin. At the greengrocer on the corner of Shore Road I saw my first ever banana, but as my mum was not a regular customer at the shop - *hey you, my Nan is!* - they wouldn't let me have even one banana from a bunch. Late on in 1944 it had been from this little shop that we were handed free treats, the most unlikely item I remember being a packet of dried milk and cocoa powder, this stuff all having been shipped into Britain from Canada. I guess it was a sort of *have this* for the supposedly *have-nots,* although no-one actually said that these were food parcel offerings. Perhaps the 2017 equivalent would be close to the stuff being dished out from food banks. On the High Street side of The Royal Burnham Yacht Club the nissen huts which had housed personnel and were offices in the War, they became home to amateur sailing clubs. In a big yard area beside the Clock Tower, between Burnham's High Street and at the very backyard of the Anchor Hotel beside the St Mary's School playground, there was a brick walled water reservoir built and filled in anticipation of any fire-fighting needs in that part of town. Previously us kids had seen it as the biggest, un-used swimming pool you could imagine, but we found other uses for it at school lunchtime breaks when the older lads launched aeroplanes they'd fashioned from newspaper, these would often crash in flames onto the water. None of those crippled planes had the Red, White and Blue roundels of course, it was only the planes with Black Crosses that got crossed off for any further action. Come the end of the War the local Fire Brigade emptied that reservoir, running hoses from their portable fire bowser along Shore Road and down the steps to the shingle beach. The surge from the hoses cut a big trench in the beach which took more than a few tides for it to infill and disappear to become all muddy tide-levelled shingle again. A sign that things were getting back to being normal? The saying then was that this had been the war to end all wars, probably with people hoping they could believe it: so who got it wrong?

Or perhaps it simply was never written into the text after all.

On the Boxing Day run a Crouch Cycling
Club tramp checks a sign pointing the way
to other pubs. The photo is also a pretty
good pointer to local places, although you
will notice that so you still will need to go
into a pub and ask "how far" as no-one has
added the digits to indicate how miles it may
be. On the other hand it saved the bother of
iron casting a whole lot more signs.

5 moving around Essex

After Dammerwick on the flat as a pancake Burnham Marshes we would have a total change of scenery about us when my dad moved to a new job at Termitt's Farm in Hatfield Peverel. There were more big trees rather than just tall elms and thicker coppices than I'd ever seen, with a hill right on our doorstep just a little out of the village from the original A12 road. We got there over a flattish railway line hump in Terling Road, Termitt's Chase soon came on the right after the dip that crossed a stream, and about here you could get confused as the road name straight away changes to Hatfield Road, although you are still travelling towards Terling! Hardly logical this, yet possibly it was a ruse to disorientate visitors and especially unwelcome ones as near where the brook flows past an old-time quarry something of a secret hideaway was lurking in the shadows. Very close to our family home in Termitt's Chase big rolls of barbed wire fully wrapped both the quarry and a small wood and straight away the neighbours told me never to go there. The truth emerged some years later, authorities had built an underground control bunker for resistance forces in the event of unwelcome arriving, either the locals knew about it and they weren't telling us or the job was done at the dead of night and in utter secrecy. It seems that slogan *Careless talk costs lives* really did apply! The one thing about the barbed wire enclosure was that hordes of rabbits were having a heyday - hay day? - masses of them scurried as I went into the field there to see the charge of the white tail brigade, serried scampering groups with their bobbing button tails. They loved the barbed wire barricade we couldn't, shouldn't and wouldn't breach.

This Lord Rayleigh farming country was when I got to become a bicycling commuter, riding alone on the full mile or so to school at Terling, where two boys attended who answered the roll call as Douglas Twin, *"yes"* and David Twin, *"yes"* in the same class. To me they looked pretty identical and I was never sure, never even asked, if they were actually twins, they may have been cousins of course; if only I had asked. The village school was just a bit short of the pub my dad knew as the Monkeys but the real name being The Rayleigh Arms, so here's another Terling riddle with the probable explanation that this came about because of a monkey in the Rayleigh family coat of arms. Story has it the pub later became the Terling Inn and the monkey sign was left to adorn the wall over the front door, maybe it's still

We all have to start somewhere, and I managed that in Burnham-on-Crouch as the boy who in his teens had no idea about beingThere other than living in this rural part of Essex . . later the travel bit would kick in and with it the pleasure of meeting people, so many of them with a real personal story to be written about.

Chris Brasher helped make history with his beingThere for the first ever four-minute mile. He's pictured at a COLA Press Lunch with top photographer Bill O'Connor reminding him he now had a bus pass - and it'd help Chris move even faster than when he won Olympic Gold at Melbourne in 1956. In 1981 he organised the first ever London Marathon event.

Giacomo Agostini: 122 Grand Prix wins, 15 World Championship titles, his Isle of Man victories included the Junior TT in '66, with his final Senior win in '72. All so very much faster than when I'd ride my scooter there on Island visits. Truth is he'd complete a 37.7 mile lap quicker than I'd get 7.6 miles to Ballacraine Corner!

Backpacking near the White cliffs of Dover, with son Michael, who has a great penchant for going quickly on a motorcycle and has been known to wear out kneeler pads at a Track Day session.

Two real chums who could bring music to the ears - Cameron McNeish and Ron Kitching, both beingThere for me at bike, hike and travel times, helping to make it such easy fun. Both have given a real helping hand to our son Craig, as well.

there although someone may have monkeyed with it and the emblem has ended up being a souvenir. It became an adventure every day when riding to school, barely past my sixth birthday and let out of the house soon after breakfast to wend a way towards Terling past a set of big farm buildings on the right. Birds in the trees, someone on a noisy tractor working in a field, young heifers with their mothers strung out across a pasture, there were guys sitting by a little cooking fire at the edge of a small pond doing their fry up, making tea in a smoke blackened kettle hung above the embers. I'd often chat to this always cheery bunch, probably casual labourers working on the estate although some would call them tramps I guess, yet real people scratching a living and not tied to anyone other than themselves, possibly escapees from the formality of towns or war work and services, perhaps even AWOL from the forces. A quite different world to this 21st century with my parents telling me it was quite ok and safe to talk to them, my dad knew one of the fellows quite well as he had been doing hedgerow work near our cottage. The guys had their own home in or under the black barn on the other side of the road from the pond, in later years I heard that one night it had burned down and there had been deaths.

Riding to school on one morning I had an eerie experience and something quite new to me. The fog restricted how far I could see up the road, being alone in conditions like this and with no-one to explain things I recall there was something of a panic session going on in my young head, and there is something about that fog and the memory from that morning that has stayed with me ever since. We all know how it happens but as a frightened youngster I had turned back towards home yet found just the same result of being in this clear bit of ground with a blanket of grey following me, but also retreating in front as I cycled. Yes, I remember it as yesterday because it is the first time I recall of being quite alone and frightened, it was scary. In the short time we lived in Hatfield Peverel I only remember other little things, like having my first ever tractor ride sitting on someone's lap, I think they were from a family called White, as it moved along the stetch and I even got to be hands on with the big steering wheel. I remember the ford in Terling with the white railed footpath where you could look down and see green water plants acting as though they knew they were being watched, waving back at you from down there in the clear water. Something else which has stuck with me is the parkland look to the fields, masses of big oaks at each field border and often standing sentinel in the wider space of a field, sometimes having another tree close by as if for company, probably all of them were related in branches of the Wood family. There were hundreds of pheasants or so it seemed, and as I rode back from school I'd often hear a covey of partridges tissick-ing away, an occasional jay would snap out that sharp warning which has earned the bright plumaged bird the nickname Policeman of the Woods. There were birds everywhere, that's one memory I have of living at Hatfield Peverel which is now much quieter in the main street with the A12 traffic thundering through on the dual carriageway that gained itself quite a bad reputation when the stretch past Boreham first opened. It was laid as a concrete road and allegedly more distinctly rippled than a fine sand shoreline looks after the lapping tide has receded down the sand to leave closely undulating ridges. The A12 here didn't exactly resemble the roof of a corrugated iron shed roof but it still caught plenty of drivers stopping to see what all the rattling of their suspension system was about.

Barleylands and a doodlebug

We didn't live so long in Hatfield Peverel which meant I changed the daily cycling to school to catching an Eastern National bus for the journey up Crays Hill to Great Burstead School in Billericay, I had company with my sister Jean enrolled in her first encounter with teachers and other pupils. On the way from Barleylands where my father said he had moved to for a better job with the Fisher family, the trip by bus was on a rural road that was much quieter than you find today. I'd often cycle to South Green for things from the couple of shops just by the Kings Head pub halfway to Billericay, the hill ahead was too steep for my little legs and it'd be years before I came back to crest it with clubmates from the Crouch club. We lived at Park Farm, today it's a well known visitor attraction opened as the Barleylands Farm Museum in 1984 with a small caravan site in the fields from where dad would call in the cows at milking time. Today's visitors can step into a tableau of rural life and learn some things about the journey from field to fork as they explore the museum exhibits or watch old farm machinery being trundled around. Mostly, in the museum presentations and tv programmes you come across are moving picture versions of The Archers, bringing a somewhat sanitised version of life as it was really lived, but then the raw and stark reality of living on a working farm even without a war going on around your ears, that is something a film-score or the playwrights could never cobble into a script. Mostly people who've actually lived amongst beasts on a farm will squirm when the salient points are over-ridden by script writers who wouldn't be able to tell the difference between cowshit and horse dung. Several times I have returned to Barleylands, this time it is a bit different though, back for afternoon tea with Tiptree jam and a buttered scone just across the road from where we had once lived. It was a busy day and a long way from being a farm I'd known seventy years or so before. This working farm then was under the German aircraft and doodlebug alley with the flight path of incoming Target London bombers pressing on in their delivery mission and being harried from nearby fighter bases with their fast reaction Spitfires and the like. Maybe quite a bit of the noisy night-time air traffic was from planes decked out in Roundels rather than having the black crosses on them, it was dark so we couldn't tell but then we were mostly sleeping in our Anderson Shelter dug into the garden beside the semi-detached farm cottage. My parents had said they had never known a more damp and dank place, but no surprises there I guess because right beside us at more or less ceiling height of our safety refuge was the tree-fringed pond, with a resident moorhen I'd raid for fresh eggs! Go to Barleylands today and the pond has gone, it's a car park! My parents decked out the Anderson shelter as best could be done in that small trench of a space with the earth covered corrugated roof arched barely above ground level. Perched on the internal brick wall shoulders that levelled with his garden plot my father set a section of wooden gate from the farm, he used it to make a bed I'd share with sisters, stepping down into the shelter we'd then climb the wooden stairs to peepies. Do people say that anymore or do children just *"go to bed"* and only last autumn when chatting about it to my sister, Jean said *"do you remember that gate, and Mum having to peel cow dung off the bars before putting the mattress on it?"* Well, someone would have had to do it I guess, dad was busy and anyway we were living on a farm!

These Essex outskirts to London meant sometimes seeing the evidence of tactics by overflying aircraft playing hide and seek in the dark, this was the stuff spotted of a morning hanging like catkins on trees and telephone lines: it was called Window, which some knew as Chaff. The little aluminium strips, precisely 2cm wide by 27cm long, were dumped into the air by planes to confuse and confuse even more, the radar equipment. The system used the specifically sized strips which effectively worked because a return radar blip from these would resemble almost identically that as from an aeroplane. Neither friend nor foe in nightime air conflicts could entirely rely on the Window tactic to identify the other plane, both were in the dark anyway so you'd just have to guess who it was you'd be shooting at in a sortie. Wartime propaganda had it that these enemy strips were tainted with poison, so *"don't ever pick them up"* we were told. I guess that was similar to the scare-mongering which circulated when I was at Great Burstead School where we talked in whispers to each other that *"the flying bombs out of Germany, those doodlebugs are piloted by captured RAF men."* Playground talk, but being said at the time when possibly it was another example of war-time propaganda exercises like *"Walls have Ears"* and that encouragement for us to be self sufficient which came with *"Dig for Victory."* My Dad was digging to help feed us, his victory was the home-grown spuds and veg on our plates! The battles and war he mostly cared about was with slugs, caterpillars, snails and the pigeons that savaged greens in the garden.

At Barleylands the farmstead had a couple of bulls, a herd of milking cows, horse drawn farm machinery for the fields, lots of blackberry bushes and by one hedge I found my first ever pheasant's nest and eggs. Beside the house was the willow and hawthorn hedged pond where moorhens and waders swam, paddled, pecked and preened among green duckweed and as summer dawned the summer migrant Swallows and House Martins filled their beaks with soft mud for plaster in their nest building. Do Barleylands' birds still return to raise fledglings who sit on phone wires before taking off and follow parents back to Africa? Does a cuckoo get heard, flighting in from the Langdon Hills after crossing the water from the other side of the Channel, just as those planes arrived with a deadly load destined for dumping and damaging things on unsuspecting people. The air raid warning which would have rattled them awake was missing when the silent killer V2 Rocket, which superseded the V1 doodlebug, announced their arrival with the big bang. Too late to duck! There were other dangers though, Barleylands had a frightener of a bull in the shape of a very large Friesian, the breed of dairy cattle originating from the Dutch provinces of North Holland and Friesland, Northern Germany and Jutland. That region is also pretty good at providing a horse of the same breed name, an almost jet black coloured beast that was originally reckoned to be good as battlefield cavalry. They didn't have horns, unlike the bull which was to scare the very life out of my mother. Dad wasn't so happy with it either, but something he wouldn't let show.

Picture a calm Sunday afternoon, my uncle Arthur and aunt Gladys were visiting from Tillingham, as always expecting that my mother would have raided the family Ration Book to feed them and my cousin Mervyn. A bit before afternoon milking time in the dairy parlour there was a knock at the door, the message was that a bull was out of its pen and was taking a Sunday wander along the lane towards Laindon. It was my father's job to go bring him back, as you would, but the bull had other ideas and was not going to be persuaded to turn for home, with the result he got smacked on the nose with dad's stick. That didn't change so much, the bull still insisted on wanting to head for Laindon and wasn't about to alter that idea even when being smacked hard on the snout, and repeatedly so. Eventually and slowly the bull did back up, head down and always leading with his rear, retreating in short faltering steps one at a time for a couple of hundred yards right to the Barleylands farmyard. At that moment in time my sister scooted out of the yard and past the bull on her kiddy trike . . . *"hello Dad."* From the house window across the road my aunt Gladys said *"that's a big bull"* but my mother was seeing it all in slow motion, very slow m o o o t i o n: the bull, her little daughter on a trike, my dad with a lot of near uncontrollable bovine anger wrapped in the moment. My father knew how to handle beasts, but *"please let's not have one like this again"* he said afterwards. Actually he would, as that kind of work came with the wage grade! But it was not only a four legged danger that came our way at Barleylands, my visits to hospital were on-going, Chelmsford was no easy place to reach for treatment and mother often needed help looking after my sisters when I was more poorly than on a few days previously. My dad got a job back in Burnham where we could live nearer to Nan and the girls went from Barleylands on the bus with mum so they could meet up with her at Wickford station. For some strange reason in this flat country Essex the train line there is stuck up in the sky which you reached along a road ramping up from the High Street. My sisters headed off to Burnham on the train, I stayed back at the house so I could help mum and dad pack for the move. It was nearly the last move I would make. That night we got the stark reminder that not only aircraft passed overhead, high in the sky above us a V1 rocket engine quietened when it ran out of the allotted fuel, the bomb stopped flying its course towards London and tipped straight down to dig a very big hole in a field close to us at the end of the lane. It was a big hole that took a long time to fill, some years in fact.

Luck had it I had persuaded my parents I'd sleep in my sisters' room and be more comfortable in their big double bed on that night. It turned out a good move, the doodlebug explosion damaged our cottage quite badly, the ceiling in my own room came crashing down to wreck the bed and the falling masonry could well have more than changed my looks, so once again I had got lucky and was simply dreaming the night away. On a day in 2017 at Barleylands we were at The Tiptree tea room and pantry for sandwiches and to buy some jars of quince jam, by the gate outside I was taking photos and got into conversation with a young lad who worked as stoker on the steam traction engine entertaining visitors to the Barleylands Craft and Farm Park, *"I used to live in that house"* I said to him. Quickly came back his response, *"I was born there."* Across a gap of seventy years and more Harry Wade and I had lived and slept at the same house, he was born there and if I had stayed in the small room for just one night longer it may well have been my very last.

Riding into Suffolk or nipping around the corner to Jaywick Sands or Clacton was our opportunity to be ferried across the Colne at Wivenhoe. But it paid to keep your wits about you. . and get ashore quickly . . .

Clive Jennings is standing on the bow, Mick Ives, Bryan Gallant, Tony Brown, Mick Wheeler and Nick Perkins will follow ashore. By getting off first and knocking on her door I would alert the lady her payees were arriving . . for some reason or other she never asked me to pay the penny fare at the tollgate.

And for the man who simply cannot afford to buy a bell Harry Routledge puts a picture to it . . . there were always super little ideas like this coming from Harry, who as well as being a pretty good cartoonist would chat a lot about cycling, which he was pretty keen ont too. The "mint sauce" threat was the frightener I'd often put on sheep as I rode past them on the moors.

6   a cold winter

Back in Burnham we'd live a mile from the Clock Tower in another tied cottage that again went with dad's job. Mangapps has heritage and history, a 16th century manor house as a typical farmstead where the main house is close enough to cattle sheds and barns to almost be an extension of them. There were black timber buildings, a brick piggery, farmyard pond, stables and heavily fenced stockyards. I don't recall there was anything so fancy about this manor of a place other than the monkey puzzle tree in the front garden, one I never thought about climbing! In 1943 the Manor was home to a group of Land Army ladies and their influence counted on a day when I was picking some flowers for my mother which has lasted right to now, hopefully for a lot longer too. Come turn of year little green shoots of Snowdrops poke from the ground, prelude to the nodding cluster of white and green streaked blooms that will air themselves in view of our front garden window at Whickham. I dug up those plants to take home to my mother when one of the jodhpur clad Land Army Ladies billeted in the big Mangapps house told me *"don't pick the flowers, they won't last long."* So each year when they bloom these little Snowdrops remind me of the Essex farm where I lived those 70-odd years ago, over the years they have been moved to a new bed three or four times and they have always brought memories and happiness, I re-planted them from Mum's garden to here that March when she died. At Mangapps Chase our front door looked onto the rutted stony road that reached the tarmac of Green Lane, linking Eve's Corner and Ostend. In the lane a thatched cottage was to one side but down the hill going towards Ostend was an old brickworks and derelict glasshouses with opposite that the ruins of a farmstead more or less abandoned to nature with shrubbery growing through brickwork. Over the course of the several years we lived in Mangapps I never saw any activity that suggested these places were ever used, and round here was where I took an interest in birds on a wire and the like: you could always spot Yellowhammers, Goldfinches, even Starlings taking a rest on electric lines or the thinner telephone cables. The Starlings were always somewhat shifty, often nervously responding at their roost on the wire when you eye-balled them from below, whistle softly and they'd get all self-conscious, hop and shift from facing one way to the other then take quick flight, diving to get up speed to where they hoped was an out of sight safety.

Sparrows though, they never cared much about anything, just swarming around in noisy flocks of quite uncountable numbers and barely resting in one place for longer than seconds till in a noisy shamble of flurrying feathers whirring to reach another spot, chattering away to themselves all the time - cheep talk! In this time of nowadays Sparrows in any numbers are becoming a rare sight and although most of us think of the chirper as being a House Sparrow, there is the Tree sparrow which can be identified by its chestnut-brown head and nape, which is grey on a House Sparrow, it also pertily cocks its tail almost permanently. The rarest sightings are reserved for the Sparrow's close relative the Dunnock, you'll hear them and if you have radar eyes may even follow them flighting at the speed of light around hedges and bushes. I've heard that the sparrows in America are all descended from the European stowaway immigrants arriving there as non-paying passengers, perching in the rigging of ships crossing the Atlantic. I wonder if their twittering and their tweeting is now American accented?

As a lad I'd find lots of sparrow nests under eaves of buildings and in the outhouses, others assembled as a mess of long grasses and bits of hay suspended precariously on little branch twigs of saplings or in hedges. Just about the most grass-graffiti example of the higgledy-piggidly way sparrows will assemble their community of homes was always seen in the trees by Burnham's water pumping station opposite Hall Farm. It seemed as though the wind had wafted piles of dried grass into space and it had all drifted down to the tree branches and become home for a flock, a big flock, of chattering sparrows. Sadly, no more is the Water Tower and quiet is the sparrow chatter although with Burnham's big school right here I doubt is as quiet as the St Mary's churchyard across the road always seems to be. As for the Dunnock, they will nest where you hardly can discover and we've a couple of resident pairs amongst our home shrubs and the garden hedges, I have found their nest on only one occasion. You know they are about though as their shrill voice is happiness and sweetness, often spoken from a hidden perch. A lovely sound to hear. The layout of the 40's community where I had lived is now changed beyond easy recognition, those days you turned into Mangapps Chase from Green Lane after passing a low thatched bungalow on the left, the lane to our house went along a high-tree lined, single width and un-metalled rough track. There were a few bungalows on the right, with big fields too, then on the other side was a tennis court in the grounds of a big red brick mansion of a place. Open fields to right and left, ringed by tall elms and some ivy clothed hedges brought you to the Mangapps estate which was marked in the lane by a single bar white gate that I never saw closed: we lived just past it. Across the road, but outside the gate lived the Willet family in a little house where they pumped water from their own deep well, and like us the electricity cable didn't stretch anywhere near here. At Mangapps we lived in both of the single brick, semi-detached farmer's cottage at different times, vacating the north side one to move into the supposedly warmer south side just in time to face the 1946-47 freeze of a winter. That's when snow piled deep and high for weeks, our drinking water normally collected by the bucket from a big tank in the field became rock solid. Neighbours who shared that tap lived in a couple of bungalows along the lane towards the Manor, all were in the same predicament and of these I only remember the one family, the Hazels. One of the country boy tricks George Hazel introduced me to was looping a thin twig twitch and tying it to resemble a capital P: this was our spider trap. We would then quarter the hedges sweeping with our trap to collect both the web and the spider then repeating it as many times as we could find victims before having the count up. At other times we watched nature at its cruellest, first we collected a few earwigs in a jam jar and why? For starters these insects can do lots of things but they can't climb out of a glass, we'd then check out an ant nest and stir it with a twig so that the ants rushed and scrambled around collecting and burying their eggs away to safety. Now to introduce the intruders from the jam jar, tipped in from above the earwig would scramble for safety from amidst the pile of ants and sometimes get away, at other times a battle ensued and I'm not sure if it was a case of *"here's a meal"* or *"let's go stop him"* that the ant army chanted. For them perhaps it was *"hey, someone's brought a takeaway."* It was quite a battle which-ever-way as the ants tried to avoid being cut down by the earwig's tail end pincer, some ants failed to avoid the danger but ultimately the earwig always lost out to superior numbers. And before you burn this book or call out the RSPCA, what we were doing in the fields as kids was learning there's so much to life that we all need to understand. As with some people going into the countryside they may be confused as they try to establish. . is that a cat, perhaps a vixen, or maybe that's a young kiddy yelping? It's a good thing to get the experience to know life outside of our type of homes can be raw, maybe too raw, but for certain people like Sir David Attenborough and his nature buddies will have been involved with animals and insects in at the kill just as us kids were. I guess what we really were doing then is a whole world away from the plastic war-games played at todays home couch by youngsters and others, who actually would have a distinct difficulty in finding an earwig, or probably being able to recognise one even when it had nipped them!

As housing goes the places we lived in on farms were all designed to be practical rather than palatial, the architects producing the template for ubiquitous farm workers' houses designed them with both a front door and a back door, upstairs and down accommodation, a living room that usually had a solid fuel range for heating and cooking, but not so very often a bathroom. Here I don't mean indoors toilet, I mean the place where you could bath that wasn't made of tin and one you put in front of the kitchen range, mostly because that was where the water would be heated and you could stretch for it, rather than call for family to help. Mind you siblings were regularly sitting and waiting for their turn in the suds, that's if they hadn't got there before you. Houses tended to have more than the one chimney pot, though: not that I recall ever seeing a fire lit in a bedroom and the Sunday room fire was only ever lit at Christmas time. That was the attraction set to get us kids all away from the kitchen and so having fingers smacked for picking at food still being readied. Other than for the cooking range, the fuel choice was coal delivered by the sack from a lorry and stored, guess where? - in a padlocked coalhouse of course. Coke was the alternative we carried across the bicycle handlebars back from the Western Road gasworks in Burnham, augmenting that with wood gathered in as fallen branches or the cut logs, old fence wood and stumps of broken gateposts we'd gather. The hardly ever used downstairs front room was sometimes known as the Sunday room, we had a walk-in pantry and an under the stairs cupboard sized space was as much for clutter as it was useful. At Mangapps we had the luxury of a detached brick building behind the house for storage of garden equipment and bicycles, it was also a laundry or a workroom depending on who was in there at the time. Separately was the non-flush toilet behind a shed type door that supported a candle holder. It didn't give much light, nor did it do much to heat the place and it was quite rare to see a toilet roll. Don't go there! Because we were country folk and living out in the country we didn't have the nicety of the so-called town night soil collection, our family got by through the deep mining expertise my father had needed to develop through necessity. Ahead of the time when urban sewers threaded under towns and villages the Night Soil Operator had a calling that included not just collecting and disposing of stuff from houses but also often the outflow from slaughterhouses, and most towns had one. It was a night-owl job, mostly Councils ruled that collections could be worked only between 22.00 and 08.00, and nary a drop of anything may be left anywhere on roads, pavements or the ground by the roundsman. Hey, I am sure that still is the case with refuse collectors today? Oh yeh . . .

Even in a normal winter all you'd want to do in a single brick walled house was hibernate to stay warm, and when the 1946-47 freeze happened it had caught us without a water supply from the field tank so Tim French, dad's boss, brought milk-churns full of water in a trailer from Little St. John's farm. The garden and everywhere was solid with frost that went deep, and so much for having a latrine pit over the next two months or so, forget it! Indoors, without gas heating and where the electricity hadn't yet invaded, the only heating in the bedrooms came from us breathing. Happiness there was though, and in the evenings my Grammar School homework was done by the light of a hissing Tilley paraffin pressure lantern at the kitchen table. That gave off good heat, too, but best of all was come the morning in frosty times when there were wonderful patterned traceries resembling fern fronds appearing as ice-etches on the inside of bedroom windows. On good days you'd pull the curtains and still not know what was going on outside, the window being so frost glazed you simply could not see through them. I tried inventiveness for my own bedroom light, our steam radio was probably a Pye or a Philips, with valves and powered by a lead acid accumulator. Local to us was the Short family who had a taxi business run from St Mary's Road by the railway, they recharged the radio accumulators to put about a week of life into them. With crocodile clips, some wire connecting the accumulator and a car bulb holder I designed and made my very own bedside lighting. It was far more convenient than reading in bed with a torch and safer and less messy than a fluttering candle that left wax all over the place. The wick of a paraffin lantern gave a yellow sort of glimmer but would stink the place out with its damp burn! There is no doubt that the Mangapps cottage was about the dampest place we ever lived, even as damp as our Barleylands air-raid shelter beside the big pond. The cold and that dampness of the place really played hell with my still mending right arm following surgery and it wasn't apparent just then but after the sequestrum, where a piece of dead bone tissue formed within a diseased or injured bone, my upper arm was in re-make mode. I can only guess that much of the pain suffered was the result of flesh and sinew being muscled aside to make space as the arm grew that replacement bone. I can promise you it ached worse in cold weather. At Mangapps it wasn't just the house that was cold and damp, it was the same out in the fields and barely a hundred yards from the back door there was a field pond where I often caught a crested newt or two in a square of shrimp net. It was a well established pond, circled with clumps of reed where dragonflies hovered in the summer and swallows would swoop, we often watched them circle the calm flat water and - wow - ripples came from the spot where they had dipped a beak: was it to drink or had they snatched an insect from the surface? Hereabouts the water table was high enough for there to be wide, often brimming, ditches and we had three ponds within four hundred yards of our home, the watercourse here was the upstream of Pannel's Brook which flowed under the Southminster road, looped past St Mary's Church and into Burnham Marshes by Dammerwick. Two ponds were on ground higher than us, too, one beside the big barn of the Mangapps farmyard and another across the field in the direction of Southminster. People on the main road would have spotted the tall pylon standing there with its blade missing on the wind vane driven water pump, and here's a thought, was this where all our Mangapps drinking water supply originated? But where else? In our time on the estate a neat gravel surfaced driveway went from the Manor to the Southminster Road, close to a more convenient bus stop than from Eve's Corner when going to school. People

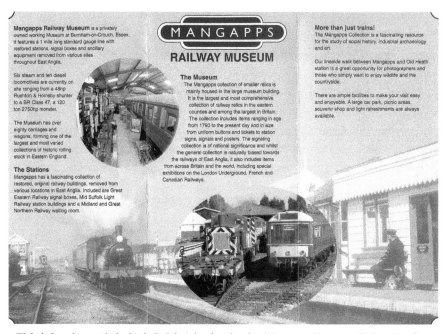

Mangapps Railway Museum is a privately owned working Museum at Burnham-on-Crouch, Essex. It features a 1 mile long standard gauge line with restored stations, signal boxes and ancillary equipment removed from various sites throughout East Anglia.

Six steam and ten diesel locomotives are currently on site ranging from a 48hp Rushton & Hornsby shunter to a BR Class 47, a 120 ton 2750hp monster.

The Museum has over eighty carriages and wagons, forming one of the largest and most varied collections of historic rolling stock in Eastern England.

The Stations
Mangapps has a fascinating collection of restored, original railway buildings, removed from various locations in East Anglia. Included are Great Eastern Railway signal boxes, Mid Suffolk Light Railway station buildings and a Midland and Great Northern Railway waiting room.

MANGAPPS
RAILWAY MUSEUM

The Museum
The Mangapps collection of smaller relics is mainly housed in the large museum building. It is the largest and most comprehensive collection of railway relics in the eastern counties and among the largest in Britain. The collection includes items ranging in age from 1790 to the present day and in size from uniform buttons and tickets to station signs, signals and posters. The signaling collection is of national significance and whilst the general collection is naturally biased towards the railways of East Anglia, it also includes items from across Britain and the world, including special exhibitions on the London Underground, French and Canadian Railways.

More than just trains!
The Mangapps Collection is a fascinating resource for the study of social history, industrial archaeology and art.

Our lineside walk between Mangapps and Old Heath station is a great opportunity for photographers and those who simply want to enjoy wildlife and the countryside.

There are ample facilities to make your visit easy and enjoyable. A large car park, picnic areas, souvenir shop and light refreshments are always available.

With dad working with the Little St John's herd we lived in Mangapps Chase, a mile from Burnham in a single brick walled house I remember as being somewhat cold and damp, we lived there in the 1946-47 big freeze when a pet goldfish was ice encased in our water butt but swam free after the thaw. My playground was the Mangapps estate, woods and ponds, thorn thicket bird nest country and with tall elms. I fell from high in the canopy of one and crashed-crashed through branches and then the thick brambles over a deep but dry ditch: at least I didn't get wet! Mangapps Farm was a collection of barns and stables, a stockyard and an un-tenanted piggery, the pond by the black barn always hosted a couple of moorhen nests. On the Southminster side of the manor the grass was chewed back to the roots by rabbits, the few of them we snared didn't seem to reduce the hordes fleeing to warrens along the gorse and thicket hedgerows. This ground is now where trains are now the big tourist attraction, Mangapps Railway Museum first opened on the farm in 1989 and is a destination that more than matches the sights of Crouch river sailing, here the tide doesn't wash out to leave shingle and mud and the Mangapps visitor can see more railways signalling kit than anwhere else in the country.

There weren't trains at Mangapps when I lived there but close to my home in old County Durham, which they now call Tyne & Wear, is the oldest railway line in the world. Running a whole 100 years earlier than the Stockton and Darlington Railway, Tanfield Railway celebrates their tricentenary in 2025. here is Causey Arch, the world's oldest railway bridge, close to Beamish Museum and the house from where Bobby Shafto once went to sea. Just past here is a mountain of a hill reaching to Stanley, it's on the Sustrans C2C route which does have easier access. The bike is Tony Oliver made, the one I rode when crossing Lapland and reaching the Lofoton.

often wandered into our lane from there, quite ignoring the white painted single bar gateway with *"Private"* on it, and just like some *"don't walk on the grass"* notice in parks and places that message was also ignored, a demarcation point just to make a point, probably.

In about 1946 time a long trench was dug in the Chase to bring piped mains water to our house, the work was slogged by hand with just two men digging and one of them was my Nan's brother Stan Boosey. Being there day after day as the trench lengthened he'd spotted birds building nests in the lane-side hedgerow and pointed some of these out to me In one nest I saw the huge and bright gape of a Cuckoo, and realised what a savage little swine this newly hatched bird already had been, with no reward gained by the pair who would keep him well parented despite he'd thrown their real babies, or the set eggs, out of the nest. The new born cuckoo has a broad cupped set of shoulders which evolution has shaped so they can easily shovel other eggs over the side of the host nest. The birds which had hatched him would also feed him well until fledging and after when his size was even more than the surrogate pair together. Cuckoos migrate from Africa and at most stay three months amongst British birds. Possibly through global warming our home species now nest earlier than when the parasitical winged invader arrives to lay eggs, that could explain the decline in reported migration numbers. Seeing all migration is a habit, if you can't start the habit because you've never hatched at the place in the first place then there is no chance that in future years you'd come back. I am sorry to tell that for the past three years I have not heard a Cuckoo call here in old County Durham. I had heard a couple in Galloway in 2016 but the previous time I had been wakened at dawn with a Cuckoo as the clock was on a backpacking Challenge trek across Scotland quite a few years back. In May 2017, by Loch Long at Morvich was the noisiest blighter not only noted by locals but one that blasted away in almost every daylight minute. Then in Wales two month later we heard a cuckoo calling by Cardigan Bay, one probably heading for a stop-over in Cornwall before crossing the water to France. But do come back cuckoo, you are not the nicest of birds yet your call carries a message that tends to tell the time, and I don't mean like the hands of a clock.

The Mangapps farm operation was run by family French, with son Tim French as dad's boss, the estate included Little St Johns Farm at Ostend and the milking herd there. Their home was at Orchard Farm on Maldon Road, an arable operation with a small orchard behind the farm, as head cowman at Little St. Johns my dad inherited yet another rather large Freisian bull, standing a lot taller in the pen than he really was. Seeing no-one had regularly cleaned out the stall but just forked in more straw for the beast to trample messily it meant a necessary long and heavy job introduced dad's tenure as head cowman and is something I remember him talking about, and not so kindly in tone. He always loved the beasts in his care and didn't suffer fools who did less than they ought when caring for animals, for me this Little St John's farmyard had an almost industrial unit feel about the place, barely a friendly vibe and more hemmed in and built tightly around than any other farm where dad worked. When I last drove by I noticed there'd been a lot of houses mushrooming, hard hats and brickies had been at play and cows were very much missing from the scene. Another farm put out to pasture, I guess. Mangapps was a time of many changes and not only for us as the War, we lived there during that 1946-47 big freeze time when in late afternoons my mother would feed birds with corn and scraps of bread to lure them to traps so they could be captured for over-nighting in cardboard boxes indoors, then released back into the freezing cold come morning. I recall Blue-Tits and different relative species, Wren, Greenfinch, Blackbird, Thrush, Sparrow, Starling and other birds all being roomed for free, a learning curve in my better understand of nature, and what my mother did then saved quite a number of birds from ending up cold and stiff come morning. Ice stayed so stubbornly thick on the pond and with snow blanketing everywhere there was little chance these feathered friends would find food, water or shelter, the farm horses were looking thinner and more ragged, the cows struggled as all their water had to be carted to them, at home with just a cooking range to heat the house that winter delivered us a cold gnawing time where the snow that had drifted away yesterday returned this morning. That's how it seemed as we endured the whiteness the farm world had become. I had never seen snowdrifts that reached hedge height, nor roads that were packed down snow yet that only on the main routes where the bus travelled and The Chase was not one of them. But there is always the Spring and it was from our Mangapps home that my first bit of commercial activity began with my earning some very good pocket money by culling young rooks from nests high in tall twiggy elm trees at the behest of the poultry farm owner. How I climbed more or less one handed, with my right arm still underpowered and mending from surgical operations, that is something I wonder about now and I guess that paid activity would probably have been classed as highly dangerous and even against child labour rules. By now they were no longer shoving kids up chimneys! Health & Safety attitudes were never a topic and would be a long time coming but my nestling murdering was paid quite well by the owner of the poultry farm in Green Lane: some years later he remarked to my father that the local crow population had recovered too damn quickly after we had moved to town, *"perhaps Peter would like to come and clear a few nests for me"* he suggested.

What I was doing in my early life as a farmer's son was very much the natural way of things. Every Spring I'd go bird nesting, adding to the expanding egg collection after that first pheasant egg was collected at Barleylands but it was all a controlled activity with one of a kind the aim except for eggs of the cuckoo which did at least stop some step-siblings being treated to an imminent heave-o out of the nest the moment the cuckoo hatched from its shell. It's a very clever bird, setting an almost exact colour match to those eggs already laid in the nest by the imminently surrogate hen, the invader eggs were a little oversize against the other's which makes spotting them a little easier. For sure, once a cuckoo hatches it gets very greedy, very selfish and in fact from birth is a bit of a monster! Mind you, that wasn't the case with moorhens, they laid eggs we ate at family breakfasts. This waterbird's eggs were harvested as soon as spring nests appeared on the ponds, after just two eggs had been laid I'd snatch one from each nest and take it home to be hard boiled and blotched with a touch of blue paint. When replaced, it could more easily be identifed when relieving the hen bird of other newly laid eggs in the nest. On most ponds the nest cache would be six or seven moorhen eggs each week, sized similar to a bantams but a lot sweeter is what I recall about them. Given a week to ten days of egg collecting from her, the mother bird was left for nature to do its thing and rear some chicks. But if - no, - when a second clutch was started, then my rotational cropping came back on the agenda. There was always a nest or two that wasn't found so chicks fledged to go on and do their job come the next spring. This was not a nest-robbing game, more an extension of a farm lad's way to help bring food to the table. A few years on I swapped searching for moorhen eggs and moved to a more sustainable supply chain provided by the flock of guinea fowl which ran amok in the cemetery of St Mary's Church. Actually, they weren't wild birds but ones straying from the grounds of the big house at Hall Farm, I didn't need to nip over the fence to nick their eggs as the guinea fowl had nested in the graveyard, such easy-peasy pickings! Guinea fowl eggs are a little smaller than from chickens, the shells are a lot tougher but the eggs are tastier, people don't trap or shoot the bird, in autumn they're sold by game butchers and they eat and taste well. Especially the ones you've caught yourself.

whatever is in season!

Hedgerows are alive with meat, berries and fruit and at the right time of year the Mangapps fields were where I started the year with nibbling at the first little green shoots showing on hawthorn bushes. I find this just as tasty nowadays - and you should try it, dandelion leaves are only rocket by another name, especially juicy when the plant is covered with a bit of slate and then picked looking creamier in colour than green, and it makes a free salad crop. That came in useful for sure when the bloody pigeons ravaged the lettuces and greens my father had sown in the garden, but we didn't shoot pigeons did we - there was never a shotgun in the house anyway. Dad told me that to be a poacher was one thing, to be convicted of using a gun when poaching was something of a crime in farm-worker life and it could threaten a cottars home so we never shot game: we simply fed well on what was snared. Rabbits, rabbits and rabbits. People don't hear a snare at work, which is not the case with a gun. More recently I came across a live-off-the-land tactic for baiting pigeons with a handful of corn and a few raisins. You need a couple of size 14 fish hook, a bit of fishing line and a stake to get the plot to work. Lay some corn around, bait the hook, then come back later and retrieve the catch. Occasionally there was pheasant in the fields around Mangapps, and like most farm people we had family-kept chickens cooped in a high sided, open topped wire pen. Pheasants were welcome to drop in to feed, as were pigeons, and as visiting pheasants needed to take-off at a longish slant to fly out again. . hey-ho they found the high sided wire pen quite an obstacle. It's tradition to hang a pheasant, which apparently makes it better for the pot but dad said if one hung around too long then that was just too much evidence to hand, it could get us in trouble so it got ate quick! Pigeons flocked well, making up amazing numbers seeing they only had the two squabs in a nest. Pigeon wasn't regularly on the plate being just a little too clever to get caught in our chicken coop but the squabs were never so wary that they couldn't be snatched when the nest was where it could be reached and just before they fledged. Pigeon breast - a delicacy.

In place of a gun this country lad developed good skills with a catapult, I still have the last one I made using a forked shaped hazel branch cut from a hedge, a length of square catapult elastic suited the lesser strength in my weaker right arm, the pulling side, and I found that this gave me much greater accuracy than with the man-strength elastic my father preferred. We hung a tin from the washing line to practice and only when hitting six cans in a row from twenty five yards we'd give the practice time a rest. Shooting for the pot meant using round beach pebbles, which could bring almost as good results as using a glass marble. For any serious play and accuracy the glass projectile was best, but could be expensive. For the pebbles we'd go to Creeksea, then on the saltings near the oyster beds looking for winkles, whelks, clams and the like but not oysters. Reputed to have been farmed in Roman times Burnham Native oysters had once been the poor persons' staple food but not nowadays and for all their reputation of being a fine dish I cannot remember us ever lifting a single one to fetch home. It is no good saying that was because if there wasn't an "r" in the months when fresh collected oysters shouldn't be eaten, it simply was not so very much the food we fancied. When Pipe's fishmongers in Chapel Road cooked their shrimp catch that was a different matter, Nan was always spending three-pence or so for a good tuck-in and we'd do the same even though the fiddle of shelling them was a tedious affair. One last mention of oysters is that they do eat well when wrapped with a slice of bacon and grilled.

Around the Mangapps fields was a crop I would harvest: mushrooms. The overnight crop I'd regularly tidy up and basket well before breakfast for delivery on the way to school. I built a good trade selling fresh mushrooms, and sometimes a punnet or two of blackberries off the hedgerow bushes to Miss Stone who ran the Station Road greengrocer shop just next to Remembrance Avenue. The early call start was easy as dad went to milk the cows at 5am time so was my reliable alarm clock! The client and I did good and happy business for a couple of years and then an opportunity struck to branch out: tomatoes were my business development. Two of my Nan's brothers lived in Ship Road, the next street to where I was born, and I knew they worked near the lower river boat sheds down past the Royal Corinthian Yacht Club, the place where Burnham Week started in 1893. I would often wander there to chat with them, in autumn picking quince which made good jam and so good in fact that I now buy it by the tray from Wilkins' of Tiptree, they make the marmalades, jam and conserves which so impressed Ian Fleming that he got James Bond onto it. One summer, chatting to Nan's brothers at their workplace I spotted a big crop of nice red tomatoes just waiting to be farmed, the uncles said ok and a first basketful ended up on Miss Stone's display which made me quite a shilling or two from that first gathering. Trade wasn't about to continue for too long though, mushrooms were not yet the seasonal crop so I'd asked if Miss Stone would like more of these juicy tomatoes, *"I didn't realise you had a greenhouse, Peter, but yes I would like more."* I thought there'd be no harm in telling her the truth . . . *"I get them from around the sewage farm . . . ."* That was the very moment Miss Stone stopped buying the mushrooms, or anything else from me!

Ride a bicycle and you soon find Essex is not flat all the way and as far as cycling in the Dengie Hundred is concerned then no road comes any steeper than where Crouch CC held an early days Hill Climb competition. The St Lawrence hill is along the road from Steeple. From the top you really can see the sea! Unless it's misty of course.

When riders from Audax UK took to the cobbles for the 165 miles of the Hell of the North Cyclo from Paris to Roubaix we won the Team Trophy, a rather large and heavy chunk of granite which had a very tired me groaning when lifting it.

My beingThere as a rider on a Journee Velocio with 7,000 or more others who pedalled the Col de Republique was an occasion to honour Paul de Vivie, 1920's publisher of the Le Cycliste magazine.

I didn't have to ride any of the route but I did get to hold the Giro d'Italia trophy!

Bernard Hinault, the 1978 Grand Prix de Nations victor and multi-champion in the Tour de France, came to Britain to help the promotion of Gitane bicycles being marketed from Moorland Cycles. With his wife in the photo here is owner Norman Mitchell and Bernard Hinault.

7   back to Marsh Road

Education had become a bit more serious that year I began attending St Mary's Church of England Endowed School under the town's Clock Tower in Burnham. I can't say I remember so very much about being at the Great Burstead School in Billericay other than there really were separate entrances for boys and girls although we all ended up sitting in the same class. The lesson I remember most there was in he home economics class and being told to always shake the very last grains from a sugar packet and make sure the wrapper on a bar of butter was always scraped dry; at the time I was still well inside a single digit age, but the message has held. Burnham was still on the War footing, Nations were battling on in Europe but we'd moved back to my home town and I was now at my fourth school. From home in Mangapps I'd often get to classes on a Monday, stay with my Nan most of the week and go back up The Chase come Friday. Burnham Endowed was the school attended mostly by children from the bottom end of town, it brought a different experience to being a pupil at Essex County Council School on Devonshire Road, but having moved away from the town and lost a place on their roster they apparently didn't want me back so I'd now be taught in classes just across the street from where I was born. I remember things sometimes being a little fractious, some of the bigger kids gave me the more than occasional kicking because of my temerity to have been born of a mother who was a daughter of a German; he'd died nearly thirty years earlier, by the way. A photograph of my school year class shows we were all pretty standard kids of the time: rumpled socks, unblinking smiles, shyness even, a dress code far from uniformity.

Mr Barker had his photographic studio in a shop near the top of the Station Road hill, at another time he was commissioned by my Nan to produce a Classic: it came over as an austere Lady beside a young boy who didn't reach her shoulder height and she was sitting! Certainly the image isn't of the Nan I knew, it also looks as though I had found someone's discarded suit. Probably she had me specially dressed for the occasion but all that is of little consequence in this treasured image of two family people born in different centuries and in a world that seemed often to be coming apart at the seams. We were not yet at the halfway point of the 20th century and certainly the subjects' eyes tell you something! In school it came as a bonus when the school headmaster Mr Mills took the care to give me extra tuition in after-school hours, spending time for me after other kids had left for home in the mid afternoon, and before his bus departed for Maldon. That near hour of attention he gave me really paid off, it meant I'd go to Maldon Grammar School. My parents always wanted the best for me, working very hard to ensure my education would help my chances in life as they knew that my weakened right arm was a limb that wouldn't lift much weight and I'd hardly be capable of doing farm work or toiling at physical jobs. Grammar School promised a new chapter was on the horizon and it proved to be something of a lifestyle change for me, few kids in my classes had our farmworker family background, most had parents working at businesses which flanked the Blackwater River such as timber importers, salt makers, boatbuilding and also at the William Bentall factories in Heybridge, manufacturing agricultural and other machinery. This was a business started in the 1700s when a Goldhanger farmer invented the plough and gave it that name, it had bolt on blades with fittings and parts that farmworkers themselves could fettle rather than having to leave their fields to visit a blacksmith. William Bentall's invention was popular enough for him to give up farming and open factories alongside the canal linking Chelmsford and Heybridge Basin, he hadn't patented his Goldhanger invention and others pinched his design. It was in 1805 that Bentall's began working, getting raw materials in and finished goods out by using the Chelmer canal. The boatcraft business was another employment area for Maldon and district workers, East Coast Sailing Barges were more the style than Burnham's yachts and sailing dinghies, ECODs was more the boat from here, and seeing that the East Coast Sailing Dinghy was clinker built they had the reputation for going good through choppy water.

Travelling to school by bus in term time gave us a forty minute opportunity of quality time meeting and greeting friends, telling of experiences and teaching each other tricks or comparing notes on homework tasks. It was time to share in our own little bubble, the prelude to a day in class although not all of us were heading to the Grammar School, a couple of my mates travelled on to Chelmsford where they were attending the Technical College. Tony Brown and Michael Burnett from Green Lanes, Pru Thrift from Stony Hills, would each board at the Eve's Corner shop stop. Further on Michael Weeks and sisters Jean and Patsy Andrews boarded as we left Southminster. Both these sisters would be appointed Head Girls at MGS, with younger Pandy ending up as a real buddy and soulmate and together we'd go off climbing trees, bike riding around the lanes and roaming footpaths. By the time we had both left school Pandy moved away to train as a nurse in Dumfries, we'd keep in touch writing letters then she returned south to marry a Fambridge lad. The options on travelling to Maldon came with two weekday buses that left Burnham just after 8am but I always preferred that one which went via Southminster rather than up the Maldon road. The ubiquitous Eastern National green bus originated as joint venture service involving railway companies which had begun in 1909 with a steam bus operation called, honest, the National Steam Car Company. At first they carried passengers in London then the National Omnibus & Transport Company came on the scene, took over the Essex routes previously ticketed by The LNER railway operation, but all on the road mind. This new transport venture was The Eastern National Omnibus Company, a service the public found worked for them. Today, at my writing this, there is a lot of debate about public transport, the high ticket costs, lack of joindy-up writing or service management and the way schedules never seem to match a passenger's needs, nor link for on-going travel. But forgive all our modern companies their shambolic deeds, all the problems can be blamed fairly and squarely on how old-time steam train operators and omnibus operators did things, they messed up and no-one, certainly not even the man who took a leap into business with the sound of Tubular Bells, can ever do better than continue to mess up: as was the case from the very beginning in 1909. The only thing that seems to work seamlessly is a bus pass: but don't expect it to work everywhere or on every service! I reckon public transport ought to be a human right, not human torture.

Other pupils at the red brick built Fambridge Road school came not just from the town but in outlying places known for Tiptree jam or the Goldhanger food plant where the cannery operated. At Maldon Grammar School my writing lessons were in Miss Joy Hulett's class, in that same class was a girl who wore her hair in pigtails and it was because of that I finished up in front of the headmaster Mr "Inky" Ingham. He was not best pleased I had deliberately shortened one of her pigtails, but it was all for a bet of course. That story doesn't quite end there, after leaving Maldon Grammar I heard my erstwhile English language teacher became Mrs Charles Grigg Tait, marrying the renowned artist father of the girl suffering an artistic hair-do reconfiguration. It's difficult to avoid more about that part of my life, as Barbara would later become my first wife, I would gain teachers as in-laws and one of them had helped steer me towards a career in writing. I made a quick exit to being at MGS when an early year term closed just three days after my fifteenth birthday, but the reality is I really let my parents down in their ambition to see me advance through educational hierarchies and it happened with a letter to the school asking them to release me from the daily school-bus trip. My mother was rather surprised when I arrived home from school and gave her some money, having sold my badged school cap and the regulation striped school tie. Unknowingly to her I had written the letter to request I left school, added her forged signature and was now free. In a week I would be working at the newspaper office at Dilliway's and what a life changer. Pitching into learning a trade meant I'd be meeting new people outside the previous round of friends and their families, the getting a wage would be new although I had always managed to do a bit of trading and earn money as I'd also sell stuff that I grew or had picked from the hedgerows. Through school years I'd also earned from odd jobs working for people using up nothing more than my spare time and turned that into shillings and coppers. What a relief that would prove to be, rather than venture into further levels of schooling I would graduate into a world using the twenty six soldiers of lead to communicate the printed word. My job at the local printers had been arranged with one of the newspaper owners George Clarke, in early wartime he had an allotment plot next to my father's on Orchard Road. I remember that place and time very well as being beside the home ground for the Burnham Ramblers football team, now I'd be going to work with the team goalie Bert Blunden. My dad went with me to Dilliway's and witness the indentures to my apprenticeship. I don't remember it as being celebrated any way special, just my Nan, parents and sisters knowing about that day really. Out of schooling for only a few days I joined a printing and publishing company, all with great excitement and the start to my big adventure that has got me right through to now. Today I am tapping keys on another important birthday, that of son Steven. He is living at the Essex village Silver End, a place where I'd later work for E.T.Heron & Sons where amongst the other publications produced was the launch issue of a magazine called *Containerisation*. It was a b2b magazine all about the innovative way big steel boxes containing goods could leave factories and travel right across the globe to customers. That magazine lasted only a few issues I recall, at that time this logistics idea was not really going anywhere meaningful, neither for the topic nor the publisher. Simply an editorial project ahead of its time, reporting a trade system ahead of its time, I'd guess. But that's b2b publishing for you!

I was still attending Maldon Grammar when we moved the bare mile from Mangapps Chase into a recently built council house where our semi-detached home shared a front gate on to Marsh Road a bit down the road from the 12th century St Mary the Virgin Church. We had no doubt when Sunday came around or someone was getting married as the six bells in the tower knew their job well. The junction of the two roads by the meadow in front of the church and Southminster Road was a little green triangle, short shrubs and gravel were enclosed by a low metal daisy chain hanging between little stone turrets. You couldn't call it a roundabout but was obviously enough of an obstacle to some people that one day it all became just the road. More impressive, towards Burnham was a proper size triangle with a metal seat encircling the broad bole of the tree: this wasn't a roundabout either. This end of town always had an arborial look about it, almost park-like with wide grass verges and regularly spaced ornamental trees. In contrast the town was just metalled streets other than Dorset Road which could have called itself an avenue and got away with it, the distinctive khaki camouflage bark of the Plane trees being nothing like others around, yearly clipped so the tops looked like a very frightened Ken Dodd hair set, all sprouting and spiky then in a year or so the barber would arrive and do more clippings. Our house at 3 Marsh Road had a huge garden which my father was going to make work for us with a few flower borders and a patch of lawn on the south side to catch the full sun most of the day. The rest of the ground gave opportunity for a lot of digging and seeding and caring for ground that'd help feed the family. We had hutches for rabbits which definitely were not pets, the hut and a wire netting enclosure kept the chickens from scrabbling about in vegetable plots and my mother tended a line of strawberry, gooseberry and raspberry shrubs. Our plum tree was only slowly maturing to offer fruit and the apple blossom on another stump of a tree never turned much past being just blossom. Across the road in front of our house was the garden along from a house where brickworks had stood, through the trees from my bedroom I could see Stony Hills and the line of the footpath which had led past us from town, from straight down Glendale Road and then crossed Pannel's Brook in the little tree cluttered hollow. There were springs in this first field that backed up towards the nave end of St Mary's churchyard, sweet watercress and other greenery grew there in the little rivulets which seeped rather than flowed towards the brook. Wild rabbits didn't seem to mind all this yet there were also clever town rabbits of course, how else would so many of them been able to avoid the snares I set in exactly the way as when I'd lived at Mangapps, too often to no avail. Our town style home was also something of a complete change from the previous three or four houses where we'd lived, the solid fuel Rayburn cooking range in the kitchen meant piping hot water for baths and there was electric light in every room. We had three bedrooms, a bathroom, the flat roofed annexe to the house had a workroom, a coal-shed and the utility room which wasn't called that! It was the wash-house, with a solid fuel washtub called the copper, but not made of that either! The famous Crittall windows made at their Witham factory for over 150 years weren't quite as stylish as the ones the Essex company had fitted at the Houses of Parliament and also in the Tower of London, but we managed to put up with that. Maybe nowadays this could all sound quite basic as far as facilities go but for us it was the real deal. My parents would live there even after we'd all married.

This new home was an Airy House, a successful development in rapid post-war home construction pioneered in Leeds by Sir Edwin Airey, his system had been used for twenty years or so and was then taken on to meet part of the post-war Government's house-building programme. Come back Sir Edwin! These homes were built on precast concrete columns, outer walls being a precast ship-lap style concrete panel, apparently the concrete columns they hung from were reinforced with metal tubing sourced from recycled and scrap military vehicles. War loot, I hope. In my mind's-eye the overlapped pre-cast concrete panels carried the look of traditional Essex clapboard barns and houses, ours had a pebbledash look rather than being built in the traditional tar pitch black timber. The houses were designed not to be used forever and had something like a fifteen year life expectancy, but these houses by far out-lasted the original intentions. There is a lot to be said for having quick to assemble housing needing less skilled labour than for a traditional build; there are lower costs so more availability to those who trying to have the home they can afford. After something like sixty years, just four times as long as intended, the home we lived in stopped being an Airey house so a new brick built house could be constructed on the plot. The house we'd lived in had taken another war to move forward the idea of housing people in good accommodation, but since then it's been a step too far for government. Time to wake up, 21st century Britain!

At the top of Glendale Road were older cottages and bungalows close to where the footbridge looped over the railway line, it's a crossing known as the Iron Bridge. The St Mary's Road that runs parallel to the railway I knew as un-adopted and unmade, muddily passing a ribbon of houses to reach Southminster Road on the northern side of the railway bridge hump. From up there you could look down at the station up and down line platforms with the up and over pedestrian bridge, on the right was a big orchard and further over were the old sandpits. They'd become ponds so full of hungry roach and carp you could bait and hook them with a soggy bit of dough on a bent needle, after all penniless kids like me and my no-better-off pals could hardly afford fish-hooks, could we. The fishing rods we made from a cane or a bough of willow or birch, the line was strong bootmaker's thread fastened

We lived twice in Marsh Road - at Dammerwick and also in the Airey house standing by the Glendale Road turning. Of the two homes this church gave us the very best sounds in bell ringing ever. St Mary's Church was just a couple of hundred yards away and for weddings, the Sunday service and other celebrations we heard just how much rope pulling was being done by campanologists at play.

to the pole end and we'd deftly twist the cane round and round to wind on the line. I am not sure that this sounds a very effective fishing, but I know that it worked better than you reckon! The fields that had become Glendale Road I remember as being where a battery of searchlights stood during the war, they gave out the sort of powerful heavens-pointing beam than would illuminate all the peace time streets in the whole of the Dengie Hundred in one go. The Iron Bridge that took you over the railway line had a short walled pavement at each end, the sloping bend in the middle lightened the gradient and over time I got to be very good at avoiding people rushing the other way as I cycled through. On the townside of the bridge at the local Council compound was the air raid warning siren and I can only wonder what the inmates at the hutted PoW Camp there thought of this War-time fixture, and were they ever woken and alarmed by that shrilling. After the war had ended that very same alert system was sounded to call out Burnham's volunteer firefighters and when I was at Dilliway's we'd rush to an upstairs Station Road facing window to admire the rush of guys pedalling furiously out of Coronation Street from the boatbuilding yards. It was rare that one of the reporting team at *The Rag* followed up to check for a story but years later, when I was freelancing for the *Maldon & Burnham Standard*, if a blue light attached to a fast moving vehicle with the klaxon bellowing was seen or heard then I'd grab my camera kit, jump on my Capri scooter to go see what all the fuss was about. Or not. When it turned out there was action I'd grab a number of pictures showing guys all decked out in black overwear topped by a hard hat, and it always made a better picture when there was a barn or a haystack flaming, smoking or steaming away beyond a ribbon of snaking hosepipes that writhed and pulsed as the water powered through. Living in that Burnham Council yard by the Iron Bridge were the prisoner of war inmates who both worked on the local farms and also were the road-builders who dug and constructed roads and pavements for a new Council estate in Burnham. Who I wonder, enjoyed such a perverse sense of humour to get the PoWs labouring to construct roads for a new bit of British housing, the roads they worked one were made with lorry loads of house brick rubble they laid on the farm fields, foundations for Alamein Road, Dunkirk Road, Arnhem Road and also Normandy Avenue. Some new homes were for people who'd suffered their own houses being knocked about a bit by the Luftwaffe along with homes needed for the military personnel coming back after their operations in Europe.

It appeals to me now that I preferred living close to a farm, the sort of life we'd enjoyed up to the time we came away from Mangapps. The railway that looped between us and the town was as close a physical demarcation line to the urban set as you could get, seeing it had to be crossed by one way or other to go shopping or for a visit to the Cinema to watch a black and white movie more often than catching ones in colour. I had little jobs in the town, one was delivering Sunday newspapers for Skipper's newsagents which earned me good pocket money and best of all gave me a big opportunity to share conversations with the people on the round and learn things I'd otherwise would have missed. On one of the paper rounds I delivered to houses in Prospect Place and there the big attraction was an Indonesian native white cockatoo in a cage and taking the morning sun by the back door. The bird is also known as the umbrella cockatoo, a name almost certainly gained because of its striking semicircular head crest which the bird raises when something catches their interest such as a new toy or even a person coming to deliver newspapers! I was told he was quite old. The newsagent Mr Skipper also ran a smallholding at Stony Hills and one of my summertime tasks was creosoting chicken houses and sheds and also re-tarring the roofs. I have a warning for anyone going up a ladder to do such a job - don't step onto wet tar otherwise you're likely to toboggan back to earth then end up needing to have bare skin scrubbed clean with paraffin and suffer long baths with lots of soap. The amazing thing is that I landed from the roof without any damage other than being covered in tar and relating that experience always made people chuckle, especially when Mr Skipper told other crew members I was with on his St George class Bermudan rigged sloop he owned and raced.

Sailed at Burnham Sailing Club on a Wednesday club racing evening in the season his yacht was one of only six built to a Roger de Quincey design as a light displacement race boat more suited to UK waters than the Dragons and Tumlaren from Scandinavia. Named as St George it was the only one of its Class berthed on the River Crouch, built as a boat that rated similar to a West Solent cruiser with cabin berths for two and being one you could sail in open water such as across the Channel. To me it looked a big boat, just over 30ft long and with 4ft 6inches of draft there was plenty of lead-line dipping to check for good water under the keel on some river reaches when the tide was a bit down or we were trying to do better than others in a fickle wind. The only time I ever competitively helmed St George was in the Club's annual Crew's Race and I made enough of a mess of the job to win a steel marling spike, a pointed tool used in marine ropework. This sort of fun had continued through after my early days working at Dilliway's but then I came to realising there was a lot of country beyond the Essex border that I'd like to explore, and the way to do it with little money was to pedal where I wanted to go. To prime that new opportunity came the new influence of Londoners John and Alf Lane who spent weekends camping at Burnham . . hey, what a great idea to try, living in a tent in the countryside! By train, John and Alf Lane came for week-ending in the tent they pitched on Burnham playing fields at the top end of the promenade, their gear they pushed along in a Silver Cross pram and in those days it was safe to send things ahead of your train travel and collect it on arrival, which saved time and was very convenient. Their tent was where I first developed a love for camping and was lucky enough to spend a night or two experiencing that new found freedom, I did need to ensure my parents it was safe to be with these two guys they didn't actually know, and I guess that demonstrates how far today we have drawn back from giving children the opportunity of engaging adventure in their own space. What a topic that makes in our modern social media driven world where no-one trusts anyone! For me in those 1950s time what I experienced with those two guys instilled in me an insight into outdoors living, on being practical about ways to travel, on trusting and sharing the good things in life. In retirement John and Alf Lane came to live in Burnham within couple of hundred yards or so of where they had first arrived to pitch their tent for the weekend. Thanks fellas for starting me off on the journey and teaching me how to live in a tent and how to be a happy camper.

Nan had got herself a new home in a new Council bungalow in the new built Arnheim Road cul de sac in about the time I was in my teens, by then she was living in just one downstairs room at Lime Street with the cottage becoming increasingly dilapidated and falling down around her ears. She still had the toilet at the end of the garden beside the tap for her drinking water, just the one little gas lamp, a cooking ring and the open range fire under that gaping chimney. That changed her life to being in an all facilities, comfortable bungalow that was now palatial in comparison and she'd enjoy that for about twenty years, but on a day visit to us at Marsh Road she walked into an armchair and broke a hip. Nan would never return to her own home despite all her hoping, living her last couple of years or so after hospitalisation being cared for by mum and dad, that came about when my aunts and uncles thought my mother was more up to the job than themselves. They didn't see just how much extra work it gave my parents, but after all there was a spare room at Marsh Road anyway so those other relatives didn't need to pitch in, did they. I didn't cry for Nan when she died, my being too sad would have not have respected the outwardly bright and independent way she had gone with her life ... *"you are my sunshine . my only sunshine . . don't take my sunshine away"* was a song she'd often be singing.

I often think about those words, sometimes anyone near enough may hear my tuneless rendering of thoughts composed into verse over eighty years ago, it is something of an anthem at the gathering of many families ever since. I have no doubt some of the sunshine clouded over when Nan died, I had now reached the end of having two mothers, who both did so very well starting me on the journey to beingThere and reaching this happy place where I am at today.

Cycling to Kent for day rides or the weekend meant we'd cross the Thames on the Tilbury to Gravesend ferry, that opened up the sight of big ocean going ships and the tough little tugs which nudged and pulled the sea giants into docks along the river. This was London's watery highway connecting the people of Britain to all around the world.

there were days when Crouch Cycling Club riders became fans of fast moving sport such as motorcycle scambles or car racing at the Kent circuit

8 sailing through the fifties

In towns and villages you catch up with the names of the locals who didn't come home from hostilities, it's such a good reason to stand quietly and read who died for our freedom. The War Memorial by the quay in my hometown High Street has some names I don't recognise there among some whose families I've known or grown up beside in Burnham on Crouch. On a school day during the war a mass of us kids stood waving our flags on the slope to Burnham railway station as a stream of uniform clad men carrying bulging kit bags rushed towards waiting families. These were people coming home for a period of leave from the struggle, some couldn't come home and are denied that chance for ever. It also happened that sons from the other side are buried nearby in the town cemetery, not in the main graveyard with that big white angel by the main gates and other memorial stones of different styles but along in Cobbin's Chase. The wartime graves of these fallen German airmen I remember as always tended by the farmer's wife there, years later a newspaper report told that on the occasion of the men being repatriated they had asked why she had kept on doing it, the lady's response was *"I was sure that people over there would be doing the same for our lads."* When those airmen were taken back to their home towns in Germany she was welcomed as guest of the families of the airmen she'd tended in their simple graves.

It is telling how not all local people were as generous of mind and that came very much home me in the early fifties when I took to exchanging letters with a pen-friend living in Frankfurt am Maine. Perhaps not everyone wanted to broaden their horizons in that way but hearing sour tones from some neighbours living in nearby Stony Hills Road at Burnham wasn't comforting. The voices persisted in forcibly advising me their kids didn't want to hear about that German lad, nor where he came from and anyway I was only doing it because of family connection with Germany. Yes, the Warnecke connection is mine and although I'd say I didn't get to caring a shit about what the local kids' parents said, I guess I did and in our more enlightened world now that would be thought of as downright heavy racialism. I'd met Heinze Timpe in Burnham, wheeling his bicycle which had a puncture, he'd been chatting with Maureen Adams who's father was landlord of the Old Ship Hotel and guessed I may be able to help. I used a patch and the sticky stuff from my John Bull

Repair Outfit to repair his Continental brand inner tube and wished him well for the ride back to Steeple where he was staying with an English family on a student exchange programme. We'd exchanged addresses and mending the puncture began a years long friendship, we both reached out to share in another's life by writing letters to the other growing up in a new world order. Both engaged communicating on things early-teens kids talked about in a world getting rebuilt after the long conflict in Europe. What else would you call that other than both sides winning? Heinze was keen to improve his understanding of us Brits and how to use the English language so the correspondence between us was putting him on that learning curve, in return I was hearing more about my grandfather's country, and his too. Today such conversations would be in an e-mail or a text message and social media, and probably in English regardless of what others in Europe may say! Back then it was the penned words, written on paper that brought us to each other's side, perhaps on the day we bumped into each other we were just two young cyclists yet sustained across considerable years was this Anglo-German friendship, the Burnham boy and a lad from Frankfurt who shared lots and of the giving I still have the Hohner mouthorgan which Heinze sent from Germany. We'd continue to exchange letters past the time he moved to Johannesburg some years later, having lived through bad times at home and in very much worse danger than I'd faced in Burnham I guess he saw the move was to a better future in South Africa. This was a time when the world all knew about apartheid but reacted in different ways, that all came home to me from a letter when he wrote about getting back to his house and finding a problem on his doorstep. *"Luckily I had my gun"* was the chilling note. I have often wondered if Heinze returned to his German homeland or of how South Africa turned out for him. Our letter exchanges drifted apart in the 1960s at about the time when *"the blowing winds of change"* were promised, and not just for the African continent. Britain's Prime Minister Harold Macmillan had given two speeches about the life changes coming to the African continent. In Ghana's Accra and then in Cape Town, Macmillan told the people it was right for them to want to run their own lives. I'm writing this at a time when in Britain and on the nearby continent the descendents of those Africans are still running hard to make better lives: so much for predictions and promises from politicians. Nelson Mandela was one man who got on the case in a good way though, working with another to help broker the end of apartheid and give everyone equal voting rights. That man was Frederik Willem de Klerk, who not only happens to be Pisces but I can even remember his exact birth date as if it was mine. Actually, it is: both day, month, year!

Looking back and not forgetting that again hostilities between nations broke out, this time with the Korean War from June 1950, a lot in the way of hopes still came to fruition for us in Burnham. So far off on the other side of the world and somewhere we knew little about that war in Korea was between the two countries which bordered the 38th parallel. North Korea sent around 75,000 soldiers to invade South Korea but they weren't left to their own devices to sort out the mess, with the United Nations and USA as its principal force giving support to South Korea whilst China aided the North Korean side, helped by the Soviet Union. Whilst the 1950 differences were kicking off us Burnham lads got on with doing things that mattered to us, growing up like there was no tomorrow, swimming in the Crouch and doing almost anything we could providing it didn't cost money, which was a quite scarce commodity! Some of us found cycle speedway was more attractive than playing football although we did both and between us organised matches with lads from other villages. For cycle speedway, locally there was a league of sorts and teams were building their own tracks with Burnham's on the town's playing fields whilst another I remember was at Latchingdon, on land that would later be used for the new Village Hall. To build our track the ground was scraped of grass and any weed roots cut out, it was shaped into an ellipse with longer flattened sides and a true semi-circle as the corner each end. I guess the truth is that this idea of sport came from motorcycle speedway and the bicycles made especially for us looked fairly close to the real thing, obviously minus the engine. For sure, at that time in bicycle fashions this was no forerunner of the bmx bike nor the mtbs of later years either, the bikemaker Phillips produced a model as a single speed machine with a looping toptube at the saddle end, rather than have straight tubing. There was a long rake to the front forks that were embellished with a bowed front fender stretching from the 'bars down to the front axle. In a way it was a sort of crumple zone although the makers promised this was to help strengthen the frame. Handlebars they described as Canadian style swept outwards and upwards and were made really wide to let you steer the most outrageous line into the tight bends on the track. The Phillips model sold for over £10, which was an absolute fortune to pay but I built my own bike, used a length of narrow galvanised gas pipe tube I bought at King & Hines' hardware store, one of the first shops of Station Road coming from High Street and opposite the Baptist Church where in earlier years I'd gone for my Sunday School lessons. The sport itself was a lung bursting sprint and then corner, sprint and corner effort repeated for a few laps, sideways drifting over the loose surface at the apex of the bend rather than scrubbing off too much speed by broadsiding the bike, and that helped you get over the line first, chests heaving with the effort. Our track was covered in real cinders, brought in sacks from the Western Road gas works, we would carry this to the Playing Fields on the four wheel chassis of an old pram.

The Burnham Boys' Club was weekly when we met in the Mildmay Sports

These photos from my album show that DuPont's Spandex and their Lycra was still a few years away from being invented. The winter picture of Tony Crickmore and I was taken when we were riding the Brentwood RC 100-in-8 Reliability Trial. Jock Wadley, editor at The Bicycle *weekly magazine, the rival publication to* Cycling, *had pictured us at Copford.*

At Great Totham outside The Bull pub our group is Gloria Short, John Dowding and Mick Wheeler, along with me on a Claud Butler track bike loaned by Tunbridge Road Cycles. No mudguards though! John was known for wearing peaked caps and industrial gloves and my cycling top is an ex-Army garment, all came in handy as it snowed, snowed and snowed.

Club in Foundry Lane. The organisers made sure there were plenty of indoor games to play at this bonding exercise of a weekday evening which brought lots of people into group sessions, much of that a rough-house from where I once went home with a reddened nose that stayed tender for some days. They called the game British Bulldog, one characterised by a physicality embodying even personal violence so intense that it was banned from many schools ten years of so later due to the many injuries to participants, or shall we call them victims! What I recall most is that the activities were based on boxing, rough and tumble scraps where mostly big-boy townies in groups scuffed up us outnumbered countryside-savvy kids. Even in this small town there were different cultures, the riverside games were different to farmyard activities, the town lads did have the Crouch mud and shingle but where we lived further out then doing things around hedgerows or in the two big woods near home was different, sometimes we played in the stackyard or in farm barns. The Boys Club numbers began to stack up when it was announced we'd have our own brick built sports hall on the Playing Fields, there was some fundraising to do before volunteer Tradesmen built it foundations up in concrete and bricks and the building became home to local youth groups, The Cub, Scouts and Sea Scouts and others like them. The town was now getting a community life back to make the long war years just a memory, one we all wanted to forget - but never those who'd died.

Sailing by - more than music

here's music to the ears: www.youtube.com/watch *link to "Sailing By" composed by Ronald Binge in 1963, here it is performed by the Alan Perry/William Gardner Orchestra. You can catch it around 00.45 immediately before the BBC radio's late night shipping forecast. I have a habit of listening to it through the week.*

Play the recording any time of day and you'll end up relaxed, by my score it's the best bit of music to hear before shut-eye and a wonderfully relaxing composition. The wave cruising tones from Ronald Binge's *Sailing By* preludes the BBC radio's late-night Shipping Forecast, something I regularly hear when listening to check what is being told about the weather. Somehow though the tune doesn't exactly match my vision of a tough trawler skipper swigging on hot black coffee, readying a pencil to take notes of coming weather patterns, but it does have the lilt of a boat's bow cresting gentle waves. Burnham-on-Crouch is at the shore of a salty flow of a river which at mid-tide runs very fast and is a tricky, challenging and competitive sailing arena for the boat fraternity, yet far away off the most northerly tip of the Western Isles the trawler skippers and the sailors in those seas have more need to know where anti-cyclones are about to happen.

  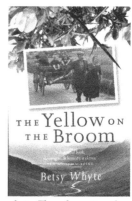

Books from John Hillaby and the wonderful story of Betsy Whyte are my beingThere favourites, the written words come with a cover pictures which invites you in to travel with the authors. Bringing places to life came with the local scenes depicted in the postcard work of J.Allen Cash from his Leica camera for "wish you were here" reminders people would send to friends and family to show bike, hike, travel and tourism is so much more rewarding when you are sharing that lifestyle.

Not everyone needs a page to make a point, this photo shows a mural on the wall of an electrical substation in the little town of Eidsvoll. Here on May 17, 1814 the Constitution of Norway was signed by the Norwegian Constituent Assembly. Clive Tully and I came back from the Rondane aboard the Skibladner, the side-wheeler (below) known locally as Mjøsas Hvite Svane, which translates as The White Swan Of Mjøsa. Here the world's oldest preserved paddle steamer in timetabled service was leaving for the return trip to Lillehammer.

Sometimes words we write don't please everyone. For one of our bicycling consumer magazine campaigns I asked that more care is given when passing a rider on the road, both the AA and the RAC supported us. EICMA loved it, shops in places such as Paris endorsed it, however voices in the CTC weren't so sure it was the message they wanted to see displayed in print.

The home waters of the River Crouch, once known as *Wholve* or *Huolve*, take your pick, are for fishermen, ferries and the sailing festivals that bring many people and a lot of business to the East Coast. In Burnham, the first of a series of competitive yachting contests took off in the late 1800's between London Sailing Club and The Royal Corinthian Yacht Club. When the Royal Burnham Yacht Club and the Crouch Yacht Club opened up things further it developed into an organised week of sailing. Burnham Week became the big event that ended the sailing and re-gatta season for those owners who would leave their boats moored to over-winter in mud berths or be lifted from the water all along Essex estuaries. Burnham town had the advantage of railway connections to London and all over, which helped secure more customers for traders, outfitters and yachting businesses in the town, the local workers toiled on a lot of refitting work that came their way for the darker months of the year. The boatyards had a high level of storage capacity too, and all sorts of craft sat out of the water on support blocks just waiting to be worked on by the yard owners. I wonder how many of them or the unsuspecting boat owners knew just how many Burnham lads courting their girl friends through the longer and darker evenings found things more comfortable when spending time in the cosy cabin of a parked up motor cruiser or yacht. Don't ask!

A lot of super sailors and magnificent boats came into local waters and one famed vessel to race on the River Crouch was *Bluebottle,* the 1948 Dragon Class racing yacht presented as a wedding gift at the marriage of HRH Princess Elizabeth to the Duke of Edinburgh. Prince Phillip liked that boat, but he didn't apparently so much like the River Crouch and expressed that view at a Burnham Week reception that it was *"rather like racing in a ditch".* Over time *Bluebottle* had plenty of suc-cess, in 1956 that included the Melbourne Olympics where her crew won Bronze. The Dragon yacht class originated in Sweden as an affordable cruiser before 1930, and today the type still is built. *Bluebottle* herself is berthed on loan from the Duke of Edinburgh at the National Maritime Museum at Falmouth in Cornwall and is often seen crewed atop light weather waves in full racing rig. During his time away from helming the country Prime Minister Ted Heath was racing *Morning Cloud III* and whilst wearing Henri Lloyd neoprenes won Burnham Week in 1972. Ted Heath was a top ranked sailor, having won the southern ocean Sydney to Hobart Yacht Race sailing the first of the five race boat he commissioned. In 1979 he got badly beaten up in the Fastnet yacht race that saw eighteen deaths and involved around 4,000 people in what is known as the biggest rescue any time outside of war. The Fastnet of that year will always be remembered as a time when yachtsmen and their rescuers together fought to the death in a harsh war with the elements. Someone who also knew about rough seas was the first person to single handed sail around the world yet hadn't always had happy times at Burnham. Sir Francis Chichester once described his famed Gypsy Moth as *"cantankerous"* after having run aground in the River Crouch and then had to abandon his kedge anchor he'd used to prise the yacht off a mudbank. Others were not being cantankerous at the time he famously managed to upset locals at Sparkes', the Station Road butcher. The ladies who had patiently waited in the queue asked him to display better manners as he'd tried to step in front of them to do some provisioning for his boat's galley. Rebuked by one of the regular customers who said *"Oi, get to the back"* it apparently didn't quite register with the sailing knight and his retort was *"don't you know who I am?"* It's legend that Doris Martin smartly told him *"it don't matter who you are around here mate, there's still a queue so you'd better get to the back."* Cowed, he relented and it was rumoured he bought one small lamb chop and four sausages.

The local boatbuilding yards have been very successful in creating craft that are quick through the water, the yacht that brought Ben Ainslie huge Olympic success was built at the Stebbings yard at the end of Belvedere Road in Burnham. With his favourite *Rita,* Ben Ainslie stands as the most successful sailor in Olympic history, from 1996 to 2012 four gold medals and a silver from five editions of the Games. In 2013, he received a knighthood from the Queen for services to sport. Next door to Stebbings' the P.Newall Petticrow marine engineering enterprise was ahead of the game with a feathering propeller for fitting to cruisers and yachts so they could more efficiently sail in races with very minimal drag on their speed through the water. Without getting my hands dirty in an engineering plant I still got close to that project myself, that happened at Bay Read's Crouch Press printing shop in Station Road when I worked on the brochure distributed to visitors at the mid 1950's London Boat Show. I know the family still has one of those brochures and it's so very much an historical document, Crouch Cycling Club member Les Martin worked on and had input in this pioneering project for racing yachts. The Petticrow's yard was one of the several riverside yacht businesses and suppliers that contributed to Burnham being the real hive of skilled activity which sustained the local boatbuilding and allied industries. Sailmakers had their lofts where smooth polished floors were often covered by big mainsails and spinnakers being cut for yachts and dinghies, and knowingly sewn to catch each and every whisp of the zephys signalled by the little mast top flag known as the fly. It'd take more than a light breeze to balloon a spinnaker but when the boat had a full one then didn't that make the boat bow cream through the water! Not all the boat workshops were on the nearside bank of the river, though and if you were near William Kings boatyard at noonish or the close of work time you'd hear a klaxon bellowing to the other shore that their work time was up so a spell of down tools. A lady came out onto the townside jetty at Kings and cranked around and around with one hand the handle of heavy klaxon she held in the other. It was something similar to the barman ringing the bell in a pub and calling last orders, but a damn sight louder and a much more ear-drum penetrating bellow. It also needed a lot more sinew and muscle.

These photographs from my cycling album tells the story of how the local scenery has changed. At the road junction by The Ford Garage business in Althorne stand Tony Crickmore, Mick Wheeler and myself with John Dowding. This was called "Ford's Corner." In Burnham the entrance to Mildmay Lane has changed quite beyond recognition, gone also is the foundry where they worked with molten metal and produced things like piano frames. In this picture are Clive Jennings, Tony, Brian Robinson and Mick Wheeler.

In many ways this really has to be where my writing career began, my first full-time job came within days of skipping out of Maldon Grammar School three days past my 15th birthday. My release from the lesson routine there came through a letter from my mother which she was unaware had been written. The signature I forged as well. My parents were not exactly over the moon about that I can admit, but there was a job waiting for me at the offices of the weekly, more or less hand-produced Burnham on Crouch and Dengie Hundred Advertiser, *which the locals called* The Rag. *From a world steeped in letterpress this is where the path began, leading me to working with a camera and the pen in bike, hike, travel and tourism, along with business reporting. Sixty-five years on it's still the thing I cheerfully do with enthusiasm.*

March 1953

Why not a Cycling Club?

To the Editor

Sir,—May I, through the columns of your paper, appeal to any cycle-minded persons living in the district who might be interested in the forming of a cycle-club?

For a few years from 1929 onwards a club, named the Crouch Cycling Club, existed in Burnham. Every week the club met to discuss and arrange the run for that particular week-end. About 30 members took part in these club runs which were also arranged for Easter and other Bank Holidays.

In Burnham alone there are quite a few "lone wolf" cyclists who go off at the week-end to "potter" about and enjoy themselves awheel. Many of these, I am sure, would welcome the company which exists in club life.

Some cyclists do not join a club because they think they would be unable to make the pace—this is not so, a club's riding speed is governed by the slowest member. Others who think their present machine is unsuitable are wrong, an "ultra lightweight" is not an essential. Packed sandwiches will help defray the cost of a day's run, which never exceeds five shillings.

Club cycling is popular mainly because of the company, but organisation is always well done and variations of route may always be forwarded for consideration by the club leader, a member who has been elected by the committee, and whose job it is to lead the run.

Any persons who are interested in helping to form this club, or who are would-be members, should advise me by post or verbally as soon as possible.

PETER R. LUMLEY
3 March Road, Burnham.

This letter appearing in the Burnham Advertiser on the 21-3-53 was later

9   getting into print

It is telling to recall that my reading about the family's shared moments in time would became the groundwork for my life and how I would later work for a living. Those additions to the family's collection of ink or pencil writings in little books helped my first reading sessions, these came from Nan or my mother. At first my scribbling was on slates they used in the cow milking parlour, easy to wipe clean the mis-shapen sentences and wrongly spelt words: *"so write it again, Peter"*. It was rather like the classroom blackboard and a teacher with their chalk, but far less dusty. This was the way I was taught, learning by example and I guess this was the starting point where I began wanting to be a writer, to write and write more. Imagining, experiencing, investigating little things and bigger ones around the place can swell in the mind and excite the heart, then wanting more and understanding it well enough to shape words on paper. In many periods of hospitalisation in Chelmsford & Essex General I found it really was a necessity to get into letter writing mode, there was no phone in our home after all and it was this letter writing that probably honed what was to develop as my preferred way of communicating: putting feelings into words and on to paper. Nowadays mostly the seeing it first on a screen in front of you is the way but not always, I have notebooks as my constant companion and one of them is by my left side now even as I tap the keyboard, that osteomyelitis altered me from having been born right handed, by the way. You will have heard about hoarders, well I hoard notebooks and quite often I come to entries in one I have taken from a box and that jogs the thought process, the memory lane reminder of stuff telling of beingThere, talking to someone, hearing things. Notebooks and paper, pencil or pen, this writing idea has been all around us for a very long time and this octogenarian just couldn't live without getting words onto the page. Which is what I was doing earlier this morning and was doing yesterday, something which had become a habit with me before I had left school and then joined a newspaper and printing company.

There was more than a little meaning in what I was being taught to do at Dilliway's and on the *Burnham-on-Crouch and Dengie Hundred Advertiser.* This was the opening of a career which would grow through the words, more words, the pictures taken then more words written. Possibly this was a brave move then, perhaps a deceitful way for a son to take on a job so much earlier than parents had anticipated, but this Burnham boy had been sure his working full-time would open opportunities to get out and about to explore and test and try ideas. For sure, it is not everything that works out quite as hoped, hiccups happen, but I guess that when you want things hard enough, and work at it, then by the very law of averages there must be things that are going to work. Without bragging I can claim a fair share of winnings, one big reward coming when sitting with mum and dad at their council flat, aptly named Dilliway Court by the way, first occupants of the new-build property on the site where Burnham Gas Works once stood. As they unwrapped that first book I authored, one in the *Teach Yourself* series, I remember my dad turning the book back and front a couple of times, taking in the cover picture of me standing above Monsal Dale in Derbyshire, not saying much until he flicked to the photos inside then looked at me, saying *"this looks a lot of fun, this walking about and camping job you've got. Is it better than your cycling?"* A good question I could ponder right now, yet the two recreational habits are part of the outdoor lifestyle that makes it so good to enjoy beingThere. I doubt you'd ever find anyone, anywhere, who wouldn't enjoy taking a walk or riding a bicycle and being rewarded for the involvement. I have got really lucky being able to make it to the next mile or over the next stile, and know I've found a niche that's provided a really satisfying and lasting way to live.

To go take a walk is a way of life that's given me some great times shared with super people, as with Derrick Booth. He actually took that photo used on the cover of *Teach Yourself Backpacking,* and Mike Marriott, he'd inspired me to pull on heavy Scarpa boots and start walking. Together we founded The Backpackers Club in 1972 and the Durdle Door front cover of a *Backpackers Guide* annual I was striding along the Dorset Coast with Mike Marriott. Dennis Noble, first secretary of Backpackers Club helped me cross England coast to coast and every step of the way on our own two feet. A year later we did the same thing in Scotland, except there was a short bus ride to go to the pub for dinner that wasn't cooked on a Primus petrol stove. Ken Ward, pioneer of Footpath Touring and the original Lord Winston of Walking Tours fame, he opened my eyes to things in the Britain's countryside which made all the difference to the day, and more days than I can count now. These are just some of the people who've helped me step forward along the walking side of my life, and that makes these guys so very special. All of us, though, we were doing this for the readers who'd be trusting us to point a way they could go.

The first edition of *TY Backpacking* sold out and was reprinted, written as a how-to manual from the standpoint of beingThere and learning. When the third printing was offered I reckoned that in the light of product development some text changes should be made, but they couldn't be done to the publishing budget so

With cycling friends I would feast on the
exploits we could only read about but
then it happened in London and we'd
watch continental stars competing with
British riders. Although it's a long time
since they rode and raced their bicycles,
every day I have them at my elbow in my
writing den. It was at Herne Hill when I
photographed Fausto Coppi on his Bianchi, in the background is Shay Elliott with
one of the Burgess twins. Brian Robinson
was racing there that same day, a British
rider who not only made history on the
road but also become a national treasure.
He has been actively engaged in the
Yorkshire cycling scene as the county has
developed an international racing flavour
which draws not just spectators from afar
but people who follow the racing on tv.

On a visit to Milan I met Gino Bartali at
an EICMA show, after talking together
through the very essential interpreter on
my part, he autographed the big picture
that's on my wall here. It's one big and
real treasure!

When in 1952 us Burnham lads,
Tony Crickmore and myself
pedalled around East Anglia that
same year Fausto Coppi was
pedalling to his win in the Tour
de France. Inspired by that it was
1953 when Crouch Cycling Club
became the reality, Fausto Coppi
become the World Road Race
Champion, Mount Everest would
be climbed and our Queen was
crowned. More good news was
that sweet rationing ended too!

no third printing happened. I was told that the book sold 60,000 copies and as the introduction to backpacking in the UK it worked to promote awareness, practice and product that people could use to do their own thing. Today it reads as a book of the time and on page 118 for instance it is on Ventile, it also mentions cold fingers can be a nuisance and that wool socks, a wool base layer or balaclava hat keep you snug. *"Don't wear jeans or cotton based clothing . . and if you do then don't expect to be anything but cold when you get wet"*. That book I wrote was based on the enjoyable backpacking being experienced, on a freedom to go do it your way, today some make sure that technicalities and people-posturing dilutes the fun, when you look around it's not difficult to fetch up on stuff from authors worryingly dictatorial about the way you must do things to be happy. It seems a lot of the scribes don't have a clue on how to straighten a bent tent peg, nor stay snug and dry when a lot of wet is abroad, yet that tell you to do it *this way*. A really enjoyable thing about back-packing, also about cycling for that matter, is that just leaving the house and getting to do it from right then is the start to being somewhere pleasing: there's always a start time but then the trick is to keep it going. It's not what you've got that matters, it is just what you do with it that counts!

It's a realisation I began my working life in a newspaper office before the litho method would become more universal in printing offices even though it had been around since 1796 after German author and actor Alois Senefelder used it as a cheap method of publishing theatrical works. Litho gradually shouldered aside the letterpress printing style born of Johanes Gutenberg in 1439, the first European to use a printing press and movable type when publishing his iconic Gutenberg Bible. This first major work marked the very beginning for the age of knowledge through the printing process. Of that book just forty-eight copies, some not quite complete portions, survive today: they are all considered to be among the most highly valued books in the world and no copy has changed hands for over half a century. The publishing which Gutenberg did was truly the dawn of the species, and for every book, any pamphlet, leaflet or page that's read, we all owe it to him and to his press time he put into doing the job. In the Britain of 1476 it was William Caxton who took the art of printing forward, his system of awareness and personal learning is something that has helped everyone share knowledge and understanding ever since. Without those two doing their bit and others sharing the workload of getting it all underway and fully used, there'd be no printing of books and the like as we know it today. We shouldn't even begin to ponder what life would be like without paper and printing, and don't even bother to give electronic media ideas a second thought in the durability stakes. Keeping with the printed word is the only reliable, durable and sustainable way of making sure fact, fiction or anything else that matters can be around for future generations to hold, read and study. OK, there is one alternative you can trust, use Oak Gall ink and slowly pen the message on vellum, write it well and legibly though. Kings, Queens and Parliament have confirmed it really works! Relying on electronic registration and collation may well be ok for now but what of the future as computers could represent only a short-term solution. Humanity has come a long way from their original painting images in cave sessions or chipping the message in stone, or inscribing on a wood and wax tablet those Vindolanda messages which intrigue us two thousand years later. In my life though, printing the words and pictures on paper is something coming as a matter of course.

The 1951 act of getting a job marks the true beginning of my career in the communications business when I stepped into that near Dickensian world of newspapers and printing in the company founded by Ebernezer Dilliway on Station Road, Burnham. That first full-time job was at the offices of the weekly, more or less hand-produced, *Burnham on Crouch and Dengie Hundred Advertiser,* the one the locals called *The Rag.* Certainly William Caxton would have felt not so far from home, looking at some of the working practices, hand presses and equipment my apprenticeship had me using. Since that fifties time I have worked nowhere other than where words to be read is the output, and that has ensured I have lived from the most rewarding of jobs on the planet: yes, I've heard that Caxton added notes to his works, explicitly complaining that often his pen was worn and *"mine hand heavy, mine eyes even dimmed"* which I reckon is so very much the same for all those engaged in writing. Midnight oil burning and note making can still the hour, stop time, even if it is not showing thus on the hands of a clock. In my den I have a time-piece that when its battery isn't flat, show the minute and the hour hands going backwards: that means I can always manage for time to show earlier at the finish of something than when I actually began!

In Burnham, once away from school things kinda just happened I guess, during those first years at Dilliway's I just got used to have a few more coppers to spend. Mistakenly part of my first pay-packet bought twenty Senior Service from Rumbles the Barbers next door. I coughed on the one I'd lit and gave away the other nineteen to Bert Blunden, one of the people teaching me the trade. Next week it was ten cigarettes bought, nine given away. That means other than cigarettes bought to give to friends or family on special occasions I have never since contributed to the Government's cigarette taxes. For me, smoking and riding a bike were simply not compatible. Work at the *Burnham on Crouch & Dengie Hundred Advertiser* brought me the sum of £1.10shillings for a week of work - today that's £1.50. Terms of my apprenticeship promised a yearly increment of 5 shillings (25p.) for the next five years. For some reason myself and the men in the company began work at 7am, broke for a 45minute breakfast slot from 8am and were then joined before 9am by the lady workers. There was all of a full hour for lunch, work closed at 5pm - but maybe it was at six? The working week included Saturday mornings, although it was noticed that a couple of the team were not in the place when Ramblers Football Club were playing an away match. The bosses' privilege!

Upstairs over the stationery shop and newspaper front office was where words were shaped together one little piece of lead type joined letter by letter by the compositor. We worked with founders type, the little upright lead letters that brought about the saying *"26 soldiers of lead."* Yes, print is powerful! Actually there are more than 26 letters in the printer set picked from little letter-separating boxes of the two trays. The upper wood case has capital letters and other special little symbols and fractions. It would sit angled away from you, and is the upper of the two trays. Upper case! The lower little set of boxes of the tray is directly at your front as you pick out the type of ordinary letters with a difference being the size of the separate compartments take account of there being a lot of some letters like *"e"* and *"s"* used in words. The setting of type is a little more complicated than just picking up the tiny pieces of lead: you do that right handed, then locate it in the composing stick, the line of type has to be spaced tightly to the row, all this making up the line of words that will be read. Each line must be tightened and to do this you can alter the non-printing lead spaces, using clumps and reglets and ems, nuts and hair spaces sometimes. Every line composed must be as taut as otherwise the loose ones will fall from the forme or galley before printing making the whole sense of the lines fall apart.

Being a compositor is a job of skill and technical ability, you have to get it right so others can get it read. Amongst the little tricks the composing type had more than just letters of the alphabet and symbols, there were also real gems like an *"fi"* and a *"ffi"* cast as the one letter. There is single spacing between the words but for paragraph openings we'd use a mutton - equal to three single spaces. There was also the two-singles nut, with word spacing first tried with "normal" ones or by using "hair" space widths to get everything taut. Yes, a technical skill, allied to knowing how a word break will work or not work, and exactly where to place the hyphen. This is the way we'd work for most of the week putting stories and announcements into the hand-held metal composing stick set at a column width to suit the pages of *The Rag*. The massed rows of type that had been composed were slotted onto a galley for the first proof-reading. After that the hours of fiddly manipulation of little pieces of type the mass would come together in a forme. This is the heavy binding metal framework that's lifted to the bed of the printing machine so that impressions

Over breakfast in the Lofoton willage of Reine it seemed quite a good idea, over five hours later we were sure all the effort had been worthwhile. Tony Oliver built our Lapland mountain bikes, beingThere and looking on the sea encircled mountains, was worth every struggle. The bike enjoyed it too!

there's been a lot of miles under my wheels in Norway, beingThere with John Potter (above) in Fjiord country, then Lapland with Tony Oliver and a Lofoten trip lasting over five weeks, for a lot of the time far offroad.

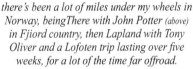

the Norwegian guide tells Dave Brown and Nigel Moore they'll enjoy a stroll on Sulitjelma König, here above the Arctic Circle in west Norway. They did!

can be rolled out, in our case on a stop cyclinder Wharfedale press. One sheet at a time Bert Blunden would feed in the newspaper sized sheets, automatically these wrapped around the rotating cyclinder so that the inked type imprinted the paper to be delivered by a set of wooden stick flyers that deposited it into a holding tray. My job was to pull the print into place so it was neatly stacked for the next part of the task, when the other side of the paper was also printed. The two of us on that Wharfedale machine had taken a blank sheet of paper and processed it into the *Rag*, a newspaper that'd be delivered and read all around the Dengie Hundred, certainly even further away too. Then less than a week into the paper's life it was old news, there'd be another *Rag* taking its place so why not now stuff last week's newspaper inside damp Wellington boots, help light the kitchen fire or even use it to wrap fish and chips, although that's now banned! There is so much you can do with discarded newsprint, I have always suggested tenters and caravanners have a little pile inside their entrance to use as a doormat which soaks up the damp from footwear. For the backpacker, pages of a newspaper become an effective method of combatting condensation and we all know that a sheet or two of the stuff inside a racing jersey helps keep a descending bike racer from chilling. As to being used as a fish and chip wrapper, no longer allowed yet a month or two back when I bought a supper of Britain's favourite snack at the chippie it came across the counter in a container emblazoned all over with newsprint images. Ah, the old days do come back!

If you want to visit a similar near Dickensian workplace to where I started out, today you can see almost the very same one in Beamish Museum at Stanley in County Durham and just three miles from where I now live. Brought to the museum from the *Sunderland Echo* office the Wharefedale printing press and the proofing press used, like so very much as in Caxton's times, reveal to the newspaper reader what the compositor and the machineminder did in their work time. At Dilliway's in the winter time we'd wear an overcoat and scarf with fingerless gloves. There was a coke stove but all the heat went straight to the brick tile roof, which unlined gave no insulation against outdoor temperatures. Forget when it was a bit warm, you could handle that, but on real winter days we'd even have snowflakes fluttering down. You suffered a bit of damp when it rained hard, too! As I put it, these were *"near Dickensian"* working conditions, truth is it was here I gained so much discipline, essential learning and the groundwork for how I work in publishing today. It was certainly a worthwhile appprenticeship.

10 scratching a cycling itch

Learning how to ride a bicycle started for me on the short stretch of road between our Dammerwick home and Pannel's Brook bridge, soon I'd encounter a swathe of stinging nettles as a solo pedal pushing session went awry. Up to then my dad had held the saddle and trotted with me, now I'd quickly discovered that staying upright on wheels takes a certain skill: but once learned it stays with you forever, nice! For all that you will fall off your bicycle at some time or other and losing control of my Moulton AM7 in Epernay brought a lower back injury which persists to the point where it pained me even this very morning: and that trip through France to Bodensee was six years ago. Gravel rash cures, joints just ache, surgeons can fettle, and when back home this was an offer but as I'd already done my hospital spell when a kid I said no thanks for the moment.

Within a little over the year of my first pedalling a bike on Marsh Road I'd ride with my dad to visit an uncle halfway across the Dengie Hundred. It'd be a five miles or so each way ride and from home we passed St Mary's Church, Bullfinch Corner with Lord's Wood just a field away on the left, past the Rose & Crown pub and through Southminster to go down and up the winding hilly bit at Asheldham towards Tillingham. The stumpy water tower at the Asheldham bends showed signs from the wrath of a Messerschmitt or possibly a Heinkel pilot, my dad pointing out the bullet pock marks indenting the red brick tower. My uncle Arthur lived by the village green in front of the church, here a criss-cross of macadam pathway quarters the grass making the scene which would be the backdrop in a tobacco company's

A tea break for two of us at Crouch Press. Along with John Rickwood another staffer was Nick Perkins, who became my close cycling buddy. They both did National Service in the Forces but left me at home so I could play war games and parade with the local Home Guard contingent. That was fun and especially as I was given Major Wilson's full written authority so that I never had to salute anyone, anywhere, of any rank, at any time! And I got to firing machine guns and rifles on occasions.

advertising shot with Reg Harris the World Champion track cyclist. A dozen or so years after this first visit to Tillingham I was back there with others featuring in our own cycling photographs, recording the first ever Tramps Run of Crouch Cycling Club. We'd been in the Cap & Feathers pub for a quick drink and then came the silly photos session where John Dowding did double exposure tricks, perhaps he had drunk too much? The snaps show a set of ghostly figures posing on the green and the photo of Mick Wheeler reminds me of Captain Mainwaring in Dad's Army, the BBC television sitcom about the British Home Guard during the Second World War. Broadcast on the BBC from 1968 to 1977 it ran for nine series and eighty episodes in total, you'll probably find it showing on one tv channel or another this very week, possibly even today! It has become one of the truly Classic sitcoms and we all get fun and pleasure watching actor Arthur Lowe perform, but sadly in 1982 his life ended with him laying alone in hospital following a stroke suffered in the dressing room of a Birmingham theatre, he was 66 years old. Switch on a Dad's Army film and they come into your time so very much alive, stomping across bits of Norfolk heathland as the credits roll.

Here perhaps I should make a confession, Crouch Cycling Club also has connections with the real Home Guard and that began on the evening assigned to collect the gift of a grand piano for their club Hall in Station Road. With a lot of effort needed to shift that piano from Belvedere Road the lads and girls thought that as I had arranged it then surely I ought be in on the action. I went AWOL, sorry, as on that very evening I'd been told to muster with the local Home Guard contingent having just that week been enlisted by Doctor Wilson. He had been in the Royal Medical Corps during the war and who now headed up a gang of Burnham's khaki clad volunteers. It would all become a lot of fun for a lad who'd been denied a place in the regular army on National Service conscription, and missed going with other Burnham lads into hot jungle places like Burma and shooting at people who were not liked. Neither was I given the chance to parade at BAOR army barracks in Germany either, as did the Essex Regiment band drummer Peter Bowton who had been a workmate at Dillway's before his call up. At about the same time John Rickwood would serve the whole of his National Service time in the Regiment's Brentwood barracks, mostly as an Officers' bar and restaurant orderly, he told me. At the Crouch Press I worked with John along with Nicky Perkins, who wore khaki except when was riding his bike when on service in Germany. They all agreed I'd done well to avoid the tricky bit of sliding a concert piano down a doorway wide passageway to the Crouch Club's meeting Hall, they also thought my joining the Home Guard was something else. It had me out on war game exercises with the Territorial Army types, throwing grenades and firing small arms in tune with the

We'd enjoy good company on Crouch CC clubruns and at hostel weekends, *(left)* Judy Little was from South Fambridge where her father ran the pub, later on she would become an air hostess then feature in films. Barbara Hext lived at the Post Office in Latchingdon, there her father was village postmaster, she was one of the support team helping to organise and run Club events.

This picture from the photo album was taken at Hadleigh Castle, Dennis De'Ath is on the left with Kathy Duke, Dorothy Philpott, Gloria Short, a lad from the Spencer family is on the right. Sitttng in the foreground are Tony Crickmore, Bryan Gallant and someone not recognised, sorry. Day rides for the Club tended to stay within Essex county borders for a lot of the year although as more riding fitness was attained and daylight hours lengthened then so did the mileages rise .

Colchester Garrison soldiers, guys who were happy to show us how. The standard .303 rifle was quite different to my air rifle or the .22 I used to frighten rabbits, but that Bren gun was fun and with an element of mastery, lucky accuracy even, I fell in danger of getting a one stripe. That meant I might be promoted to the rank of Lance Jack, however, my right elbow problem had earned special *"excused duties"* status from Major Wilson and in the end that promotion wasn't going to happen as I was quite unable to salute anyone properly, anywhere and at any time.

Judging by the medal ribbons being worn a lot of saluting should have been the formality on the evening we got inside the perimeter of the Wethersfield USAAF, a complex opened in 1944 as a bomber base. It had been closed after the hostilities ended in 1946 but in 1951 re-opened as a result of the Cold War, we were on station to learn cold war stuff, which we were expecting would happen but there was much more than a certain menace in the brass hat's voice when he told us *"you will all die."* It was a very dark night, we couldn't see too much of the secret bits around the place before being shepherded into a big hangar at the base and shown how to miss getting shot in the heat of the moment. But only providing we did as instructed. The way to rescue a pilot from a crashed plane was plain and to the point: watch your step and *"always approach from the wing tip ends, that way you will avoid being in the line of fire if their guns start up, accidently or otherwise . . "* All so very re-assuring of course but the man in the uniform took us even closer into an orbit of fear as he elaborated how we would be deployed when the hostile Russian invaders parachuted onto the Dengie Hundred and Burnham Marshes. This was the cold war era, remember, and the much-ribboned American played it big and strong and so very clinical with his portrayal of impending battle that he clearly believed would become the real thing *"it is your job to be there in position to welcome the Russians to Britain"* he told us Home Guard guys, *"you must shoot at them to show they are neither invited nor welcome. When the Russians land you will all be killed of course, but soon after that your Territorial Army friends will arrive to hold the ground as best they can. A lot of them will be killed before us Americans pile in to send Ruskie packing back to their homeland."* It really was entertaining stuff and I have to admit I felt so proud dressed in the British Tommy khaki, surrounded by gum chewing Americans and even being told I would not live very long once I was in battlefield action. *Wow!* The Yanks would then save things as they would get the measure of Russia, we just got on with things, assumed it was not likely to happen, in fact it was beginning to seem all a bit Hollywood here in Essex surrounded by America military types: inside ten years of course there would be the big Cuban showdown and as the world wondered what next. In October 1962 the American president John F. Kennedy and Nikita Khrushchev stoically waited for the other one to blink, behind them in the wings waited stuff for the nuclear showdown. Luckily it all got sorted out which was good news seeing by this time our Home Guard had been stood down, we'd handed in our rifles and put corks on the sharp bits of hay forks so were no longer having fun on training exercises. It was good the Cuban fuse was snuffed out, after all it saved us being late on parade to help get matters settled, that is before we all got killed of course.

Like a lot in Burnham and around we were getting on with doing things that really mattered and getting about on bicycles was growing in popularity, one annual club outing was that Tramps Run which became the way we'd celebrate Christmas with a different line in revelry. It goes down in the Club's annals as the time we'd put on fancy dress, cycle to a pub for a drink and once inside do a quick swallow before riding on to the next pub! The Boxing Day round always took more pedalling time than we had for quaffing, but a sobering thought is just how far the group of riders would get in the short midday opening hours during which landlords could legally pull a pint. For the rest of the year the Club was getting around Essex quite a lot, we'd venture into the neighbouring counties and generally attract the right sort of following to build the local cycling culture. From memory I recall this as a no-pressure period although just about everything you needed to buy was in short supply, and so was the money! I'd guess Crouch Cycling Club came about because bike riding was a good way of sharing things and doing it despite quite meagre resources other than ingenuity. This was the way of life amongst people I got to know in my hometown as I grew up, we needed to make the most of opportunities so worked between ourselves to broaden friendships around the local communities. That's probably why the cycling habit was getting a good following from the day our club was founded but actually it was less the founding but more my finding when scanning pages in archived copies of *The Burnham on Crouch & Dengie Hundred Advertiser* newspaper where I worked. The reports described tours and events enjoyed by members of a Crouch Cycling Club active during the mid-'30s. What they described for their cycling times was so very much in the pattern of my going on trips and tours with Tony Crickmore, and that brought me to write a letter *"to the editor"* at *The Rag* asking if anyone would like to come and share the cycling experience. The plea drew the responses where people turned up, they rode with us, raced with us then in 2018 the Crouch Cycling Club reached the grand milestone of 65 years continuous bicycling activity since the founding, having an appropriate name change 50 years back to help gain members from the wider catchment area with it becoming Maldon & District CC. It was great to be there that evening.

It's Sunday lunchtime and what else would you want to do other than ride an Old Ordinary cycle at Canvey Island. On the left is Les Martin, giving a push from behind is Nick Perkins and trying to help Mick Wheeler balance on the saddle is Tony Crickmore. It's all obviously a lot of fun because others also tried their hand and that amused onlookers too!

Derek Bacon and his wife on the roadside at a club time trial with, probably, Dorothy Philpott holding her babe in arms. Derek Bacon was the first chairman of the Crouch Cycling Club in 1953.

The original membership card was printed at the Dilliway's office with a bicycle logo found in their printing stock!

Dekko the candle! One of the Chittenden lads from Southminster tinkles on the ivories at the Crouch CC hq. Molly Richmond with Barbara Hext and Nick Perkins put in a relaxed rendition although I suspect that Nick could be warming his hands as there was no stove for heating. The Hall did come rent free from Mr M. George, though.

It's easy these years later to forget that in 1953 Britain wasn't big into the cycle race scene, Tony Crickmore and myself talked about happenings in France and other places where cyclists did their thing, in 1952 Fausto Coppi won both the Giro d'Italia and the Tour de France so it was mainly this Italian rider who inspired us although it is fair to say that neither of us had ever seen a Bianchi bike painted in the Celeste colour that is the trademark of the maker. In Burnham even before the local newspaper carrying my letter had hit the streets others were asking for more news, I'd quickly found backers for the Club idea with the local sports enthusiast Bert Hawes helping with sponsorship and Maurice George, the owner of Carter Yachting Stores, ready to give us sole use of his large pavilion Hall at the rear of 59 Station Road. It took only a short time for the Club to become fully formalised, Mr George was asked to be the first Club president and the events programme began almost straight away. People who had been cyclists with the earlier Burnham club joining our quite brash and young group and from the peers we adopted the original Crouch CC shield shaped badge. Helping me, my dad's sister Eve gave me a Club badge and my uncle's original pre-war black Alpaca jacket which time trial riders famously once had to wear. Time trial rules were that long sleeves could be rolled up to just below, but not above, the elbow, and long black tights were legitimate wear as long as they stretched to the ankles. Only a small maker's logo should be visible on the bicycle frame, trade publicity was not allowed, no Trade connection and certainly no race numbers were to be worn. On crossing the finishing line the rider had to shout their name, so save some breath fellas, and all race courses were known only by a number. Derek Bacon became our first chairman, a full daughter complement of the Short family joined and Gloria was our treasurer, there were Spencers and a Robinson, a Beard and a Rees. My first post was being the Club secretary and supported by a lot more than just the names recalled here. Burnham people were joined by members coming from Southminster and Latchingdon and other local places, the long standing MADcc president John Philpott was originally a Diss & District CC man coming to live in Burnham. Riding tandem with Doris after a visit to Suffolk he was hijacked on Latchingdon's main street and asked if he would join the Crouch, they both did and the rest is history.

Socially that grand piano became something of attraction in our Club hall, now refitted back onto its ornate and bulky legs that had been unscrewed to thread the mahogany box and its tuneful ivory bits down that narrow passageway from the road. It became a well used feature on Club evenings, inspired ivory bashing by Mick Wheeler and others showed that musical talent abounded in the Club. Once, when Crouch riders stopped in Stisted Church for a look around All Saints Church the organist and the vicar encouraged Mick to try his hand at the church organ, and he played *Sugar Bush*. It's a number recorded by Frankie Lane and Doris Day which, music charted in 1952, also had the distinction of being sung for HM The Queen by Eve Boswell. On their touring and weekend cycle rides the Crouch club met other clubs and people with similar interests which enhanced our sharing the experiences and hearing what was going on in wider circles. Cycling was coming over as good-news, we'd celebrated Ian Steel from Glasgow becoming the first and only English speaker to ever win the Warsaw-Berlin-Prague race, a year on from when he had triumphed in the Tour of Britain. The hard Eastern European classic he won was known as the Peace Race and it had taken place as us Burnham lads and lasses were beginning to make war on the convention of being told what to do. We were striving to make our young lives as independent as hell so it happened we didn't go asking very much permission of anyone, really. Our first programmes of Sunday club-runs caught on with mostly in their teens locals wanting to see what taking off on their own was about. People who had done little more than a few short trips locally, round the villages or to the shops, now they would join a Sunday run to clock up forty and more miles on the rides to places other Burnham folk normally visited rarely, if at all. This was when thos occasional trips for towns people of parent-age were organised by social clubs and the likes, when church followers and darts club people alike would go off for their day of fun and leave the younger generation to their own devices. I know about that because my parents occasionally disappeared for a day out in one of Fords of Althorne's coach trips with friends: it wasn't that we were envious but later we even tried that idea ourselves once, a day trip by bus to Great Yarmouth: but only the once! Come 1954 some of us cycled to Great Yarmouth, five of us came out of Burnham cinema just before ten at night and on the spur of the moment decided it'd be a great idea to see next morning's opening stage of the *Daily Express* Tour of Britain. The long night ride was interrupted at Ipswich by a night patrol policeman, on his bike and wearing a short cape. He asked what we were doing, us sitting under a lit road-sign having a sandwich. I guess he didn't believe our tale but come later that morning we'd be tucking into a big fried breakfast before being amongst the throng at the beach side waving off the riders in the bike race. Our club treasurer Gloria Short was especially smitten by the Ellis Briggs rider Brian Robinson riding in a team that included the previous winner Ken Russell, Eugene Tamburlini of France would be overall winner of this round Britain race and on the final stage on to the summit of Alexandra Palace in London the Club was among the cheering crowd seeing Essex rider Dave Bedwell win the sprint to the line. The big national newspaper story about him was that in his jersey pocket his road feed was always a sweet rice pudding his mother had baked.

The Sunday rides went mostly further into East Anglia or across to the

Alex Moulton changed the face of the cycling scene with his innovative small wheel machines, Jack Lautterwasser was building wheels for Moulton bikes when he was over 90 years old and he is also remembered as the man who won two Olympic medals in the same bike race.

" FOLLOW THAT CAR ! "

Hertfordshire border, when most times at a lunchtime stop we'd play crazy golf, hire a boat to row, as at Flatford Mill, drink Mackeson Shandy to slake a thirst and be home in time for late tea. Always we were visiting ancient monuments and churches or daring ourselves to bow-wave our wheels through fords or climbing castle ramparts, building a collage of touristy photos along the way. In number terms, after just a few weeks in our first season the enthusiastic following had grown to over thirty riders joining a day away from Burnham and you can believe it that a group of that size didn't go un-noticed by other road users. Funny how car drivers even back then in the 1950s made their view known that they thought roads were built only for them, but wrong! For touring weekends and our multi-day trips we'd go away as members of the Youth Hostel Association, stretching our only small wages by staying at their accommodation offer which meant us meeting a lot of new people and friends, extending the range of the distances we could go in our time away. Some would ride out to a hostel on a Friday evening, although most could only start away Saturday afternoon as a sixth working day in the week was very much the norm. The hostels favoured mostly took about three or so hours pedalling to get there, Houghton Mill in Huntingdonshire, near St Ives was one; we'd go to Nazeing by the Hertfordshire border, or Cambridge which often felt just a little too urban but was handy, we liked the old barn at High Roding whereas at Saffron Walden there was a peach of an ancient half-timbered YHA hostel nestled in a street close to the Parish church of Saint Mary the Virgin. Reckoned to be the largest church in Essex and with ourselves being so friendly and asking so nicely, we were even allowed on to the roof high over the nave. The church stands tall with a spire that soars 193 feet into the air, but is not quite as long with the nave stepping out to 183 feet. Saffron Walden lies in an area of rolling Essex chalk folds where

Mr Maurice George became an immediate benefactor of what the Burham teenagers were doing to reach out into the new world emerging from WWII. In todays terms it was a brave move to give us unfettered use of a Hall in Station Road which became the Crouch CC hq. We'd join together there to plan our next outings and the agenda, which clearly was always to enjoy beingThere. In the picture Gloria Short and John Dowding listen when the Club president welcomed visitors from other cycling groups to the annual dinner held at the Ship Hotel on Burnham High Street.

Club chairman John Dowding is seen here at a less formal time adding a high level of decorum to one of the Club's Tramps Runs when braces and a ciggy added to the askant titfer and a bearing which would later see him elected as a Town Councillor.

Light and Peace   DAY 2
Every time you allow yourself to be disturbed by outward conditions you turn towards darkness and away from the light. You cannot afford to live in shadow Let nothing dim the inner radiance of your peace in God.
" Live in peace." 1 Corinthians 13: 11

this is Kersey in Suffolk where people first wove Kersey Cloth. I've seen Tony Brown lay here with a camera photographing ducks in the ford, so when I found a tattered little book with this picture then memories of our touring times together simply came flooding back.

the ground is good for crops and the town actually got its name from the cultivation of saffron several hundred years ago. When Middle-east traders started bringing their saffron to Britain the Essex growers could not compete with the cheap imports from Iran and Kashmir and so they went out of business. Saffron is the world's most expensive spice, but fast forward to around ten years ago and you'll find it again being harvested in Britain after a local farmer began the fight back with English Saffron. Starting from scratch his trial and tribulation times were helped when he came across an old manual from the 1600 time which confirmed he was doing things right with the bulbs he'd planted. Other advice in that book outlining how harvesting should progress that sealed the deal. Today you can buy the English grown spice that has speared its way from the ground in Essex and not from some far-off land.

Further over to the east, in the area where Essex bumps into Suffolk our Club weekends also led to Kersey, with the ford in the village approached when plunging straight down a hill. I was intrigued, when on my first visit there I saw a whole window full of curing hams hanging in view. What struck me was the shop looked almost derelict, the windows were far from clean and there was no butcher's name, nor any name on the door. Our local stop-over hereabouts was often at the Naughton Mill hostel in Nedging Tye, close to another East Anglian base for the USAAF from where the flyers had the showy trick of noisily jetting a tight vertical climb above us, switching to engine after-burners and rattling your eardrums even more as they became the ever diminishing little dot heading in the direction of Mars. With Dakotas and other prop driven planes cloud hopping around the place too the urgent sight and sound of a jet war machine was extra-ordinarily awesome and an unmistakeable sign of that cold war era gripping us. Amidst an evolutionary spectrum of airwaves, tensions and noise we'd then enjoy a reminiscence from a calmer age, tonight sleeping at a YHA hostel conversion in a tall, several floored granary and mill where the upstairs floorboards creaked, if you did a little exercise jumping on the spot then those on the floor below got a good dusting from their ceiling, our floor: have our flour! I can remember clearly the fun we all had and as to occasional headwinds, on a ride we shared being at the front and rarely got lost except on the odd occasion when it was always someone else's fault. We were in Bury St Edmunds one Sunday and following the main road home after a hostel stay, leaving the mid-afternoon tea-stop we followed the road number with Dave Rees in charge. Next thing was for all of us break into a sprint for "bonus points" awarded to the rider being first into the home County. It wasn't. Instead of Essex the sign said Norfolk, oh well, time to turn round and head home across all of Suffolk.

Clubnights for the Crouch were a midweek affair that gave the opportunity to have our programme slipped onto the pages of *The Rag* published on the Friday, although we often changed our sociable weekend plans on the spur of the moment and rather than cycling off towards Suffolk we'd hop the ferry to Gravesend to be in Kent. The ferry would thread through boat traffic on the River Thames and that could be anything from the biggest of ocean liners or past stumpy little tugs with the single funnel and with the power of a whole string of Suffolk Punch horses helping the big ships berth at Tilbury or further upriver in the London docks. With a Sunday start from Burnham we could get in a round trip to Rochester on the Medway, or to the chalk caves at Chislehurst past the top flanks of Kent's North Downs. The caves at Chislehurst had been dug for chalk and flint from as long ago as the 13th century, miles long in a network of avenues underground where bombs have been stored, mushrooms grown and Crouch Cycling Club members even played hide and seek. From Burnham a two day round trip reached Canterbury for a stop-over then ride back through oast house country, often we'd head to Kemsing down by the Pilgrims' Way to stay at the hostel. This hostel was the perimeter of the cycling range for those who worked through Saturdays, but Kent was still a very do-able destination. Working on a Saturday morning, and remembering that for five and a half days in the Dilliway's workroom and office I was paid £1.5s - that's 102.5 pence in nowadays money . . it was never going to be a big-spend weekend. It cost sixpence, half a shilling which today equals two and a half pence in metric money, for a mid afternoon ferry crossing from Burnham quay to Wallasea.

Riding towards Rochford gave plain sight of 360ft high wooden pylons further up the river at Canewdon, these were part of Britain's strategic defences against air attack that the Government had started to build in 1936. Radar arrived just in time to be part of a defence screen and this main structure would last through to about 1960 when it was dismantled. On the way into Southend the road passes the aerodrome established in 1915 and a year later named RFC Rochford, it was from here that sorties would be launched against incoming Zeppelin raiders. After being a centre for balloon flights in the early 1920s and then a civil airport from 1935, four years later Rochford again became a fighter base, right at the WWII frontline and ringed by dozens of concrete pillboxes just in case foreign paratroopers arrived. The defence system was backed up by a huge underground control facility to link with air operations. London Southend Airport is there today and *Which?* has listed it as the best London airport several years running, perhaps in 2018 too! Landing in Southend after the dozen or so miles cycling from home was my time for a Rossi ice cream, the tastiest and the creamiest ice cream money could buy. I'd be on schedule to greet Club member Judy Little when she finished work at tea-time closing in the town's British Home Stores shop, then providing we didn't hang about on the way we'd be in Kent pretty soon. There was first the road through a rural Basildon then past the Bata shoe factory, close to a little place the locals called Stanford No Hope and then on to the Tilbury to Gravesend ferry. If the wind was in the right direction we could get to Kemsing YHA early enough to have a late supper in the members' kitchen before lights-out time.

The whole experience and discipline of the YHA set-up brought us as close to being co-operatively independent as was possible, members were responsible for looking after their own needs as well as doing jobs which helped others staying at the hostel. You made your bed in a dormitory using your own sheet sleeping bag, the bunk-bed style often meant late-comers never managed to get the bottom one! The YHA supplied bed blankets and a pillow, folded and tidied next morning, whilst you had your own sheet sleeping bag that theoretically saved you from actually laying directly against the blankets or the mattress. It was a sheet, it was a sleeping bag, it wasn't anything more than that and sometimes in colder times you needed to find more than the regular allocation of blankets. Still, we were pretty hardy!

Normally it would be a community breakfast; porridge and a fry mostly, loads of toast and a big kettle of tea. Or you could fight for space in the kitchen and prepare your own. The resident Warden allocated the hosteller duties of tidying or cleaning the place - which was less of a chore than it reads although you just hoped to could avoid doing the breakfast dishes, which would make you late away from the place. I've peeled spuds, washed cook pans and dishes, emptied trash bins, swept yards and yards of corridors and dormitories and even had a garden tidying task. Some people reckoned the hostel Warden was there to make their life difficult but hostel life was a well honed system that needed to be faced with a smile and some humour, and anyway what could you do, Mick Wheeler, if the hostel warden really was out to get you? This became a regular thing with Mick, Kemsing was a popular destination for us but over time it became clear he could find problems or problems found him - and if you mixed the words bull, red, rags and eye to eye, then that more or less sums up the way Mick and the hostel warden interacted. It was something we laughed about! At hostels a certain discipline was the key word, and when that need was fully understood and accepted then weekends were just made to be happy for everyone. Those members who arrived late at the hostel often ended up with being given the scrag-end jobs that sometimes were less than the easy ones, but you still had to be off the premises before 10am, and you'd want to do that so you could begin to wend the way onwards and homewards and have fun on the way.

more than wheels - it's life

When the bicycle arrived to change how people got about and lived that is when

As a lad growing up in the countryside and living mostly on farms I had little idea of how big and wide things were over the horizon. I'd break the family mould and take up work in print and publications rather than being in the fields or with cattle. After a time of moving around print shops, newspaper and magazine offices and the like I settled to working in London. The call of the countryside beckoned though, and I was the editor at Practical Camper *when the market-leading monthly notched up ten years helping readers get the best out of outdoor activities. The launch of* Backpackers Club *was our game-changer at the magazine, it also was good for for the outdoor industry which found new opportunities and new markets to sell their camping and travel kit.* This page first appeared in *Practical Camper* magazine.

Now we're ten

Ten years is a long time by some standards and as you'll see on other pages we're celebrating ten years of 'Practical Camper' with this issue.

For my part it seems only yesterday when I was offered the job as editor, and worried about following John Cade's footsteps. John, alas to die a couple of years after leaving Haymarket, was going off to start up his own camping newspaper and I couldn't see how I was going to match his knowledge or reputation on the camping trade.

I was lucky with editorial assistants, and can always remember the reaction of the first — Fred Dawkins — when I said we'd go camping in that first November in office. 'It's up to you, but you are going to be *!**!!* cold, so I'd bring some winter woollies'.

And cold we weren't because it snowed and everyone knows snow is a great insulator.

In that first year we also tried a new game and called it backpacking. At that time the word was just an import from the USA and Mike Marriott used this title for one of his series 'What's the pitch?'

We all went camping in the New Forest, all four of us that is, and Backpackers Club was born, to be launched at the 1972 Colex exhibition when John Hillaby, Derrick Booth, Dennie Noble, Mike Marriott, Fred and myself had an Indian feast in the Hunza Restaurant just across the road from Olympia's halls.

I suppose this is the biggest event, in development terms, which we have experienced in the camping trade and Press over the last ten years. If you take our February, 1972, issue and check out advertisers who were offering equipment specifically for this 'new' lightweight craze you'd be surprised.

There were four of them, two retail outlets and two manufacturers.

The YHA Services advert., was based on their lightweight lines and Mike Marriott's shop, The Practical Camper offered equipment for backpacking and adventure camping. For the manufacturing side Robert Saunders introduced the Lite Hike (at £19.50) and G&H offered a good range of waterproof equipment.

Nowadays it is a different story and you will see many companies, mostly established well before that 1972 introduction on the idea, who have the word 'backpacking' in their trading name or advertisement.

But one good idea like this doesn't add up to a complete camping scene — which is what I strive to get over all the time. I have a great hope that just round the corner there is something just as big about to break. Other journalists on other papers have the same idea and that is what makes time, like the first ten years of Practical Camper, pass quickly.

WITH PETER LUMLEY

Modern threat

Mountains are lovely when there is snow on the peaks, I think they are even lovelier when the snow gets down to the lowest parts of the valley, too. Certainly I can remember no other week of camping which has been as rewarding as a week I spent in the Central Highlands in early December.

We missed the cold, though. It was a cool 30 degrees of frost on the night before we arrived at Aviemore but never dropped lower than about 10 below for the next week. A pity! The idea was to walk from Aviemore to Fort William, and we almost made it, too. No booze, in fact no pubs. Not a lot of daylight, it gets dark up there at about 3.45 p.m. And no problems with crowds or midges. Just lots of deer, hundreds and hundreds of them including a big herd (a staggering number, perhaps?) of real, live stags.

You know, the sort they picture on the postcards and which you don't believe are anywhere but in a zoo or game reserve.

Snow all the way, and weather which made us feel life was really worth living. We didn't hear a peep about IMF negotiations, inflation or strikes. Just whooping swans, coughing roe deer (not a cold, it's their bark) and an occasional sheep bleat. But we also heard a sad story of commercial intent.

Why did we go to the Cairngorms in the first place? Why is it a National Nature Reserve? Why is there peace, quiet and just Mother Nature looking after herself and those around her? Was this mountainous area put there to relieve pressures of modern living, or was it put there to be exploited by all and sundry? I realise that our party, three of us, exploited the potential for a long walk. But we left nothing other than footprints and took nothing but pictures. And I am not looking for praise for doing no more than I think is essential at all times. But how I would have hated the experience to have heard a raucous helicopter chattering away to the inner glens.

It is bad enough being frightened out of your wits by the rare flash of a screaming RAF jet, such as we heard around Loch Erich. A play-thing of the sort which has been proposed by Travel Centre (Norwich) Ltd. has no place, as far as I can see, in this particular environment.

The company have made a planning application to Highland Regional Council to operate a helicopter service at Aviemore. My information, from the Badenoch and Strathspey Conservation Group, is that this company would anticipate flying for 4 hours each day on five days in seven. The flying would be pleasure flights of three to four minutes for joy rides and for 'private charter to and from the Cairngorms'.

The company are making an application, and this would be considered on January 12, to the Highland Regional Council but even if approved the matter would have to be referred to the Secretary of State for Scotland so there is plenty of time to object if you wish.

For my part I am on the side of all those deer, birds and other creatures who won't understand what it's all about. At least I can read! And I hope you, the reader, can write in support of their cause.

Write here, by all means, but another interested party is the Conservation Group, their Convenor is Victor Russell, of Drumcluan, Kincraig, Kingussie, Inverness-shire. He'll keep you informed, too.

Trumpet blowing,

I hope you'll excuse the commercials but there are some new camping books which I think you ought to read and in case you hadn't guessed I'd better also mention I've written both.

Hillwalking is a new Venture Guide published by Spurbooks. If hillwalking and camping high is your idea of fun I hope you'll try this one.

Then for the family man, and all those who want to get the best of their holiday there is a Continental Leisure Publication called Your Camping Guide. These titles will be in your camping shop or bookshop this month at 75p and 95p, I hope you'll find them useful.

●Editor Peter Lumley, in Scotland recently, and Wendy Hilder (centre) the Assistant Editor. Right: John Cade editor of the first Practical Camper

5

life began to gain real meaning, yet when it first came on the scene cycling was an expensive luxury. Today a bicycle is affordable across all of society: match the purpose to a style, pick your steed, pay your money, take it for a ride. Originally a plaything of the rich, ermine and a tiara were as much a part of cycling garb then as is Lycra, tweed and a peaked cycling cap or helmet today. To choose and gather a cycling wardrobe you can be a follower of fashion, although to practical people it is function that matters most, some makers will tell you they sell clothing that repels the effect or rain: I am more interested in finding cycling garb that helps negate the headwind or reverse an upward slope of the path. Wouldn't that just be great! I do not recall Nan ever riding a bicycle but my parents always had their own and by the time my fifth year birthday came around I was well and truly riding wheels. The first bicycle I had was fettled together by a Mr Tunbridge, who lived in Lillian Road and other than being a bicycle mechanic was a taxi driver who ferried kids to school or drove one of the buses from Ford's Garage at Althorne. The bike my parents bought was small wheeled and called a Pavement Cycle, something that the name suggests it was for a *Child* to ride whilst accompanying *Nanny* as she promenaded a baby carriage to the shops. When I was taught to ride mine my Nan was family and never called Nanny, i's no surprise that around home now, seventy-five years on, there is a lot that depicts cycling, cycling people and even some of the bits we used to go cycling. On the wall in my den at home is a photo of Tony Crickmore and myself taken by Trevor Davis after a Crouch CC time-trial, beside that a cartoon by the famed *Cycling* magazine cartoonist Hemmings. His Baz character is signing on for a race and in the artist's word-balloon the race steward says *"I hope you can ride better than you can write."*

This and a lot of other stuff is the scene of how life has evolved for me I guess, always trying to be positive about riding a bike - as illustrated in the Harry cartoon of an un-mistakably bearded me hurtling downhill past sheep on a narrow road . . . *"mint sauce, mint sauce"* is the warning cry. Happily I will admit that cycling for me has always been a happy passion, yet looking at bicycle riding as more than leisurely recreation I'm sad that the machine and the habit has become a sort of political tool, a myriad of bodies jumping on the saddle to peddle - yes, peddle - environmental and political alignments that are not at all quite like the label I first saw on the tin full to the brim with bicycling life. For some the bicycle is a tool wielded rather like a pike or a battering ram to push an agenda, or spear things they don't like. Luckily though the majority amongst of us simply love the bicycle as the constant companion, the unfailing one that gets people to go places, doing to-getherness as it educates, motivates and exercises both body and brain. I cannot see it ever much of a problem in recognising that the bicycle is the friendliest mode of transport ever! Perhaps the bicycle is seen as a threat to motoring habits, being too perfect a solution for sustainable travel, perhaps people hate it for its noiseless and neutral impact on the community and the environment when people cycle by at the speed *they* want to travel. The bicycle itself is so good for us all that the obstacles put in its way and the objections against its viability or doubting its sustainability are but a grain of salt hidden amidst all of the sand in the Sahara.

My being born a Burnham boy was a decade or so before when the bicycle began to lose favour with some because of the influence of the infernal combustion engine, yet in the wings bicycles were standing there for those who recognised it as the absolutely useful, essential and universally shared necessity of family life. In the time I was growing up the norm for the near neighbours of Holland across the North Sea was for a family of six like ours to have nine bicycles. That tally came so spare bikes were the ready replacement for one with a puncture, or just parked up waiting in case there was a thieving invader looking for a bike to help them retreat homewards more quickly. That recalls how our bikes where quite often borrowed, especially when we lived on Marsh Road just out of town. If a puncture got in the way of someone from a farm on the marshes needing to get home late at night, it would be one of our bikes as likely saving the day for someone. Such borrowing or sharing was the norm really, and the bike would always be returned home, often personally and it wasn't so rare for there to be a knock at the door with someone standing there saying *thanks, sorry, I hope you didn't mind . . . thanks again.* A while later someone else, or perhaps the same guy, would again borrow a bike, probably it was a sign of good understanding, of honesty and responsibility towards others. This was a local thing, sometimes happening with a dinghy moored off the Pound or tied up at one of the jetties along the Burnham river front. Rowlocks were left in place, oars shipped ready, easy to borrow but it was very unlikely anyone would do anything but use it, row it back and tie it up again. But that was in the fifties . . a different time and a different set of people going the rounds today? Probably, and more's the pity. This was in a time when I was so lucky to grasp the realities of cycling opportunity, using two wheels to grow my own independence, something which seems so much denied to UK kids in this 21st century world.

Cycling began for me as the necessity, then through work and through leisure times not just as the rider but professionally too, I am so aware of how the bicycle has again become a nation's favoured tool for personal leisure, pleasure and healthy living. So when the oil runs out we'll all have something more than a horse to ride, won't we? You have got to admit it, if anything was made to be immortal then, definitely it is the bicycle. Those mid-to-late '30s through to the ' 50s in our part of the world was well before a time when people parked a family motor car outside their homes; in all his life my father never owned a car, gaining a license to drive only a farm tractor yet not even a motorbike. He always cycled to work. I was born before the Kingdom was Nye with a Labour Party's Bevan-inspired NHS jewel, the real and unique gift to the Nation's health in a war ravaged, ration book imposed era for Britain. It meant my being born into a lifestyle that had to be sustained through personal effort rather than twisting a throttle or hoofing the loud pedal. Tilmann Waldthaler who became a friend is my idea of a cycle tourist, he reckons to have ridden a bike for more miles than to the moon and back, he met his wife Renata in the Sahara on a trip to Europe from Oz and seems never to have suffered a puncture to his ambition of carrying on riding. My journeys have taken me to destinations on the Scilly Isles, to hilly Welsh Wales, to the Wolds and to the Fens, a lot of Europe and the dream birthday celebration in Scandinavia and looping down the Lofoten. That's a part of the world from where Bill Betton once sent me a postcard, on one of his tours the Mercian Cycles boss was well north of the Arctic Circle and the note said he was reading one of my articles in the *Bicycle Times* magazine, "*has anyone taken a copy this far north?* he asked. That is the sort of question I cannot answer and simply all I'd ask is that anyone who gets out and about on a bike, anywhere and at any time, then they do it happily and come home safely. Remember that when stopping to mend a puncture, or pretending you have one, then here's the opportunity to have a rest, to take a look at the scenery around

Here's a destination for spending time pondering and wondering about the amazing world that is cycle sport, beingThere in Novi Ligure to soak up the story of man, woman and machine where efforts have been pitted against both the strengths and the weaknesses of other riders, more or less since the very first competitive stroke of a pedal. On show in the Hall of the Winners are the Campionissimi who rightly are revered with Fausto Coppi following in time the winning wheel tracks of Gino Bartali, Alfredo Binda and Constanti Girardengo. The museum lives in a former factory and once inside you will see how the manufacture and componentry of the bicycle has evolved through from basic engineering, the use of wood and simple fabrics right to today and the super technology of space age thinking and materials. Here is a temple of bicycling.

The roadside signs point the way, they tell you of the local opportunities to be a tourist, where to eat well and stay close to where Fausto Coppi lived and trained. On street corners and houses there are murals and photos from his cycling times.

The spectacles we wore were so near being replicas we had to double check . . I am at his home with Sandrino Carrea and holding that first ever Yellow Jersey to rise over Alpe d'Huez in the Tour de France. That was in 1952.

Three times a Giro winner in his race career Fierenzo Magni *(centre)* was reckoned to be the third man of Italian cycling alongside Bartali and Coppi. Vittorio Adorni *(left)* was the Italian race ace who followed them a decade or so later with his 1965 Giro d'Italia win and victory at the 1968 World Road Race Championships . They are seen with Costantino Ruggiero, the ANCMA boss who helped me find my way around the Italian trade scene and to understand more of how two wheel riding was essentially the lifeblood of Italy.

11   wheels set a world alight

tears were in my eyes at the breakfast table on the day Senator John Kennedy said
he'd seek the Democratic nomination as President of the United States. When
asked why I was crying I told my mother that Fausto Coppi had died.

There's a village in Italy where more pictures of a cyclist on a bike adorn the walls
of buildings than you'll often find in the latest copy of a favourite bike magazine.
This is no ordinary village, Castellania is where Fausto Coppi was born and lived,
where after getting his own two wheels he took a job in a nearby town as a butcher's
delivery roundsman. From birth to boy to man, this is where he grew up, today
the house where he lived is open to visitors, still more or less as when the family
home. There's a smart coat on a hanger, newspapers from that time are in the room
where he slept, there's a bicycle in the room too! The tableau in the kitchen shows
his brother Serse and blind masseur Biago Cavanna amongst as friendly a group of
riders just as you'd find when cycling clubmates visit another's house today. My
beingThere at the house was with an Italian chum Stefano Doldi and local mayor,
people who calmly admit an undeniable aura sits around the place to suggest that
1960 didn't actually happen, did it - *and did you see that rider just flash by . .*

From the street of Casa Coppi the roads around Castellania, where just
about 90 people live, doesn't offer much in the way of easy cycling and it was these
twists and turns and drops and climbs which moulded the local farming family's
boy into the racer who became *Campionissimo.* When you are there soon you'll
discover an ambience which confirms the legend, just as I felt Fausto Coppi was
right there at my elbow in the small town and places around which embrace you, the
walls and the street signs and the livery in the coffee house and cantina hereabouts,
they demonstrate a lasting strength and a reminder of his will to win and his winning ways. From the colour of the life he led until he was forty years old there are
so many photos and so much writing about his exploits that there seems very little
more that people could know about this world revered Italian cycle racer who died
in 1960. Go to Castellania, though, and that's where your feel and understanding for
the man intensifies. The World Cycling Road Race Champion, the winner of Giro
d'Italia on eight occasions, Tour de France champion twice, the first rider to win
both big Tours in the same year, holder of the world one hour record on the track, a

superb palmarès but the question must always be how much more would he have achieved if the war of 1939-45 had not got in the way? What more would there be to tell of his riding and racing if the hostilities hadn't ravaged Europe, keeping people apart and poor and stopped people riding races or watching them. He was a rider who didn't just win races though, he was the hero who dominated social awareness through radio and in newspapers, on film and at a myriad of cycle events. At races crowds lined roads six and ten deep to see him ride by, and to witness history being made in the smartest Brylcreem manner, his hair slicked as with the Birmingham made cream emulsion of mineral oil, water and beeswax. Fausto Coppi dressed in a way that made him the best known sportsman in Italy and abroad, despite all the show of Holywood cinema screen idols, fantasies, music and adventure stories.

For the public Fausto Coppi brought the glitter of a film-star, with the revolving media set ensuring he needed to do nothing more than press on pedals to dominate the news of the day. His powerful riding style and that race winner's fashionable lifestyle was what other riders and racers wanted to emulate, but they couldn't match him and his matter of fact way with a bicycle. He triumphed in ways others envied, but was also a person that so many in the world have emulated with their own love triangles. When it comes to reasoning how and why this man endears us so strongly, and to regret that he died when so young, that it is like wondering just how it is that people can actually love cycling so much. Racing a bicycle against others is physically hard, a near mentally impossible sport to predict and much less the game, more the war when competing with others who would love to beat you, perhaps by any means. On the screen in films, in books and on the pages of a popular comic it is the hero who always wins: Fausto Coppi was born to be nothing less than the cycling hero of all time, the real life person the winner. Campionissimo and so remembered. The unique thing about his Castellania and its quiet streets is the images of the rider we see gracing the place here, he is pedalling serenely and breathing easily, well at least Fausto Coppi looks to be doing it that way! The battles of road and track where he competed are related in volumes of reporting yet it is a single picture from the 1952 Tour de France encounter that identifies a world-aware rivalry of two famous racers remembered for coming together to forge epics: Gino Bartali with his countryman Fausto Coppi. Every day when I go to my writing den at home I am with that famed photo showing the shared bidon filling moment, and yes I will again check: Fausto Coppi is passing to Gino Bartali riding at his right, a glass bottle almost full of water. The bidon tucked in Fausto's left hand against the handlebar is newly filled, you can see there water splashing from an un-corked bidon showing as flecks of white against the rider's black race shorts. That photo which I see every day brings a personal and cherished link to that cycling era when my own involvement in the sport and activity was beginning to blossom.

The picture reminds me of Gino Bartali autographing that photo image during one of my times visiting Milan, and of meeting his wife Adriana and their son Andrea, who so often was at EICMA gatherings and other events I visited when in Italy. A lasting memory is from 2012 when I was with local bicycle sport people at dinner, Stefano Doldi and Faustino Coppi among them and then going to the home of Sandrino Carrea, Fausto's favourite lieutenant who'd been the very first racer to crest Alpe d'Huez in a Tour d France Yellow Jersey. That very jersey Sandrino let me cuddle, sitting with him at his home. All of these things give a connection to that 1952 picture from the Tour de France, the one which has had probably more than a million words written about it. So many people have attempted to interpret the message, such as the end of hostilities, a re-unification of a country, confirmation of the new champion, and perhaps others will understand how I feel about the two people who are part of that scene in the photograph on my wall. Actually, weren't they simply two thirsty racing cyclists sharing some freshening water on a hot day when riding in the Alps?

It is written history that Gino Bartali also won the Tour de France twice, a World War and ten long years separated those wins but what took years to become our knowledge is that during the Second World War from 1943 he courageously saved the lives of many Jewish people living around his native Florence. In wartime he had carried counterfeit identity documents between Florence and Assisi where they were printed covertly, the false documents being hidden in the seat tube of his bike. As a champion cyclist who had trained on these roads so often a lot of the soldiers manning the checkpoints would have been fans of his and they knew it would have been wrong to alter the settings on his machine so they never slid out the seat post to search for that hiding place. Gino Bartali was involved in his style of war effort after Elia Dalla Costa, the Cardinal of Florence had already shown an anti-fascist stance when he absented himself from the city's welcome for Adolph Hitler during a pre-war visit to the city. Knowing that Jewish people were in danger from the Nazis the cardinal had offered them protection and that had led to Gino Bartali being asked by him to help to carry papers and information which could be used to help those being persecuted. He rode thousands of miles by bike, travelling the roads between cities as far apart as Florence, Lucca, Genoa, Assisi, and to the Vatican in Rome. All of this was known to but a few people until a book written by Aili and Andres McConnon was published by Weidenfeld & Nicholson, describing Gino Bartali's life as *"an irresistible combination of sports comeback story and the tale of a humanitarian who helped the Jewish community."*

Talking of comebacks, when Gino Bartali raced the Tour de France in 1937 he managed to lose more than ten minutes before the Ballon d'Alsace stage. In the Vosges he recovered all of that and led by 1m 14s over the peleton when taking the leader's jersey that night in Grenoble. It was the end of his race though, after tangling with crashing team riders he rode into a wooden bridge crossing the river Colau and fell into the river. Gino Bartali won the Yellow Jersey and the Mountain Classification of the Tour de France in 1938 and again in 1948, between 1937 and 1950 he won twelve stages of the race. Giro d'Italia he won in 1936, the year I was born, then again in 1937 and 1946; he was first home in 17 individual stages of the Giro and took the Mountain prize seven times between 1935 and 1954. Tour of Lombardia, the Race of the Falling Leaves, he's won three times. What a man - and his face I see every day in that photo with Fausto Coppi here in my writing den.

A few years back I met a photographer in Monza who told me his father helped organise the Tour de France togetherness session of these two great riders. The Press guys were looking for a special picture from a Tour de France day when they anticipated things would be relaxed in the peleton. So there you have it, a rider in his Yellow Jersey handing a drink to the one who'd been there and done it before, a tough racer who was just two years off retirement time. This day, riding as his team mate, Gino Bartali was following the younger combatant's wheel doing something which was now happening more often than when he'd beat Fausto Coppi to the line which means this picture is probably the monument to the end of an era and the confirmation of the prowess of a new champion. There are other opinions in the questioning of how the picture happened, of course, and one is that this 1952 photo defined the last of the Bartali and Coppi skirmishes: the King is dead, long live the King! Gino Bartali would live for 40 years after the passing of Fausto Coppi, then after a heart by-pass operation he died of a heart attack. Some will see political overtones in the picture too, Fausto Coppi winning the French tour in 1949 and now in 1952 was the final signal that bad blood between nations in Europe was now ended; others suggested that these two Italian cycling giants so renowned in their own country were celebrating together a more unified Italy, their homeland.

Of the signature he put to that picture, and the word *amigo* he added to the inscription reminds me how much I enjoy being in Italy and with those people there I so dearly love. I was so lucky to be trackside and take those photos of Fausto Coppi from when I saw him race at Herne Hill in London, this wasn't the ultra-fit and so full of energy Italian rider of earlier years but his riding and the parading of the winner's garland would lift our hearts and intensifying the excitement of having seen the *Campionissimo* racing his bicycle on our English patch. No dream this, it really happened and I was there and in a way seeing it as 1952 all over again, Fausto

Coppi making the press headlines, us grabbing every moment of it we could get. He'd set the bar very high for us, Tony Crickmore and I, right from the Tour de France race we'd follow in newspaper reports which fired us up even more so, then into the next year it encouraged our following more closely the cyclesport scene. The 20th time of the World Road Race Championship saw Fausto Coppi win in Italy in 1953, that year we did big-miles riding time trials or as cycletourists, all of this helping some sort of bike rash turn out to be quite contagious. My founding Crouch Cycling Club was an itch I scratched, fifteen years later the club name changed to Maldon and District CC and a member who began his riding career there would make a big mark in Italy himself. Alex Dowsett won Stage eight of Giro d'Italia in 2013, that happened to be the year Crouch CC reached being 60. A terrific year!

Montains loom around the rider on the bad surfaced roads which were the regular feature when the Tour or the Giro was being raced. A late evening shot of just one of the many photos hung in walls in Castellania showing Fausto Coppi in action.

The Isle of Man International Scooter Week was a destination attracting me to ride and write about roads made famous by people travelling dangerously fast on two wheels. In motocycling's Isle of Man TT the mountain circuit and the Tourist Trophy races bring to the Island spectators by the thousands who witness more seat of the pants hairy moments and insane derring do than Geoffrey Chaucer ever envisaged in one of his poems. Today, it is an onboard camera from a motorcycle that sticks to showing you the near impossible passage of humans drawing the finest line through bends bordered by brick buildings and stone barriers. With my scootering mates we did our best to follow suit, Eddy Jubb took this photo of my quick passage through the ford halfway around the Druidale course which was a ride coming as close to heaven as you could ever get on a scooter. This centre spread was in the Classic Scooterist Scene *magazine of Dec/Jan 2010, at the same time a reader's picture and letter told that this Montpelier epic can no longer be experienced as the little river is now diverted through a culvert. Dry the tears!* The magazine is published by Mortens Media Group Ltd, their other titles portray life with Lambretta and Vespa scooters in the ptw scene. Scooter riders simply love it!

Refuelling during a Lambretta 12hr Snetterton trial. I am with co-pilot Jim Wistow as he gets ready to ride the next section. Work all day, ride all night then after the trial try not to fall asleep on the long drive home as there was a story to write up.

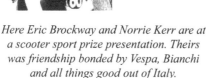

Here Eric Brockway and Norrie Kerr are at a scooter sport prize presentation. Theirs was friendship bonded by Vespa, Bianchi and all things good out of Italy.

12 turning on engine power

There came a time when pedalling a bicycle just couldn't meet the needs of the moment, in the early '60s I realised that for reporting and photography assignments with local newspapers I'd need independent transport that'd more quickly get me around the Dengie Hundred. Nowhere near monied enough to become a car owner the solution was to buy a slightly battered Capri 70cc scooter, the L plate on the back didn't stand for Lumley but the scooter helped my beingThere at community events on sports fields, in village halls and reporting the Blackwater sailing scene. Sailing matches on that stretch of water weren't quite the regatta size of Burnham Week but the events seemed friendlier occasions which brought into play both my camera and the reporter's notebook, and the opportunity to sell pictures was welcome. Another scene changer came when motorcycling friends Ted Yeldham and Rodney Wallace suggested I joined outings with Maldon Auto Club to motorcycle scrambles, so more fun and spectacle bringing good opportunities to sell photos from the action and reports for local newspapers. I wasn't doing so much youth hostelling but when freelance work didn't get in the way I'd get out with the Crouch Cycling Club and there were still photos to take, touring stories to log and the follow-up articles and reports to write.

An assignment on the Blackwater was to report the very first Old Gaffers Race sailed from The Stone in 1963, working with the Old Gaffers' Association organiser and for the specialist yachting press. I sailed on board *Sugar Creek*, the Colin Archer boat owned by Mike Peyton and his wife Kathleen, well read authors. After the most fickle of winds and turns of tide our boat wallowed in at best a sultry and calm swell for a near full day and a long night, I went ashore in Harwich at around 5am in the morning and took a train journey home to go straight into the darkroom and process my pictures for the newspapers and magazines. Mike Peyton wasn't into using a camera so much, he didn't need that tool as he had not only come through the war as a military artist and prisoner of war, a while after sailing with him I discovered we both had a mutual friend in the backpacking scene. Mike was a colleague of John Hillaby, working as illustrator for his articles in the *New Scientist* periodical, in that author's *Journey through Europe* we read how John steps off a crowded ferry into Belgium, but that's quite a long way from the original idea where he'd have crossed from England on board *Sugar Creek* with Mike at the helm, coming ashore somewhere in polder country to begin a walk all the way to the Mediterranean. Sailing, fun and the beingThere in a boat is what Mike Peyton illustrates on pages and across the decades there has been a tide of hilariously funny cartoons in magazines and his books, always bringing more than a chuckle from every page. Mike's wife Kathleen is the renowned writer who has produced more than fifty novels including the Flambards stories about the Russell family spanning the period before and after the First World War. Her book was made into a much watched Yorkshire Television series in the late '70s.

A lot of my time was spent following the opportunity to photograph other beauties on salty rivers with sea water lapping their sides, the images from East Coast Sailing Barge matches worked my YashicaMat roll film camera hard and if ever a subject enthralled then it has always been the sighting of red ochered sails. I'd first seen these years before when I watched men reworking the big sails laid out on meadowland behind the Royal Corinthian Yacht Club at Burnham. When barges are on the water their wind-catching sails seem to fully link the blue of sky and sea with their enormous red exclamation mark, often a full five thousand square feet of rusty-red colour flax sails. That hue is a traditional dressing made up of red ochre, cod oil, urine and seawater. One big sail, no engine, a huge cargo with just a man and boy in charge of the barge. So how does that rate for sustainability in our world now gone wrong where people have a pattern of life where they won't make the time nor have any inclination to wait for the right conditions of tide and a fair wind? Don't go there, it'd be a one sided argument running into the tide!

On my 70cc engine Capri scooter I'd get to assignments on the Blackwater river for Saturday dinghy racing, check the practice list for boat numbers and crew names, shoot photographs then spend a late and long evening processing film and working in the darkroom to produce pictures to sell next day at the sailing club. Photographs of the Sunday racing, along with collecting the result sheet to help marry captions to the pictures, then an evening typing up my report before riding a dozen miles to get the package on the London train from Chelmsford. The stuff I did went to both one of the nationals and to the new sailing magazine being published out of Elm House, that one would hit the streets midweek. Next day another report and more pictures would go to magazines such as *Yachts & Yachting* in Southend on Sea and the yachting monthly. The photographs with the reports or displayed at weekend sailing club meeting would often bring in repeat orders for the pictures over the month ahead. Photographing people as well as boats was the job, and when Keith Musto raced his Flying Dutchman at Maylandsea Sailing Club he showed us the Silver Medal he'd won with Tony Morgan at the 1964 Summer Olympics in

Japan. That photograph of him with the big Medal earned well with private sales as well as to newspapers and magazines. Alongside the specialist magazine market I'd get reproduction and reporting fees from *Essex Chronicle,* the *Maldon & Burnham Standard* and occasionally the Colchester, Braintree and Witham weeklies in the Essex County Newspapers chain. The boss and owner there was Hervey Benham who had pioneered newspaper publications from the garrison town, he was also the author of at least fourteen books and among them the best known are *Down Tops'l,* the *Last Stronghold of Sail* and *Once Upon a Tide.* Reporting on the sporting side of sailing meant slightly producing different words for the papers and magazines, although a carbon copy version of a write-up was often taken by news editors. And that carbon copy? Yes, this was pre-computer days by a long way and when writing a story you'd punch hard on the typewriter keys to impress the letters not just on the top page but through interleaved sheets of carbon paper and the next sheet of paper itself If you managed to get a third page impression to read ok then you'd got lucky! For travel to assignments I needed to move quicker than cars were going, and seeing how Sunday traffic nearly always backed up across the Dengie Hundred I'd done the sensible thing and bought a scooter. That also opened new doors for my writing and photography and after I'd submitted a touring article about chasing after rather than tilting at windmills around East Anglia, which linked a different form of sails than on boats and with mill stones and a Dusty Miller or two at their work. The feature was accepted for the Link House magazine *Scooter & Threewheeler* where editor Dennis Dalton liked the style and asked if I'd take on reporting jobs.

One of the first commissions was to ride the Esso Scoot to Scotland event, run as part of the Motorcycling Club's Edinburgh Trial. This Classic rally had begun in 1904 with the start in London to a finish line in Scotland's capital Edinburgh, the event was for two, three and four wheel automobiles and motorcycles, some with sidecars, all navigating wild country, old packhorse tracks and various muddy places along the route. Things hadn't changed much when the Trial I rode started at Findern in Derbyshire and for those who didn't fall by the wayside we'd wine and dine in Ayr, on the West Coast. I managed not to fall by the wayside but arrived far behind schedule after my stopping to interview people at checkpoints and taking photographs, it was early evening before I signed off at the event Arrival in Ayr. This part of Scotland was as far north as I had ever ventured yet as appealing it was to stay and tour around, instead I headed for Prestwick Airport to check out the way home. A year or so previously this was where Elvis Presley stepped off a military flight to mingle with fans on the journey back home after duty in Germany. My idea was similar but wouldn't include flying the Atlantic, a much shorter distance meant I'd fly with my scooter to end up west of London at Heathrow. That flight with my Capri could be done they said. In the morning they added. And the cost wasn't so

(Left, top) R. Sedgley, an Epsom club Junior, leads R. Hewitt, another Junior from Luton. (Left, centre) The crater always attracted a big gallery of spectators. (Left, bottom) Pete Meads, a Luton Senior, in action before he pushed the bike all the way round the course on his last lap to qualify for championship points.

REPORT AND PICTURES BY PETER LUMLEY

(Below, left) Mick Mannings, final victor in the Ray Collins Memorial Scramble, on his first day as a Senior rider. (Below, right) Standard-machine riders caught in a typical poset

MANNINGS WINS ON FIRST DAY OUT AS SENIOR

RAY COLLINS MEMORIAL SCRAMBLE AT BRANDS HATCH

In the first meeting since being upgraded to senior status, Mick Mannings won the race of the day at Brands Hatch to take home the Ray Collins Memorial Trophy to Luton. Riding his DKR special in atrocious conditions he had followed Bob Jarvis for three-quarters of the way through the final, then when the Noys Stingray-mounted current holder of the Trophy made heavy going of a gear-change he went through to lead to the line.

There was little close racing in any of the fifteen or so events that remained from a programme that had to be shortened because of adverse conditions and lack of riders with the strength to get round the muddy 900 yard course. With only one combination entry that class was omitted from the schedule which

had, for the first time, included Lambretta scooters in road trim. Over 20 hopefuls had entered their standard machines in the meeting, but although they received a handsome bonus of a lap start on the scrambling specials they just did not have a chance.

On the day before the meeting the clerk of the course and his helpers had laid out a testing circuit, which included a fair straight on good level grass, and a climb into the shrubbery. A rough track brought the riders to a crater that held one large muddy puddle and then back on to the grass again. Somewhere between the roping-off of the circuit on Saturday and the practice laps on Sunday about 2in. of rain fell and that made the course into a quagmire. With the "spud" tyres on the scramblers

there were times when I'd take my camera to muddy places and need to wear wellingtons - at other times I'd wear a dickie bow to present awards, as at Bromley SC in Kent. above: my *Scooter & Threewheeler report.*

Two riders I met on my first Scoot to Scotland I reported were from Mansfield Deerstalker SC. Jim and Jeannie Wistow became lifelong friends and here's a photo from an Isle of Man Scooter Week, with them taking part in the Scootering Couple competition at Noble Park in Douglas.

prohibitive I discovered. First though I must drain the petrol from the scooter and let down the tyres. It all sounded not a good idea!

That evening I would forsake an in-flight meal for supper at a lorry drivers' b&b stop-over in Cumnock, after the big Sunday morning breakfast I started south and by lunchtime was in the English Borders around Penrith in amazingly sunny weather. A new countryside was rolling towards me as I travelled.

First opting to pootle along to Scotch Corner, instead from the spine of the Pennines I slid off the A.66 into the Yorkshire Dales and past the Tan Hill pub, little realising I'd be coming back here to listen to the quiet of the place quite a lot and in that future time I'd be shouldering a rucksack and listening to curlews call. At Richmond I emptied a pot of tea and devoured sandwiches and cake, hearing Frank Sinatra's *Strangers in the Night* on BBC radio, the song and his album marked a return to a Number One place in the pop album charts and a Number One place in the singles chart. Even better, at the 1967 Grammy Awards Frank Sinatra garnered two prizes - Record of the Year and Best Male Vocal Performance in a song. His entertainment career that spanned seventy years gained Frank Sinatra two Academy Awards, a Jean Hersholt Humanitarian Award, two Golden Globes, twenty Grammy Awards, an Emmy Award, the Cecile B. DeMille Award, a Peabody, the Kennedy Centre Honours and the Presidential Medal of Freedom honour by the USA with the Congressional Gold Medal. Old Blue Eyes was pretty much an Italian, just like my new Agrati Garelli 125cc Capri, with the engine singing well as I turned out of Wensleydale onto the A1 after Bedale, headed south to hang a left after nearly 200 miles or so of the trunk road. I was in Huntingdon an hour or so after midnight and made in to home in Essex a bit later than 4am, after eighteen hours of riding.

Yes, a long way, a tiring trip but just consider one which Vespa rider Norrie Kerr repeated and repeated on his 90SS. He rode about 460 miles from Glasgow to compete at a Torquay scooter rally three years on the trot. Departing Glasgow mid afternoon then at Brian Morgan's home in Birkenhead stopping for some food, he grabbed three hours shut-eye to get on the road for Torquay again at 2am. On Sunday afternoon it was back to Glasgow, which is a leg closer to 100 miles further than my own trip from Cumnock, but then he was quite young! What happened next was a bit unexpected, just as I had got my freelance feet firmly under the table at *Scooter & Threewheeler* the magazine closed and editor Dennis Dalton moved on. Link House had pulled the plug on their publication but a Nottingham printer & publisher looked at the prospects, assigning me the editor post for a new magazine *Scootering & Lightweights*. When I went back to Scotland the next year it was on a more powerful 180cc Rally Vespa model and from that ride with Chelmsford

Vespa Club guys I'd be able to produce another article. The whole trip was easier, I'd gained the experience of beingThere previously but the weather was inclement beyond belief, softened a bit as our Club picked up the Best Vespa Team award, at a price. Alex Hunt, son of a Witham motorcycle dealer rode his Vespa GS 150cc all the way to within ten miles of Ayr until he misjudged a tight left hander. Arrested to a dead stop just short of steep drop, the wire support strut to a telegraph pole failed to garrot him although as it snapped into the gap below the scooter headlamp it redefined the chassis configuration. Alex Hunt didn't get up and dust himself down, the ground was far too muddy for that, but quickly realised there was now a much shorter gap between his handlebars and the seat of his GS: well over a foot shorter in fact, all showed by the big crimp across the metal footboards of the bodywork. After the finish at Ayr we stayed at my favourite Cumnock b&b where the hostess took all our very wet riding gear to dry, then in the morning I'd head from Ayr to Arbroath and do things on the east coast other than eating Smokies.

Going homewards after a day meeting family there I had my first ever glimpse of the Forth Road Bridge and chased the A.68 road south, past bewitching purple haze of the heather in the Borders to the climb over Carters Bar. This was a final view of Scotland I'd get for a while, but I'd be back a lot and as this time see fields white speckled with gambolling lambs in a good time of year with trees lightly greened and some patched black with the nests of crows built noisily on high. There was May blossom in the hedgerows, appropriate as it was May I guess but of the yellow gorse colouring in big clumps on slopes and in hedgerows, that is more than just a spring clump you are seeing, the gorse bush flowers every month of the year. This was soon Hadrian's Wall country and ahead of me where miles of tarmac laid over where Romans had often travelled, into and through Corbridge I'd cross the River Tyne past the signs of a successful Northumbrian County Show - or rather all the muddy tracks onto the road from where they'd held the County Show in the riverside showground fields.

Mud on the road is a real bane for two wheel riders, manageable when at Corbridge this once but mud and sugar beet together littering the Great Baddow roundabout on the way into Chelmsford one day didn't just hurt me, in the crash it split open my helmet and the clear visor sliced my cheek. The brand spanking new Capri 150 scooter on road test and with just 158 miles on the clock lay battered after meeting up with a strong railed fence, it then screamed and rev'd itself into a frenzy that painfully ended as an engine seizure. I lay at the bottom of the road banking, seized by pain all over as a lady cradling me said *"it's ok, the ambulance is coming."* I recall she looked quite worried, at the hospital their worry was the head injury but I was much more concerned about the flat indentation of a camera body imprinted at the top of my right thigh - wince: in the groin area, neither headlamp, Leica or my body had enjoyed the meeting! I self-discharged from the accident ward and limped home on the bus: someone would collect the scooter and take it back to Nottingham where Garelli were very good about it, regularly asking how I felt. They couldn't have felt bad about things as very soon after they asked if they should put together a 50cc Capri for me to ride in the Isle of Man International Scooter Week. For a buzzing bee it still was a real go-er, at just 49.5cc and revving to 13.5k revs a minute they reckoned, I rode from Nottingham to Essex then across to Liverpool for the IoM Steam Package ferry. On the island I'd pick up the only Gold medal for the Under 50cc Class since a Polish rider was awarded one in the very first year of the Scooter Week. This would be the last time I rode a competitive scooter event, *Scootering & Lightweights* magazine was folded by the publishers and no longer was there the editor's job. Twice. Strike. Lightning: re-arrange the words and you'll see coming for me a *"between jobs"* spell that too regularly is the case for freelance operators. And as there's one freelance born every minute, they say, it can't all be such a bad time to endure . . .

This hadn't been a very long-term job, Milward took the monthly print run to the eighteenth issue before shutting up shop, yet that magazine didn't disappear from trace nor die in people's minds right there and then as a lot of people kept in touch. Almost thirty years later at the EMSA and Federation of British Scooter Clubs "End of an Era" celebration dinner in Nottinghamshire the *Scootering & Lightweights* magazine made headlines with a presentation of *"the best ever scooter magazine"* award. Their words and a nice accolade of course, but from what I have since seen from Sticky Round, Andy, Stu, Mortens and a few others the scooter titles of today thrive with a different reader profile and content need. There's a lot of new machines around, in fits and starts people buy them but that market sidles up against fashion and transport trends, there is business and pleasure in renovating old but very expensive Classic scooters, whilst the scooter sport following is now different to the 1960s, although it could not be any more competitive than when we were wringing the throttle open. Of the Mods & Rockers era I'm sure much of the newspaper reporting of those scooter times had a lot of the Quadrophenia feel and screen flamed sensationalism about it. For sure I'd blame a lot of it on the way the tabloids set up one side against the other, encouraging social divisions for their publications' sake. I never experienced aggro amongst the motorcycle friends I rode with from Maldon Auto Club, we may have been riding at a different speed some of the time but we'd be together at the destination and with plenty of friendly banter. None of these guys resembled a scooter-opposing Rocker element read about in national newspaper reports and neither did I dress up like a Mod! Nice thing was them being tickled pink that I would go ride and compete on my scooter somewhere then bring back silverware to stick on the snooker table at Althorne Village Hall, our Auto Club's weekly social meeting place. *It's not what you've got . . it's what you do with it that counts!*

industry matters . . .

When Nottingham's branch of the Motorcycle & Bicycle Industries Association staged the National dinner in a big hall it had buzzed all evening with business banter and chatter between people involved closely with two wheels, amongst them were some people I had not seen for years. The start to the evening was quite thought provoking, this was early in our *tradeandindustry* b2b days when I was staying nearby in the same hotel as Norman Court the big boss at Falcon Cycles. I asked if he'd like a sherry before dinner then as we chatted he noticed there was an un-opened bottle of Malt on the table and Norman came straight to the point: *"are you an alcoholic?"* I quickly moved the notion that although journalists may be inclined to take a tipple or three, the mostly full glass a writer sets out to instil in readers didn't actually add up to alcoholism, did it? I'd always considered this was reciprocal socialising but I took this as a warning shot across the bow. Whilst my enjoying leisurely and social sharing was one thing, obviously not everyone saw it as I did: oh, I'm no secret drinker, by the way!

That Nottingham Trade evening with the industry association enhanced renewal of some old friendships, the Puch distributors Fred Green and Peter Bolton were there, and of the charismatic Peter Bolton himself I have a York Rally memory where he had come to see bicycle people at the York Rally on the Knavesmire . . *"flew up, you know, called a farmer friend who said it was ok for me to land on one of his fields. Flying back later."* With Fred Green I'd been at the Puch operation in Austria meeting Herbert Kropf who lent me a lightweight sports bike built around a Reynolds 531 frame to go ride on the cobble roads in Graz. On our way home through Vienna we all rode the Ferris wheel that loops 212 ft into the air, the one remembered from *The Third Man* film which stood tallest of all in the world until 1985. That was just two years short of the hundred since being built by twenty-three year old English engineer Walter Bassett who was a Royal Navy man. The Wiener Riesenrad, the proper name of this Ferris wheel, was built to celebrate the Golden Jubilee of Emperor Franz Josef I. The film itself was voted the greatest film of all time by the British Film Institute in 1999 where core to the film is racketeer Harry Lime's black-market dealing in diluted penicillin, the drug that had played so much importance in my own life. Fred Green would soon be doing great things at the

*Press clippings and all that - amongst piles of papers, mounds of pictures, tape re-
cordings and more stuff torn from magazine and newspaper pages than we ought to
keep, are reminders of changing roles that come with beingThere as a reporter and
a rider. The International Scooter Week held on the Isle of Man was hectic, thrilling,
daunting, relatively dangerous - but a lot of fun that has kept friendships in touch
and alive amongst us all for several decades. About it, we all laugh a lot!*

*plenty of people were adding their voice to
what scootering was about - including press
coverage of people getting airborne on a
hump back bridge near Danbury - it seems it
was considered anti-social behaviour!*

Moore Large operation with two-wheel brands, also initiating in-house marketing at the John Moore family business in Derby by opening the company's photographic studio and using his camera expertly and effectively to their promote brands.

The MCIA Dinner brought together people from around the country, including some of the East Midlands people who had been real rally mates in my scooter sport days. In those times I'd join activities on motorsport race tracks, in Kent it was Lydden Hill and we also met up at top country circuits of Brands Hatch, the Midlands' Mallory Park circuit and spent hours of competition at Snetterton in the wholly, holy Lambretta sessions. People will say *".. what, all that on a scooter.."* but in reality it was all a lot of high-octane, two-stroke revving, scooter screaming fun. As for the Leicestershire circuit it is the one place where for me bicycles and scooters meet, it registers for cycling as the time when Les West almost gained a Medal in the World Cycling Road Race Championship. He'd got into the break with the likes of Felice Gimondi, 1969 amateur world champion Leif Mortensen of Denmark and Belgian Jean-Pierre Monsere. When they came into Mallory Park for the finish it was fourth place for an arm raising Les West, surely him showing sheer frustration at missing a Medal. Yet, it must be remembered that of our senior cycle road racing giants it is only Tom Simpson and Mark Cavendish who have done the real job for Britain in The Road Worlds than Les West in 1972. I live in hope.

That evening in Nottingham would reset my interest in ptw riding and scooter events when that blast from the past cry came from amongst this 1980s time dickie-bow wearing diners at the industry Association dinner. The smoky air wafted aside as I heard *"blimey, that's Peter Lumley sitting over there!"* This was from a guy last seen on the Isle of Man at the International Scooter Rally, a rider from the Glasgow Vespa Club who'd become a Championship Winner of the week long competition, somewhere I had also ridden and competed. The voice was from Norrie Kerr, who remembered when I'd ridden the IoM Championships with a *Scooter & Lightweights* magazine Team of the Kirkby-in-Ashfield living Lambretta rider Jim Wistow and the west London scooter dealer Pete Hasler, who was more than an expert in making Moto Rumi and little Vespas scooters go very fast, and even faster for their size. In the sport and scooter activity of those days I rode as a country member of Mansfield Deerstalkers SC, as well as being in Chelmsford VC, which meant I was travelling around a lot in the post as magazine editor at *Scooter & Lightweights*. During an EMSA Road Trial I remember one check-in point was on a bridge overlooking a muddy mess that was destined to be the M1 motorway reaching North past Junction 27, this was in the period between when it was quite legal, and then not only illegal but also thought of as being very noisy at nights and dangerous during the day. That was when the scooter scene was often engaged in frantic all-night rally affairs where navigation mattered a great deal.

A lot of the events worked at squashing at least three days of a weekend into just a Saturday night and Sunday morning; we'd go to work weary and bleary eyed on the Monday! On the epic Western 250 Starlight Trial run by Birmingham Cherubs Scooter Club the start line was at a pub in Oswestry at 10pm. The late Saturday evening start was handy for a lot of us needing to ride all the way into the Welsh Marches, myself coming from Essex. Geoff Burns and Pete Hasler came up from London. Between us we were the magazine Team that individually tore around very unlit, narrow, switchback lanes, across odd bits of farm or forest track in Wild West Wales to finish at breakfast time in Abergavenny. When the morning finish arrived I had already put over 450 miles of riding on the clock since last in bed, but luck had it there was a family friend living just across the River Severn and I could rest up there before the evening 190 miles ride back to Essex. I am told that I arrived at their home a shade travel worn in appearance, two big white circles around rather reddened eyes after spending hours peering through the race goggles we all wore in pre-visor days. I was probably quite road-grubby, too.

Despite the kiddies of the house playing and visitors to the family home stepping over a log-dead me crashed out on the lounge carpet, I slept and slept well without being aware that our Team had won a shed-full of awards in the Night Trial. Fun and fame! The evening ride back home, out of Gloucestershire, across Oxfordshire then the other counties north of London through to Essex finally meant I'd ride over 650 miles in the two days. The reward was that we'd later collect the Starlight Trophy Team cup for *Scootering & Lightweights*; the Under 125cc Trophy went to Peter & Dot Hasler, I picked up both a Best Newcomers Award and the Over 150cc Trophy on the Vespa 180SS. Five of the six major awards came our way, with the other one going to Bob Young of Glasgow SC, a Lambretta riding close friend of Norrie Kerr. The fun hadn't yet ended though, Pete Hasler took us to the Birmingham Cherubs' Dinner and Prizes Evening in his Morris Countryman come a December weekend, on the return journey he was stopped by Police on the M.40, *"just a routine check, Sir, may I look inside"*. Five shiny Silver Trophies wrapped in a blanket needed to be explained: the Policeman kindly said . . *"congratulations."*

Nottingham is a place with the reputation of being big on the wheel scene, locally in a pub you could spot fame-framed bicycles, one being where Gerry O'Donovan the Ilkeston Raleigh Speciality bike-builder showed off Joop Zoetemelk's Raleigh racer in a glass cabinet. The Dutch rider won the 1980 Tour de France, a race he finished on 16 occasions from 16 starts, then in 1985 he became

LOWER DEPOSIT FOR SUPERVAN!

You can still buy Reliant's famous
5cwt Supervan III for a deposit of only 20 or
25 per cent–with up to three years to pay.
The sturdy, all-purpose Supervan
has emerged as better value than ever from
the Government's latest economy measures.
At the same time, Reliant have given it a more
powerful 700cc engine for 1969–without altering
Supervan's legendary 65 miles to the gallon.

RELIANT SUPERVAN III £437.10
(no PT applicable.)

Sales Division (SL) Reliant Motor Company Limited Tamworth Staffordshire

*In case you'd thought this was an advertisement - sorry, it isn't. The price
has gone up! My father had only the license to drive a tractor, so never onwed
a car and it was only after I needed to carry more gear than I could with a
bicycle then I bought one of these three-wheel but very handy carry-alls. Like a
lot of things people did in those days, I bought the pre-used version . . actually
one that had been pre-unloved, too.*   Advrt from *Scootering and Lightweights* magazine.

---

the Worlds Pro Road race champion at 38 years old. TI-Raleigh and Peter Post's team had continued what Reg Harris, the world beating track rider had begun in those early days of my own cycling: both those guys raced Raleigh. Lots of business consolidations had joined local bicycle brands more or less at the bottom bracket, with makes such as Humber, Carlton and Rudge and other Lenton House banded and branded together in the TI-Raleigh operation. There was often something of a corporate aloofness from the company in the slow-recovery years when bicycle product simply struggled to appeal and two wheels had lost so much ground in the public domain as tin boxes took over everyday transport expectations. As far as Raleigh business was concerned it needed something of a Chopper act to gain a bit of glamour, after the leaner, less peddling opportunity with pedal product. For the 1963 high street Raleigh had produced the RM6, a motorised runabout bike with basic suspension but not too much in the way of stopping power: in reality little more than a petrol engine driven bicycle. There were goodish sales figures for the Raleigh Small Wheel model, riding 16 inch wheels - hence RSW16 - then in 1967 they acquired and added the Alex Moulton bicycle model to their range, in a way it was lucky for them that the Chopper arrived in 1969.

The bicycle flow out of the Nottingham factory came mostly with their sluggish small wheels, these bread and butter town bikes were staple diet through retailers although back in 1930 the Raleigh company had thought engine powered lightweight delivery vehicles were the future. They began with a cargo cabin and a covered in driver compartment all built around the steering and the controls of a motorcycle engine, the company developed this into a two-passenger version which morphed into a Raleigh car, the three-wheeled Safety Seven. It as an idea which had limitations and the Nottingham company stopped making these powered vehicles to concentrate on bicycles in about 1935, when their chief designer T.L.Williams took the Raleigh manufacturing equipment to open a factory in Tamworth and started production of what became known as the Reliant brand. I've driven Reliant Regal vans and saloons for thousands of miles, and yes, it is a car!

Earlier than when I had bought my first Reliant the company was fitting the new Regal 3/25 with what was Britain's first mass produced all-aluminium engine: and it was made in their own factory. The first Reliant engine is reckoned to have been test-run on the very morning that news of World War II broke - September 3, 1939 - and other than a few examples having been completed it was 1946 before Reliant went into full production with it. That delay came about because a lot of Britain's factories turned to making things for the War Effort. The Reliant car has always been misunderstood, which is why I will repeat, *Yes it is a Car* - and it's been

has a very distinct advantage over my usual two-wheels when the roads are like that.

Morning starting was not bad but it was erratic and right through the time I had the Bond I was not *sure* it would fire first time. Much of the trouble seemed to stem from damp, the rear engine cover seemed to let *some* water in especially if for any reason it was raised, and that water always seemed to settle on the distributor cap. If I needed to park out overnight I got into the habit of laying an old jacket over the plugs and electrical

Bond 875

—impressions after 5,000 miles in a lively three-wheeler

Driving a vehicle for a week, a thousand miles or sometimes even longer doesn't always tell you all you need to know about that particular model but take any machine and use it regularly day in, day out over three months of the winter and you're bound to find the weak spots.

I've been driving a Bond 875 since early December and with regular runs from my Essex home to "Scootering's" Nottingham address as well as regular trips in London traffic, to various sporting and social events as well as the normal run-of-the-mill journeys I've clocked up over 5,000 miles. My initial impressions appeared in the road-test report published in the November issue after a fortnight's driving, at that time I appear to have been in love with the power and speed which the car gets from the Hillman Imp engine. Bond's three-wheeler has more than that.

No-one will deny the ability to go off the clock at ninety can have some reward—if the law doesn't catch you—but much more satisfying is the comfortable gait with a light foot on the throttle and 55 mph on the dial. Fast enough for comfort, over fifty to the gallon for economy. It is this virtue which *must* appeal.

The front of the Bond hasn't much in it other than a petrol tank, the wheel and your spare. This isn't in itself a drawback but can tend to make driving in windy conditions a bit hectic when you're on your own and have an almost empty tank. Put four gallons of juice in the six gallon tank, take on a passenger and at 55 to 60 no-one would guess you've got a £10-a-year-tax car. Not that the passenger is *so* important but seeing that the Bond will seat four, driving it on your own is a bit pointless.

In some of the winter's worst snow—around this part of the world, anyway—travel was possible in the Bond if others could get about. It didn't get so bad that travel by any means was impossible but I wouldn't endorse the remark I've heard that one front wheel is an advantage in such conditions. The Bond is light—it has to be to be classed as a motor tricycle—and it is that lightness which can be a nuisance because there isn't the weight to crush the slush or snow and it gets to being a case of following in other tracks. Piles of slush form just where the front wheel goes and that is another nuisance, although nothing more.

To sum up I found driving in those conditions required plenty of care but not *more* than I would have given travel on any other sort of vehicle. And the Bond

bits and found that I had cured any trouble I might have been heading for.

Tyre wear can only be described as remarkably light, the set of Michelin X fitted to the car show no signs after over 10,000 miles. Tyre pressures are very important—I would say almost critical—and a very uncomfortable ride results from over or under inflation. I tried to vary the pressures but found the recommended 26 psi the best, in the rear.

Petrol consumption has already been remarked upon —a very economical average of a shade over 53 mpg— and during the full 5,000 miles I have only put in six pints of Viscostatic oil. During the time I was driving the Bond there were no other "hidden extras" than a fan-belt which needed replacing and three pints of Holts anti-freeze.

There are times when the handling characteristics of the three-wheeler—and the Bond in particular—can be downright frightening but that only occurs when the roads are rutted and pitted. Potholes don't matter so much, it is the infuriatingly difficult-to-see ridge between one strip of machine laid road and another which catches you out. Corrugations caused by heavy loads or trench-work is by far the worse and I have yet to find an answer other than to be extremely wary whenever there is a possibility of these conditions occurring.

At all times the general handling is safe and sure even if the front does twitch a bit—in other words it might feel a bit hairy but those three wheels are firmly on the ground and there is never any chance of anything wayward happening. Cornering is sure but *is* an acquired art if you want to be a bit brisk.

If I was given the brief to improve the Bond I believe the first thing I'd do would be to fit some sort of mud-guard over the front wheel and utilise the bonnet space which surrounds it. Next on the list would be a window which opened nearer the front and so improved ventilation and the ability to stick out a mit when necessary, after that there isn't anything I'd really *worry* about although I think I'd like a courtesy light and something done about the steaming-up of the windscreen.

After those 5,000 miles I'm still back to my remarks last November—"It must be a good buy for anyone who wants something sporty . . . cheaper road tax . . ." there's no doubt about it—I grew fond of that Bond.

28

Bond made their threewheel car by wrapping a lightweight shell onto a Hillman 875 engine, it was a bit quicker than quick. I drove it on a full motorcycle license, had a few scarey moments as it was so light that when going a bit beyond legal motorway speeds there was a tendency for it to drift around rather like a wind plagued feather . . a few of my friends declined a second trip. Someone persuaded me to test a luggage van attached to the rear wheels through a constant knuckle joint, with no drawbar was needed . It worked very well although the Bond solo front wheel lost some of its light steering. Quite hairy! Article from *Scootering and Lightweights* magazine.

a popular vehicle despite Jeremy Clarkson's inane spoofery about a threewheeler not always staying upright on the road. It has always been an under-rated vehicle but what brand wouldn't just love their product to be watched by 24.35 million people as when the *Only Fools And Horses* duo of Del Boy and Rodney drove their famous yellow Reliant Regal three-wheeler in Monaco, and being featured in the TV Special *If They Could See Us Now*. That BBC1 programme tops of the list of the UK's most viewed TV episodes of all time: 24.35 million people watching three wheels on a wagon! In November 2017 that van sold for almost £42,000.

As an economic carry-all the Reliant would also double as our cabin on camping weekends as when Fred Dawkins travelled with me *up North* to report our first Harrogate COLA Show for *Practical Camper*. People were liking the *practical* name a lot it, and on our travels we went to the Mitchell's Practical Camper shop, owned in Dewsbury called by Jos Mitchell, a member-elected Councillor of the Camping & Outdoor Life Trade Association. That Trade body was well respected for the way they achieved good things with a Committee and Board member-elected through a voting system overseen by the Electoral Reform Society. COLA worked to achieve a community spirit, on the way aggregating a big war-chest of coffers built through member energy and owning and organising the Harrogate outdoor show. Later there'd be changes in the association's steerage leading to marked big-boy and littl'un differences, a name change or two and some struggling to see the wood for the trees, means today it's a different industry ball game being played.

As Fred and I toured our three wheel way further into Yorkshire and the Dales we followed our noses from Dewsbury on a drive which ended up at the very snow covered Howgill Lodge camping site in Appletreewick. It was dark, it was snowing, no-one else was camping there and we wondered what it'd be like in the morning seeing we were in a part of the world with lots of hills and narrow lanes. *"Would we ever reach Harrogate"* came from Fred, wondering aloud, I confidently said we'd eventually arrive whole and happy at the Show, after all a Reliant three-wheeler could legally be driven on a motorcycle license, and I had one. I assured him that I'd practised a lot with a Reliant in all weathers, and I was hardly going to let a couple of foot of snow worry me. I'd survived my late-20s crisis realising a bicycle didn't always deliver transport needs I'd got myself a scooter, then invested in a Messerschmitt, aka a bubble car able to transport two people sitting tandem-like or alternatively carry photography gear, tripod and such, even camping kit. I'd moved on and to gain even more shipping space bought my first Reliant van. It wasn't new, it wasn't expensive, it wasn't exactly road legal either. The supplier in Middlesex arranged I did that first journey right across London not realising that the vehicle indicators managed to flash to the opposite direction of the intended left hand or right turn. We got to Harrogate of course, overnight someone had nicked all the snow laying around at Howgill Lodge, Wharfedale was fully aglow with late autumnal hues and green grass was everywhere. At the COLA show John 'Tony' Anthony, the *Practical Camper* advertisement manager was confiding to his clients that his new editor of just over two months was actually camping during COLA, rather than booking into a hotel as nearly everydody else was doing.

Downside to all this came when bosses insisted I used a company car and took to test-driving motorhomes from the like of Oxley and Danbury. There was something of a problem, first I'd need to pass the motorcar driving test: luck was it I bagged a cancellation slot at the Braintree test centre and to everyone's amazement I gained the correct piece of paper to say I could drive big things like motorhomes. I found how big they were when negotiating across London from Brixton to visit Suffolk and Norfolk for a few days of camping with a Winnebago. It wasn't the *big* part that was the worry, it was the width of the vehicle and someone had also put the steering wheel in the wrong place. But it did have a huge bathroom!

Training on the dump

MEET one man who is NOT dissatisfied with sporting facilities in Maldon. He is magazine editor Peter Lumley, who has been making good use of the saltings to the east of the Promenade, to get into trim for forthcoming scooter and motor-cycle races.

A member of Maldon Auto Club, Peter has not raced for six months following a serious accident. In recent weeks he has been putting in a few hours practice to shake off the rust before he takes part in the Brighton Mondial and Snetterton 12-hour race.

Most people in the country complain about training facilities for scootering and motorcycling — but not Peter. He reckons that the clay and rubble covered salt-mounds and tricky ridges, provide an ideal training ground.

During the last week he has been test riding a new Lambretta for his monthly magazine. The scooter has been designed as a cheap-to-ride commuter and fun bike, but the makers probably never envisaged it as a training bike on Maldon's Council dump.

13 pictured in Italy

It was going to Italy on a Lambretta which introduced me to riding on the *other* side of the road, it also taught me a lot about how to sit in one place for hours at an end and twist a throttle to wind in interminable strips of dual carriage highway, first it was Belgium, then came Germany, the habit slipped a bit in Switzerland but once over the Alps we soon discovered Italy had caught itself the same roadbuilding rash. But it was all worth it as after the longest continuous road journey I had ever made we were in Milan, a city as near the centre of the two-wheel universe as you can get. We were there to join 20th anniversary celebrations with Innocenti and the XIX Raduno Internazionale Motociclistico. At the end of WWII a company in Milan had launched the Lambretta scooter, and at different places nowadays it is not only available to buy new something that resembles the original thing but personal fortunes will also be spent putting new life into an oldie. It may well have become a rust-bucket or a deteriorating mechanical mix of parts that don't wish to co-operate with other parts, but the result is often a glamorous, smartly decorated two wheeler which then is magnificently distinct yet still with that sameness of an exhaust note defining it as a Lambretta. In 1968 I rode overland to Milan with Ken Peters, a director of Watford based Arthur Francis scooter dealership after he'd outlined an idea thrown into the pot by Mike Karslake that it'd be good to celebrate the full twenty years of Lambretta and write it up as a *Scootering & Lightweights* feature.

It didn't go exactly with a roll at the beginning, engine seizures bringing heart stopping moments almost from daybreak on the first day. It was preparedness that kept us going, Ken had a bag of tools, a pack or two of spare piston rings and was adept in that task, as with sorting clutch slippage his little machine suffered and encouraging more in the way of determination out of a small, and elderly, engine. Think long miles and the climb over the Alps for his 1948 Type A original Lambretta that completed our round trip of over 1,200 miles: there were obviously lots of guts inside that little 125cc two-stroke engine. It was an epic trip, Lambretta guru Mike Karslake had met us at the Rochford airport where we embarked for a short cross-Channel flight in a British Air Ferries Carvair plane to Ostend. The scooters were loaded onto the plane by a ramp that lifted us into the bulbous nose of an aircraft, a brainwave of Freddy Laker who had produced a cardboard model of his idea to show how a converted Douglas DC-4 low-flying plane could whisk people and their

For their trip to Milan (then Rimini) in 1968 Ken and Peter first rode to Southend in Essex where they caught a British Air Ferries flight on a 'Carvair' plane to France.

Peter Lumley and Ken Peters somewhere in the Alps, 1968.

was hit with this knackered feeling, plus the fact that I couldn't use my hands properly because of the vibration caused by the lack of silent blocks fitted.

What was your time from London to Milan?
It took me 16 hours, 50 minutes. I didn't take any motorways throughout the journey, it was all A- and B-roads apart from a small stretch of Autostrada just before Milan.

The route was critical, I had it taped to the headset! Because most of the riding was going to be done at night you could take direct routes through towns without worrying about traffic too much. I can't remember exactly but it was as direct route as I could to get to Geneva, through the tunnel, then Aosta and down to Milan.

Where did you go from Milan?
Well we were meant to be riding down to the Lambretta rally in Rome after that where Bob was to meet the Pope. But when I got to Milan I was the only one of our lot there, no one else had arrived yet! They'd left on Monday, me on Wednesday, and here I was on Thursday in Milan on my own. Anyway, when we were ready, because I had no feeling in my hands still, Rex White and Bob Wilkinson had to run

alongside me to let the clutch out because of my fingers and I had to crash the gears when riding because I couldn't use the clutch! We did that a few times when they had to refuel or we all had to stop. But once we did stop at traffic lights for example, I couldn't get going again without their help!

Back in the UK now and you mentioned earlier the Bultaco Lambretta...
Yes, Arthur had come up with the idea that we could graft a Bultaco cylinder and cylinder head onto a Lambretta engine. There were a lot of technical problems we had to overcome with it though to even get it to run.

I can't remember everything about it but Alan was involved, Arthur and myself – we talked about it, got the frame prepared and got a 250 Bultaco road-going top end for it. We even made up a crude 250 badge for it which we riveted to the front legshield. Anyway, the first problem was that the Lambretta is force air-cooled and the Bultaco was plain air-cooled, so we had to get all that Bultaco finning machined off to fit into the cowling so it would both look like a normal Lambretta but also have a chance of being cooled. It was made of

alloy so it had that benefit, but there weren't many fins left.

Then we had to do the crankshaft as the stroke for the Bultaco was different from any Lambretta. I think we took a 175 Series 2 crank, dismantled it and stroked it by machining a different pin. The fear we had was overheating and I think even then we knew it had a limited life. I mean, how do you keep the damn thing cool? But it did run. Our calculations were that at the crank it would develop 30bhp, three times the power of a normal Lambretta. I remember it running, we got it out on the road and I think our fears for overheating were justified and we all made the commercial decision that it was good to try but that it wasn't a goer.

What other conversions were done?
We'd do most things I think, but the biggest we went up to for Lambretta was 225cc. You couldn't take the Lambretta barrel out any further than that.

Did you do much testing of products?
We all mucked in for that because we were all riding places. If you were going away for a rally at the weekend you'd bolt on stuff to see if it worked, or to make sure it didn't fall off!

Brussels, en route to Milan 1968.

Ken (pictured here with the hotel manager) checking them in to his regular Milanese hotel from his Lambretta Concessionaires days, near Linate to the east of the city.

My first ever time to Milan, reached on a scooter trip with a difference, our departure from the former wartime airstrip at Rochford, now reckoned to be the best London airport for service and friendliness. A Freddy Laker inspired transporter plane carrying cars and our scooters got us to Ostend. We didn't sleep very much during our ride to Milan, nor on the way back either, but this was an Innocenti celebration and a rally with a bit of history. This is a page from *Scootering* magazine when they interviewed Ken Peters about his record Lambretta riding between London and Milan and other times with the Arthur Francis operation.

vehicles to European destinations. The route I chose was Southend to Ostende, in Belgium, Ken arrived from Watford on a rattling Type A Lambretta already needing some roadside fettling to reach Southend. He congratulated my choice of Ostende as a better place to land than Le Touquet, seeing this was another day when most of France was in utter turmoil with strikes, civil unrest, demonstrations, student riots and the like: no planes were landing there. I admitted my map reading had let me down, rather than my being bright enough to predict Gallic temperament: we flew to Belgium. Things weren't good after we landed, the 1948 scooter had fractious tendencies which Ken Peters tempered by maintaining a speed closer to 39.5 mph than the 45mph which would play havoc with piston rings of the single cylinder scooter. Any faster travel on the dreadful tilted concrete slab highway with jarring joins that endlessly vibrated us, wouldn't have been safe to man or machine anyway. Getting to Milan was easy, we'd been told: drive the main road through Brussels, turn right at Aachen in Germany, follow that road to Basle in Switzerland and after climbing through the Alps and over the St Gotthard Pass you'll be in Italy. Milan is not much further on, and you can drive past Como on an Autopista. *Yes!*

We left Southend Airport before midday, at tea-time we were threading through heavy home-going Brussels traffic and then outside Cologne, some time nearer midnight, the pfennig coins I stuffed into a drinks dispenser delivered me a kolsch, rather than a soft drink: wrong button! We pressed on, took a breakfast stop somewhere near Baden Baden then come darkness for the second time since leaving England - all without a proper rest - we booked into a zimmer-frei close to William Tell's town of Altdorf. The kind owner let us safely garage Ken's valuable scooter in the corridor outside our bedroom, upstairs: don't ask! Next day was uphill a lot, along corridor roads hewn through snow reaching higher than a house either side of us, then a twisting tunnel and out into a blast of searing sunlight with hair-dryer hot air that soon softened Ken's Barbour and my Belstaff waxed jackets. The sun turned refrigerator cold riding to sun-blessed bliss in seconds, it was still Switzerland but did we care where we were, we'd begun to feel human again. There was not much in the way of greetings and welcoming humanity at the Italian border, though, after looping and looping even more down the multi-hairpin road we discovered that sun is often followed by rain, although crickets still chirped and the tarmac steamed as would a good dash of water onto the coals in a sauna. Milan just couldn't come soon enough - but even that was cruelly dashed from us because our scooters were banned from driving on the Autopista. It took a pistol butt gripping man in uniform to persuade us it wasn't more money he was talking about, it was our engine size was below what was allowed on the main route. It also continued to rain, so heavily in fact that piles of young leaves ripped from the branches of roadside trees blocked gutters and culverts, turning them into a green river for us to bow-wave through.

Our hotel was at the outskirts of Milan, a little distance from the wide gates into the Lambretta factory at Lambrate. Bed was bliss, three days at nothing more than 40mph had been tortuous and just the one nap in a bed at Altdorf hardly brought noticed recuperation: but now I must work. This began at a desk session with Dr Guido Candello, the company marketing and Press boss who welcomed us with a pile of Lire, dosh we really needed as this was when Britain allowed residents to leave the UK with no more than fifty pounds Sterling. Petrol was rationed in Italy so we were also given a signed and stamped document that licensed us tourists to refill the tank of our scooters. Mechanics at Lambrate took our weary scooters into a restricted factory area to make adjustments, there was nothing much needed to do for the aged Type A, but my 1968 model needed serious attention. The rear hub and brake certainly needed real tlc as on zigzags from the St Gotthard Pass my scooter had slowed to almost walking pace despite plenty of throttle twisting. Stopping, I took off the covering side panel to discover the obvious giveaway of burning, bubbling paint on the rear hub as it blistered to brown: it was my going ahead to photograph Ken Peters sedately cruising his Type A through the multitude of bends and then my catching up with him again had been an experience. It also heated up the brake pads and slowed the scooter to a near halt.

I wasn't told what the mechanics did but as they worked I was getting to enjoy riding Lambretta's latest powered two-wheeler, the Luna. It carries the legend of having been designed by fashion house Bertone, the studio which in the future would also contribute to product for other two-wheel interests with the K20 helmet for Swiss bicycle and motorcycle helmet manufacturer Kiwi. On the new Lambretta I felt you sat a little higher than the available conventional scooters, and had a distinctive profile showing off an open frame style that would later appeal to riders wanting a sporty machine that could be thrown into corners and used at off road sporting events. In the Italian market the models were called Lui, whilst all exports of the 75cc versions were called Vega or Cometa, Dr. Candello impressed upon me this was the first time it had been ridden by anyone from England. Since 1960 the Italian company had progressed a collaborative deal with BMC, who wanted a slice of the somewhat restrictive Italian market. Innocenti's car producing ventures had started in 1960 and of the to-ing and fro-ing of car parts and scooters between Italy and England I asked Dr Candello if Ken Peters was the first and only Englishman to actually move by road any fully completed modern product from either maker in either country. If that was the case his riding a 1948 made Lambretta all the way back to where it had been born in Lambrate would also be some act to follow! Of the things I heard about Innocenti was their history of engineering expertise had begun

Biked@ys
INTERNATIONAL FORUM ON BICYCLE TRENDS

PRIMA SESSIONE (giovedì 17 settembre-ore 15)
BICI E MOBILITA'
Confronto con le città, i cittadini, i politici

Chairman: BRIAN MONTGOMERY, Presidente del COLIBI, Francia
Introduce: HANS VAN VLIET, Sales Director Shimano Europe, Olanda
Sintesi: OLLY HATCH, European Cyclists' Federation Conference Director

Intervengono: parlamentari europei, parlamentari italiani, le città "pensilata" con Milano, le città aderenti a Cities for Cyclists, al Club des Villes Cyclables, all'Associazione Italiana Città Ciclabili, rappresentanti dell'ECF (European Cyclists' Federation) e della FIAB (Federazione Italiana Amici della Bicicletta).

SECONDA SESSIONE (venerdì 18 settembre-ore 15)
BICI E TURISMO
Italia in ritardo: esperienze di altri Paesi

Chairman: ANGEL TONA, Direttore Editoriale di Luike Sportpress, Spagna
Introduce: LAUREN HEFFERSON, Direttore di Ciclismo Classico, USA
Sintesi: PETER LUMLEY, Direttore di "Bicycle Trade & Industry", Inghilterra

Intervengono: esperti del settore, operatori turistici, imprenditori e manager di Aziende di vari Paesi che organizzano viaggi in bicicletta, utenti del turismo in bici.

TERZA SESSIONE (sabato 19 settembre-ore 15)
BICI E SPORT
Come promuovere il ciclismo tra i "giovani" attraverso i "vecchi" campioni

Chairman: VALENTINO CAMPAGNOLO
Introduce: VITTORIO ADORNI
Sintesi: FELIX MAGOWAN, Direttore di Velonews, USA

Sono stati invitati: Fiorenzo Magni Presidente degli Azzurri d'Italia, Alfredo Martini, Eddy Merckx, Felice Gimondi, Francesco Moser, Giuseppe Saronni.
È prevista la partecipazione di numerosi campioni, giornalisti sportivi e opinion leaders.

FIRST SESSION (thursday 17 september at 3 pm)
BICYCLES AND MOBILITY
Meeting with cities, citizens and politicians

Chairman: BRIAN MONTGOMERY, President of COLIBI, France
Introduction: HANS VAN VLIET, Sales Director Shimano Europe, Holland
Summary: OLLY HATCH, European Cyclists' Federation Conference Director

Talks by: Italian members of the European parliament, cities twinned with Milan, cities that are members of Cities for Cyclist of the Club des Villes Cyclables, of the Associazione Italiana Città Ciclabili, representatives of the EFC (European Cyclists' Federation) and of the FIAB (Italian Federation of Bicycle Friends).

SECOND SESSION (friday 18 september at 3 pm)
BICYCLES AND TOURISM
Italy far behind: experiences of other countries

Chairman: ANGEL TONA, Editor-in-Chief of Luike Sportpress, Spain
Introduction: LAUREN HEFFERSON, Director of Ciclismo Cycling, USA
Summary: PETER LUMLEY, Director of "Bicycle Trade & Industry", Great Britain

Talks by: experts of the sector, tourist operators, entrepreneurs and managers of companies from different countries that organise bicycle trips, biking tourists.

THIRD SESSION (saturday 19 september at 3 pm)
BICYCLES AND SPORT
How to promote biking among "youths" through "old" champions

Chairman: VALENTINO ADORNI
Introduction: VITTORIO ADORNI
Summary: FELIX MAGOWAN, Director of Velonews, USA

Guests: Fiorenzo Magni Chairman of the Azzurri d'Italia, Alfredo Martini, Eddy Merckx, Felice Gimondi, Francesco Moser, Giuseppe Saronni.
The participation of numerous champions, sports journalists opinion leaders is expected.

the ECIMA shows in Milan brought more than product to the table, here Costantino Ruggiero introduces Brian Montgomery and myself to an international Trade audience at the Biked@ays forum.

In 1968 the Italian company Innocenti gave Ken Peters and myself a reason to ride Lambrettas to their 20th anniversary bash. A bonus came with the opportunity to see how the new Luna rode in a trip from the the factory at Lambrate (right) after I had steered an overloaded 125 on a long trip and over the Alps.

In the heart of Milan at the huge industrial style exhibition centre ANCMA staged their bi-annual Show in tune with IFMA Cologne, a deal which ended when another organiser entered the product fairs programme to upset cordial arrangements. Here's a Tony Oliver picture of one happy editor emerging from the full works and delights of an EICMA Press Salon lunchtime networking session which had involved fine food and much cork pulling.

in the 1920s, since when they had maintained good and able production capacity: in 1943 they were actually the largest supplier to the Italian Ministry of War of bullets, making over 36,000 bullets every day. After a day or so we shot off to Rimini, although the opening salvo was more like a damp squib following someone at the hotel managing to juxta position 05 and 09. Being four hours early for the train departure meant devising a battle plan for sleeping on a Lambretta scooter at the noisy Milano Centrale station. Yes, the train would leave 09.05 the ticket office confirmed, yes you can take your scooter to the luggage loading point after 08.30. *"Yes, we'll load it for you"*. The positives in all that secured the moment although there were a lot of negatives in draping legs over the handlebars scooter to balance yourself on the dual seat. The battle began around 04.37 with the hope of staying warm enough to sleep. Comfort level was nil. Rimini is on the Adriatic coast, at about back of the knee position on an outline map of Italy: my back of the knees were numb. The coast finally showed up as miles of golden sands, in 1843 they built the Kursaal especially for the rich people who require something more sumptuous than a sandy shoreline, though. From our hotel balcony we could see the sea but weren't swimmingly in the mood for entertainment of any sort seeing we had been up and about since before 4am, soon we'd be going on parade. In a gaggle of Lambrettas we left Rimini, then Italy heading up and away for little over seven or eight miles to the multi-party democratic republic of San Marino, Passports weren't needed. The enclave lacks any flat land, has no national debt and runs a budget surplus. Roads twist, turn and soar more or less to the summit of Monte Titano and the fort there which stands at 2,457 ft (749 m) above sea level. Through WWII the place remained neutral, but poor military intelligence meant it still got bombed, first by the RAF, then in 1944 it was briefly occupied by German forces, who were defeated by the Allies at the Battle of San Marino.

The mass of scooterists were celebrating the forty years of Lambretta at the XIX Raduno Internazionale Motociclistico, with music and speeches, awards and trophies presented before engines sparked or spluttered and to San Marino we rode. Then it rained: our British weather beating Barbour and Belstaff clothing was back at the hotel so we joined the rush on a local hardware store to buy six feet lengths of heavyweight clear plastic. With shared scissors a hole was cut to poke a head through, a strap secured the sparse shield from flapping and the whole exercise went so smoothly then this must be the normal practice for locals. Next morning the 200 miles back to Milan was hardly seen likely to be a happy prelude to traversing the Alps again - we opted to board from Rimini the cross-European train that starts in Rome and ends up in Amsterdam. Someone made it problematical to board though, the message was not understood by the Stationmaster who preferred we left our scooters in his safe keeping, they'd follow on the next freight train to Milan. That didn't seem a sensible idea to Ken or myself as everything we owned in Italy was standing right there in front of us on wheels, it was very unlikely we'd be getting on any train to anywhere without our scooters and luggage. The platform guard wanted us aboard, we wanted to get on board, the train driver wanted us on board, the Stationmaster already had one hand on our scooters but no-one appreciated what was being said in plain English and strained Italian from our side. No panic, just to make the point I resorted to sign language, and with two fingers made the motion of cutting a throat. I looked the Stationmaster full in the eye, *"Innocenti will not be happy. Innocenti kill!"* accentuating my words with further throat passing fingers. A train luggage porter jumped from the carriage to the platform, then without any help from us heaved first the Type A then my scooter through the open door into the luggage compartment, we climbed aboard, a green flag waved, a whistle blew, we waved back as the train moved from the station.

Back in the metropolis we ate early, went to bed early, rose early and left Milan steadily, trickling the morning traffic to retrace our route through Como and towards Switzerland. Como has managed to connect me to history several times, first at the Hotel Villa Flori, the place where the Italian general Giuseppe Garibaldi was married, here I silently watched a tv screen reporting that Freddy Mercury had died of pneumonia that day, in 1991. Further along the lake Villa d'Este is a rather comfortable retreat at the lake side and with private grounds which will keep you amused all day. Here in 1998 I heard an international energy expert tell a conference attended by two hundred or so engine producers and people who were making top Italian motorcycles that *"when crude oil reaches 50$ a barrel you are all going to be out of business."* The story was spun with facts, figures and lots of information about hydrogen power and how things would change once we embraced fuel cells. The presentations were all very convincing, crude prices have topped 160$ since that conference but have been pretty steady at 60$ or so, perhaps we are too much in love with having wet fuel in the tank to react - at present. We'd need to refill our tanks several times on our long and slow journey out of Italy, through Switzerland, Germany and then Belgium. As it was pre-Euro days we needed to scrabble inside four different purses for small change, although Barclaycard had been around since 1966, two years earlier than our trip to Lambretta, so was handy for petrol and the zimmer frei stop. There was quite a bit of uphill and during the day we experienced an example of hare and the tortoise progression as two motorbikes with passengers passed us not the once but three times before reaching St Gotthard. In that final overtaking, something like three hours before we'd seen them the first time, they noisily rattled by with their exhaust notes accentuated in the confines of a short section of tunnel but once through there the high snow walls on either side muffled sounds as quickly as it brought the colder air bit. As evening darkened as we rode into Altdorf and the same little guesthouse we'd already used. The St Gotthard Pass itself has a stretch of cobbled road that was no joy to drive even in our car on a later occasion when we toured to Italy, but we won't talk about what it does to you when riding two wheels. The alternative for people is to get through the mountains here on what is the longest rail tunnel in the world, nearly 36 miles of it, built in June 2016 following 134 years on from the very first near ten mile tunnel constructed to handle early rail transport. The water which flows on the Gotthard Massif has a split personality, some ends up reaching the Adriatic, flowing there as the Po, the water heading north helps the Rhine flow all the way to Holland.

We passed Basle, turned left at Aachen on another all-night trundle before showing our passports at the Customs when leaving Germany to enter Belgium. Ostende was reached in time for late breakfast but before that there was an amazing and frightening encounter: an unrecognised wild-looking creature stared back at me through the mirror over the washbasins . . . this sight one I'd seen never before nor since, a Panda face in reverse but deeply grey not white, with red centred blobs of eyes on the round of white where dirt from the highways had plastered thickly. This ride to Innocenti and back would finish happily, it had been the classic *"you must do it"* journey which demonstrated fully that it ain't what you've got that matters, it's simply what you do with it that counts. Two very small engined scooters had been quite as determined as the riders to turn an idea into reality. It made a good story for *Scootering and Lightweights* magazine then, and a year or so back from today the Mortons monthly scooter magazine brought it all back to life with a story about Ken Peters, Lambretta and his love for scooters. These were powerful words about powered two wheelers and what you can get them to do if you set about it with a good idea to mind.

14 b2b habits

"existence is a blessing to those beings endowed with perception" Richard Steele

Writing about people who work to provide sustainability and a personal lifestyle for themselves or their brand, that is a topic; the how, the why and the materials employed on the way to reaching the market with their wares, that is the story for writers to craft. The reporter or feature writer who engages inventors, producers or providers in the supply chain, they are deploying b2b journalism and it's a job with many hurdles. Becher's Brook on the Grand National horse race course at Aintree near Liverpool, that is the same sort of obstacle a word jockey can encounter as the marketing or pr operator punt the anticipation that you will be happy to ride with the entry called Wheel Re-invention. We all know what happens at Becher's Brook is horses for courses, another hurdle in the editorial stakes comes as the input lobbied in the shape of a hoop from those where their advocacy is to influence decisions on just how you should word a story in their way to please a client from whom they are taking a wadge of money to organise media matters. Print, social media and the internet are two way streets in the journey to a written page, or should be, the wary must watch out for potholes as in 2018 there's a new one on the path: marketing circles, some of them based inside or working for the big brands, look to identify the friendly *persuader,* who will take on the word syrup they want spread around. This positioning is not a pothole, rather the deep pit that would-be media manipulators can only dig for themselves along with the reputation of a client or brand. When short of originality or ideas themselves, they'll blindly spend a client's promotional budget on quite the wrong function in the mechanics of building brand awareness.

That recalls my experiences from the '70s when in the members' lounge of The Press Club at Shoe Lane, EC4 I'd regularly chat with a Fleet Street man who'd earned a solid reputation for getting to the nub of things in the business world, him writing the stuff people noticed. The Press Club was the platform where you'd meet real media people in relaxed mode, with some in a corner huddle doing what they now call networking, and occasionally someone thumping a table or the bar to show passion, or possibly their frustration even an annoyance. Out of that regular mix Stan became a mentor and talking to me about making close friends with people in

beingThere to visit Eddy Merckx at his new factory was followed by meeting him on the company booth at EICMA, then later at Shows and places in Britain too.

TI-Raleigh in Nottingham's Lenton Bouvelard: Howard Briercliffe, Andy Sutcliffe, Chris Hill, Yvonne Fisk, Alan Clarke,amongst others and myself at a product briefing for the coming model year. At one time 75% of UK bike business went through their hands and with sister companies. Under the Tube Investments Group the monolith lost money, with the operation taken over in a management buy-out.

a community you are likely to be writing about, he firmly told me *"don't."* There is nothing wrong with being sociable in their company, he said, *"never compromise your integrity, and make sure people are aware you are a journalist. Your job is to always relate to the reader, you are writing for them so get answer to the questions they'd ask. The goal must always be to respect and treasure readers, without their trust you are worth absolutely nothing."*

Pointing to the time when business to business communication first began is somewhat like seeking the pine needle hidden amongst a stack of hay, so just how b2b publishing came into lives is a seriously un-fathomable question. The motive for the writer working with makers and suppliers is to put people in danger of doing business, the Stone Age axe-head my Father gave to me after it had been dredged from the River Crouch is very much a product skilfully produced by an artisan. As a product it was almost certainly manufactured to be traded on, then being sold as an important tool for workmen. It could have been used to put somebody in danger, maybe chop branches for shelter or turn deadwood into fuel, and if that stone could talk then maybe you'd be hearing how a b2b journalist of that time would have asked the maker how this piece of flint was shaped. Its flat edges and bevels took hours, days, and weeks to transform a rough chipped out piece of stone into being a thing of beautiful usefulness. To know how that axe head had been sold or traded, and how it had ended up in the River Crouch then into a fisherman's net - that's the sort of story about product, people, purpose that I like to write.

The axe-head, as quite the earliest made product I own, shares a place in my den with a book printed in 1562 that has also managed to serve as a useful tool for its readers. It was printed in the year Spain stopped English ships from trading at their New World ports, something of a protectionist stance after John Hawkins had initiated the English trans-Atlantic slave trade to traffic people from Sierra Leone on the Guinea Coast across to the Caribbean. You may wonder if a b2b reporter would have been reporting that as the news story, or about that book where some-one had added their finely inked pen-work as footnotes, Latin inscriptions and dates that were obviously important to the reader at the time they'd opened the pages. I wonder where that book found its first buyer, who printed it, who was the seller and just as importantly, who was the first reader. Such a riddle, and it would so nice to have answers about these particular stone and paper treasures which already carry for me an importance beyond what they actually represent in value as artefacts. You can admire and envy the skill of the person who scraped and shaped that piece of flint, just as I ponder what was in the mind of writers who have inked their thoughts on the printed pages and the backplate of the leather bound paper jewel. Similarly, in another set of books I have collected are the writings of Joseph Addison and

Richard Steele reprinted from *The Spectator* of 1733, these chronicles also have on the pages the added readers' thoughts and questioning written into the margins. All this shows for me that even from that early time of reportage and writing there has always been the reader or two who has wanted to add their own two pence worth to what had been written, perhaps as a correction of fact, perhaps as a reminder to an opinion they've had? Another book I have is hand written all the way through, *"Two Cyclists Ride to London and Back"* is the impeccably scribed November 1909 work telling how Mr J. Outhwaite and his friend Joe Wrightson left York just after eight on a May morning, riding through the East Midlands and south to London. The book is more than their diary or a report, it's a personalised travelogue with words wrapped around a collection of picture postcards bought along the way which show a different time to our own. Written with close personal observations, often both pleasing and unsavoury in turn for themselves, this book was never intended to have a b2b styling but the business of beingThere and doing it with bicycles is the real worth from the pages, these two riders discovering and then relating for us a part of England now long gone, but an important part of our lives as the collation encapsulates our heritage.

The responsibility to use words without fear or favour can be interpreted however you will, and then there is the *never write for money* remark oft voiced by those who would teach others how to write. Probably this last one is a tactic to hide the truth that *"how to write"* lessons won't easily lead writers to be earners, because that isn't how journalism works. Like many in the profession which sustains me it is routine to write almost every day, after all that's the job! Most days open for me with an hour or so of scribing before breakfast, not for money but to satisfy the craving to be *wordly* productive after some hours of snoring. For me the job works, just as nowadays I don't normally look at emails and the like until around the time for late morning coffee, also you'll notice that I term writing as *"the job"* and that is because I mostly am working out how words and pictures can meaningfully be assembled to tell the story on the page. Probably this comes from the way news reporting and tourism topics were shaping my future when working on *The Rag* at Burnham. I'd learned from watching how Mr Savage, the acknowledged editor of the weekly paper, would walk across Station Road from his chemist shop on the corner of Coronation Road carrying a tight little bundle of worked on letters and papers he'd typed up or handwritten in his special 1940s speed writing style. Those words went into the printer's composing stick one letter at a time then into the column-width galley for proofing and reading before the newspaper was printed and delivered into the broad market place. To explain, the stone is the base of all letterpress printing, being the solid and honed flat foundation where the type of the to-be printed word passes from the hands of the typesetter then onwards to machine printing. There can be no chips in this stone by the way: to have any would degrade the written word, effectively obscuring a clean impression and spoiling it for both the pre-press reader and those who follow. In today's terms the proof reader doing that job is the equivalent of the spell-checker of a word processor, but I'd reckon the human form is certainly more able to grasp nuances and feelings than any electronic device could hope to manage. At a pinch, this octogenarian will accept some readers may want to see stories delivered to their Smart Handheld, yet I know nary-a-one who doesn't appreciate paper is tactile and that thoughts put on paper will always gain a more indelible impact. I bet you often do it that way.

The one thing to trust is there are many ways of spoiling the message, and one of them comes in the form of a reader's interpretation of what they are seeing on the page, or think they are seeing on the page. It's always worth taking a second turn through a paragraph or even the chapter, that's a reason why so much of the good reading which people have about them can appear well-thumbed. A note being written in the margin of a page is another clue that they have actually had thoughts about what the words meant! Of the printing shops and publishing offices where I perched following my escape from Burnham, an ink-stained printer's apron often partnered my creating stories and features or spiking stuff at the editorial desk. It was local newspapers, specialist magazines and the like that attracted me to being based in Essex, Norfolk, London, and at other places on our island as well as for international publishers, by far my longest lived-in writing den though has been here in the North East. I enjoy the urge to create from a glimpse at a panorama or of stuff encompassing a subject to deliver more than just words to help inform, inspire or encourage others, that is why a camera figures so much in the way I work and it matters that the camera is always at hand. I chose to travel mostly by bicycle to get to grips with the topic of tourism and how it impacts on all people, walking can be a slow process to unroll a vista, but the bicycle does it at the pace you can control. It was after bicycling a lot I then came to spend time within the scooter scene, a bit quicker moving than a bicycle perhaps but still two wheels which park up easily to garner photo images. Reporting the sport and tourism opportunities with a scooter brought the realisation that small wheels can still cover lots of ground, go fast and also be a convenient form of commuting. I was then introduced to the thinking that city life could be so much better with electric vehicles, this particular engagement coming with the electric car scene in the '60s when I was working at the Gavin Starey operation. His office was promoting London built electric battery powered Enfield cars, today the electric vehicle is all the rage yet there at the thick edge of fifty years ago we were telling readers this style of transport would soon - *soon!* -

bring pollution-free City streets. Many a leaf has fallen over many years from many branches to a 2018 which sees workers in Sunderland, amongst other places, rolling electric cars off production lines. Some things take a long time to break through, don't they, and I have seen that with the way that in the UK the e-bike is bravely stating a good case but a message still not being heard very clearly.

Leaving that first London job where Gavin Starey's office overlooked the frenetically traffic-cluttered, pollution riven Fleet Street and Ludgate Circus I moved up West to a new editorial office in Oxford Street. Here it was equally cluttered with a long line of engines still running in stop-start mode, mostly halted traffic reaching to the east beyond Centre Point and west to past Marble Arch, hither and yon belching a purplish haze all the way. My new desk was in a more than busy place but also one with character, Gillow House has architectural and heritage charm, built in 1905 for furniture makers Waring & Gillow this was where I'd first write b2b stuff for horticultural types. The Haymarket Publishing reception area demonstrated a true printing connection with a panel wall covered with magazine front cover copper letterpress printing plates, some in the sequence of the set of four used to complete the letterpress printing of a colour image, for me this signified you really were right at the heart of publishing. By the lift doors from our upper floor you could see people waiting below, and quite recently I was reminded of the hullabaloo after the golden locks of the company top dog standing below had been a target for dribbles from a coffee cup. I had listened at an OTS event in Warwickshire where Simon Baseley mentioned his being at Haymarket in the time I worked there, and had I heard someone had got sacked for the coffee dripping episode? He told us *"it was the wrong guy who was accused and then got the push, I was there and right at that spot so I know . ."*

The b2b *Gardeners Chronicle-HTJ* move from Gillow House took Colin Parnell's editorial team to a Foubert's Place office in Soho in the time before I'd then go to working from Regent House on the *Practical* titles, based by Piccadilly Circus. My first year or so spell of b2b reporting the horticultural scene brought some really rewarding episodes dredged from opportunity of being News Editor at the weekly *Gardeners Chronicle-Horticultural Trade Journal.* The b2b didn't just do horticulture, it was the weekly bible for professionals such as market garden people, amenity and garden centres and those growing flowers, shrubs and the like at Authority and Council establishments. Circulating as the house-magazine for the Horticultural Trade it was published Thursday and carried the latest market prices for that week of trading. We didn't have internet, there wasn't a fax machine other than a rotary copying gadget linking us to the printer down on the Medway sending back page proofs. We did have a runner who came to the office to collect our manu-

It was in Accrington when I first met the touring cyclist who has ridden as many miles as it is to the moon and back. Tilmann Waldthaler has been just about everywhere, preferring a bicycle to jetting between Australia and Europe! He has written books, given talks and above all put heart into encouraging people to take up cycling simply by his travelling to explain how good it is for you. On Bodensee I picture him with Albrecht von Dewitz who's VauDe travel gear has kept Tilmann comfortable and safe on many of his journeys.

a Nottinghamshire business making a name for itself in the new backpacking era was Banton who imported and sold Fjallraven tents under SeAb. They made high quality duvets and sleeping bags, amongst ones I trialled from them was a down inner bag zipped inside one with synthetic fill to combat damp. Banton also made some very wearable insulated clothing in Nottingham. Boss Alun Daley is on the right in this photo on Pen-y-Ghent where Derrick Booth and a friend were along for the day. (TOP) This double skin tent from Fjallraven had an alu-minised flysheet which could be reversed to match the vaugaries in seasonal use. This was good for temperature control.

scripts and the photos and the page design we'd want followed back at the Medway printers. Generally the job was all phone, phone, notebooks and networking with the Trade and our retained freelances who used Royal Mail to get their stories and news to us: that or they telephoned over their copy, which was such a laborious exercise! Those stringers were our eyes, ears and nose who we'd take time with to develop the story, the result would often be an honestly won scoop for which they'd get the credit and a top-up to the retainer payment. Today journalism isn't quite like that: if you let it our game is dog eat dog with too little time to digest properly facts and nuances which can then turn a story on its head. How too often that's the case with readers suffering through people publishing ahead of getting it right. Some stories are a dream to write, and they'll always turn out better when energy is put into checking how your readership will tune into the item you are writing.

Plenty of people were, and are, quite aware that Agent Orange was dropped on the Vietnam battlefields following the British use of it previously in the Malayan Emergency, but do readers appreciate that it also contributed to other environmental and human tragedies. On the pages of *Gardeners Chronicle-HTJ* my story was about how this broad leaf defoliant 2,4,5-Trichlorophenoxyacetic acid, also known as 2,4,5-T, had been widely used from the late 1940s in the agricultural industry. That was until concerns about dire toxicity saw it phased out. Research confirmed that a production accident in 1963 at the Philips-Duphar plant in the Netherlands did a real deal in damage. Six workers employed to tidy and clean up afterwards got seriously intoxicated and developed chloracne, an acne-like eruption of blackheads, cysts, and pustules. Of these workers four died within a dozen years. Those lines in the story were compelling but dreadful, and needed writing, just as detail of when during the chemical's manufacturing process trace amounts of 2,3,7,8-tetrachlorodibenzo-p-dioxin (TCDD) occur - nastily that brings long-term environmental effects. With proper controls during production of 2,4,5-T, the levels of TCDD can be held to about .005 parts per million, yet ahead of when scientific evaluation and control were properly in place findings from some early production batches tested later were found to have as much as 60 ppm of the toxicity. In this case, my writing that news story got to tell how God's planet is now processing the deadly effects, although that can't be said of people themselves: the health effects on humans from 2,4,5-T at low environmental doses or at bio-monitored levels from low environmental exposures are unknown. But no worry there, the side effects are nothing other than bodily weakness, headache, dizziness, nausea, abdominal pain, myotonia, hypotension, renal and hepatic injury, along with delayed neuropathy. Oh, so far, so good!

There is the saying that what goes around, comes around and how scary that from those days of my b2b reporting for *Gardeners Chronicle* I would also bump up against other worrying environmental episodes in coming years. With guys publishing the outdoor and environmental magazine *Footloose*, I was threatened with probable financial ruin by people who didn't like the portrayal of our story that CFC containing products were giving the environment a hard time. They objected to a fact filled feature written by Nick Brown who was alerting our readers to the depleting ozone layer. The British Aerosol Manufacturers' Association became very upset, asked for a retraction or apology but gaining short shrift on our pages they phoned me as the magazine publisher to suggest I was shortly heading for a day or three in Court, and it'd cost me more money than I could imagine existed. *"No matter"* I told the man, *"the story is quite accurately and factually reported as you well know, however I am recording this telephone conversation and your threats and will hold it as part of the evidence I will present in Court."* The line went dead. Some years after that it was my writing *"What has China Got Against Fish"* that left me accused of being something of a fanatic when our *tradeandindustry* b2b reported in depth the Greenpeace Dirty Laundry exposures. I was gobsmacked to be labelled that way, after all it was at an OIA agm bash where we were hearing about the effort the European Outdoor Group were putting into building awareness of our need to care more for the environment. The story I wrote was fair reporting of what was happening through Greenpeace and also being said out there in a world which is far bigger than any of us; Mark Held's comment left me uneasy then, and since. My reporting approach also touched nerves in Nottinghamshire, a place where roses generally smell good. It didn't really please 1898 born Harry Wheatcroft, himself a man who was real and big and although sometimes quite prickly in dialogue, he was a very colourful person who also grew roses like no-one else could grow roses. Trouble came after he had managed to kill off a fair bit of rose root stock, and that had me digging in on a *Gardener's Chronicle* story before coming face to face with the Rose Tycoon himself. His company had advertised through a magazine Box Number to acquire lots of replacement growth, unaware of how far this story would stretch I discovered that Mr Wheatcroft was not about to co-operate, in any shape or form. After over two days of continuous phoning around I luckily discovered where the fault lay: a borer of wells from East Anglia confirmed he'd managed to dip into a water source that pumped the water that killed the roses that Harry had planted. With those facts confirmed I telephoned Harry Wheatcroft for his comment: he sounded very prickly - *"clever little boy aren't you"* he said, and rang off. Come Press day those many hours of bb2b reporting made just four paragraphs in *Gardener's Chronicle*. It was never confirmed that the well borer had tapped into a derelict NCB mine, but you can bet your bottom dollar something down there didn't taste quite right for the likes of roses!

cycling with Mike Marriott in Wensleydale

Living happily outdoors was the ethos carried beyond the pages at the monthly Practical Camper *magazine and when Mike Marriott and myself founded Backpackers Club it stemmed from our beingThere in the great outdoors where we hiked, biked and toured at our own speed. We used tents and worked on the topic from a base we chose for the occasion, too.   John Hillaby, the first Backpackers Club president was no slouch in getting about and he told us to walk as though dancing, watch out for nature and the countryside but have fun on the journey too. In the picture below my son Antony, on a saunter along The Ridgeway, he remembers it as getting good advice from people in the know.*

snow in Scotland when with Ken Ward. Tents made by the Ultimate brand in Northumbria at a pitch near Wooler and the The Cheviot hills

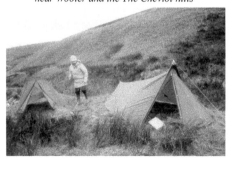

Backpacking is an in-tent time, the ones shown on the left are from an age when Saunders, Karrimor and Ultimate pushed the boundaries in every aspect.

I really have been so lucky to work with good journalists, and for sure *GC-HTJ* editor Colin Parnell was one who was very good at maintaining office and deadline discipline, and above all he respected editorial freedom. None of us ever got cowed by messages from the advertisement department's Staff, Colin's calm manner ensured those people were always out of sight, out of mind, which helped writers and reporters just get on with the job of reporting and working up the stories. It's a good maxim to sustain that style and habit editorially, being independent in your approach will deliver honestly for the reader, and these people who pay for the magazines are the most important cog in the wheel of any publication. Readers are there to be informed about what is going on, they deserve to have journalists diligently reporting the scene rather than playing at being a parrot with pervasive wordslick carrying just as much real fact in it as there is still air near whirring helicopter blades. My sidekicks at *Gardeners Chronicle* office included trade trained horticulturist Barry Hutton; Geoffrey Bateman, who knew off by heart the Latin name of any plant we needed to mention and a guy aka Roger Gentleman from Hampshire who had connections with Irish horse breeders. Roger Newman often took long weekends across the Irish Sea visiting places like the Dublin Horse Show and other Guinness-land jollies, yet from all that socialising with the horse racing scene he never once gave us a decent tip on what to back at the bookies. It's worth noting this was in the early 70s time when he was to-ing and fro-ing regularly to the Republic. At Haymarket Colin Parnell would move his horticultural desk to *Wine & Spirit International* magazine and take on an assistant Tony Lord, an Australian who had been working in London for about four years. The magazine did what it said on the tin, and that word international encouraged Tony Lord to investigate wine making in far-flung places and on a visit to his family in Oz, sitting in a bar in his hometown and doing what journalists do in bars he was approached by an old schoolmate who said to him, *"Tony, do you know I haven't seen you in here for a little while, mate."* It took a few beers together for him to fathom why.

Colin Parnell later launched his own magazine *Decanter* along with Tony Lord - that was in the very year Britain voted to join the EEC, 1975. The first issue of their magazine sold for the modest sum of 40p or 12 issues for £6 a year, and had the cover line *'How to buy Bordeaux and keep your bank manager happy'*. There was also the *'Confessions of a Lady Wine Bar Proprietress'* which clearly indicated the magazine wasn't only about popping corks and things. These guys represent exactly what I mean about "good journalists" and the way they have a nose for the story so can spot angles. In my time working with Colin Parnell he helped me become more independently minded, trusted me to develop lines of enquiry and to gain the support of reliable regional stringers who were our eyes and ears out there.

It often meant working late evenings in the London office but I was then rewarded with the roving editorial assignments that took me out into the countryside and away from London for a day or so. The nice thing was Haymarket paid me better mileage expenses than it cost when using the new Reliant and they also gave a solid subsistence allowance which more than covered my moving around in search of stories. Colin Parnell was the ideal mentor and a boss who helped me step up the ladder to advantage and I guess his way of doing things and trusting a writer to get stuck into the topic and telling the story honestly and true is so meaningful and valid. This way of working he instilled were the best lessons in journalism I ever encountered, he's remembered well, sadly I missed his going.

Working in central London played hell with us having to lug prototype or press sample camping equipment from the office after delivery by brands. Luckily there was the car and when I needed to drive to the office it would be for a 7.00am start, escaping early afternoon or in the evening hours after traffic for the theatres and Shows had eased enough to make travel around the West End a little easier. You don't get that today! Our Regent Street offices had the advantage of being next door to one of the most legendary addresses in London: when we caught a taxi back from an interview the habit was to say *"Café Royal please."* Upon arrival our taxi door would be opened by a liveried footman who then swept us through the foyer of the hotel. Unlike Oscar Wilde who chose the place for the unmatched selection of wines, or Winston Churchill who favoured the steaks, stilton and champagne. We'd just wander to the bar for a nip or whatever then exit to the street by a back door, which was right next to a service lift reaching our office floor in Regent House. At busy times of day and leaving the office for a reporting assignment the plot was to wander into the Café Royal bar, at the front entrance the alert and top hat wearing footman would spot our signal so he could hail the first available taxi!

A bit later on in time this hotel was where the Munich ISPO people would brief us about their upcoming shows, Roger Sherman and Wolfgang Klein, Peter Bond too, they'd help us make an evening of it with their suite having a balcony from where we could overlook the view from above the goings on in Regent Street. Down there were the little dots of people striding along the pavement, so strange to see the tops of their head jerking along and see below that swinging arms, their legs and feet pistoning forward like the drive rail rotation of a steam train's big driving wheels, left, right, left, right again, again. Then along comes a big red roof expanse of a double decker bus, stopping then moving, competing in the traffic flow with the dart of taxis. Looking down you'd notice just how tight a circle the Black Cab can turn: 25ft and do remember a taxi driver isn't obliged to stop for you if you shout *"taxi"* - raising your arm rather like kids do in school, that is the right and proper manner. After our 1997 evening dinner together the other ISPO guests either went to find their own amusements or went home replete but Peter and I wandered into Frith Street and the Ronnie Scott's jazz club. It's reckoned to be one of the top dozen in a listing of venues to have made the most important contributions to jazz music in the United Kingdom. Peter Bond was impressed with the music just as much as I was with hearing about how the Munich mission to develop a big cycling Show was going, their idea was to run it alongside their 1998 Intermot which was heavy into motorcycling and scooters. Today, the ptw show of that very name is established in Cologne, ISPO still are doing their thing in Munich, not overly big on things two-wheels but one for the outdoors equipment and clothing suppliers.

From my Haymarket desk or when visiting various Trade exhibitions I met Paddy Moloney, doyen of the recreational and outdoor publishing scene with his *CSE News* b2b, he was an exhibition organiser who had the full trust of the industry. He asked how the outdoor Trade should view the emerging backpacking market, and would I write a column for him. This was the generous offer which helped forge a real friendship which went far beyond Trade matters and magazines, a dozen years and more later I was still working with Paddy, Ellen and *CSE News*. Paddy knew how to help a contributor feel at ease, giving me full rein to develop b2b stories and features for his periodical, and it became what you'd call a plum job. When I delivered features and stories to his office near Paddington he'd glance through the copy, put it in the tray to open his desk drawer and pull out a cheque book asking *"how much?* Then at a local watering hole we'd discuss Trade matters over a nice claret and some lunch. In London I was working with inspired people who were making the Haymarket Publishing's clock tick, my job amongst them wasn't just with the *Practical* titles as I had grown into responsibilities in our Group for other consumer and b2b periodicals. That brought a big bonus too as over a good many years after I had moved on from London there were still good contacts on the Haymarket publishing floor think-tank who confirmed by their offered advice and help that we'd all been together as a team in this peer publishing environment.

After Haymarket I made not the best decision ever about who you should trust though, I'd spend the early months as a freelance helping a small publisher in Kent better his running in the leisure trade both with b2b and consumer papers: until his green eyes prevailed. I was working with the KSA writing and publishing firm, contributing to their guide book series for travel and for the businesses that provided the means and services to be a tourist. The North East England company had con-nectivity with the camping and caravanning scene in Europe, their strong affiliation with Siegfried Heinze helped keep the stories and the annuals rolling. The Spanish scene had become my editorial speciality and when King Juan Carlos 1 conferred upon me the Medal for Services to Tourism I'd head further into the camping and holiday travel market. It would come as a real surprise to some that I'd begin my first full year as an independent operator by regularly leaving the UK for longish periods of time, but at least I was also wearing out camping gear, riding a bike and simply discovering over weeks the ambience of a region which eludes those who travel in a hurry. I met very little rain on the plain in Spain! Pushing the envelope of b2b and sharing groundwork with a small team at the Whickham hq of KSA later led the Tyne & Wear business to launch a bicycle trade paper, still running after 38 years. The company also acquired *COLT - the Camping & Outdoor Leisure Trade* b2b from Outrams in Glasgow after my short tenure there as freelance editor. KSA turned it into the successful and longest running b2b for the outdoor trade, adding a scooter market b2b magazine. The ethos of involvement is the way KSA have worked with projects and initiatives involving hike, bike, travel and tourism, the goal is always to identify opportunity and to encourage take-up by readers.

Being a journalist is as much a Trade as taking bricks and building the walls of a house, everything must always have secure and firm foundations. The groundwork is key, and in that all I ask as a writer is to be excited by discoveries and developments so that a story can be told. For certain the scene we frequent today is too often shrouded by rather more smoke and mirrors than is decent. Sometime in 1733 Richard Steele wrote of having frank entertainment at the table, little incidents of mirth and diversion he'd relay through *The Spectator.* He also wrote of having insupportable afflictions though, being tormented with the narrations of a set of people who having thrown away their own propriety expected him to do the same. I'll let you read those words again, to reflect that just because someone decides to communicate to you a marketing message, being a parrot will do nothing for your reputation, worse it could become a cranial canker. A last word from Richard Steele, *"existence is a blessing to those beings endowed with perception."*

15 one step then another

Where did the backpacking idea originate? The answer is it all could have had something of a saving grace about it, although to be honest there was never a point in time when . . *zing* . . we knew there had to be a Backpackers Club. Certainly one idea progressed to the next, we then sorted another idea till it all more or less fell into place. Finally *Practical Camper* magazine and Haymarket Publishing said they'd sponsor the project and that confirmed we had the platform to introduce a game-changer to the UK outdoor Trade: the hard work would now begin. This new approach to lightweight camping and travel had first been seeded at the unlikeliest of places, in the editorial office for the b2b serving professional horticulturists. The Group publisher for the weekly Haymarket title came by the *Gardener's Chronicle* office one morning and casually asked what I knew about camping? To my boss Jimmy Hopes I answered *"done some"* although if I'd added *"but not a lot"* then the reply would have been much more truthful. Together, he and I had often talked about being outdoors, of weekends visiting the Coquet Valley in Northumberland and having a love for visiting the Outer Hebrides. Then just as when I had first come to Haymarket's offices in Oxford Street, here was I at the other side of a desk being quizzed by John Houselander. First question was how I would handle being editor of the UK market leading consumer magazine *Practical Camper?* The bones of his offer indicated that instead of hectic schedules as a weekly b2b News Editor I would spend time travelling around the place to check out camping sites and equipment, all the time enjoying myself between the publication dates of a monthly consumer magazine centred on outdoors living and recreation. I took a few seconds to think about it: *"when would you like me start?"*

He then alerted me I was in-line to inherit something of a sticky wicket, the problem being Haymarket needed to replace the talented, but just-left, *Practical Camper* magazine editor John Cade. He'd resigned his post to do things camping and publishing with his own new company. *Ooops.* The sting in the tail with the offer saw him admit there was an over-riding brief: "we expect you to keep the magazine circulation right up at the high end and also ensure that our advertisement manager John "Tony" Anthony has editorial stuff to keep advertisers wanting to pay, and pay right through the year". Say it quick, no problem and no pressure! I

Enlightening authority

AS a generalisation, County Councils in Britain are anti-camping. A few are vociferously hostile, whilst the majority merely pay lip-service to the Government White Paper recommendations for increased leisure facilities which of course includes more camping sites. They frequently obstruct provision of new grounds (particularly in the private sector), often on the flimsiest of excuses.

Heartening indeed then, to add one county name to our pathetically short list of enlightened councils; that of Cheshire. We carp not that they have just woken up some 25 years late. We gratefully stifle our incredulity and thank heavens—and the pressure of outdoor leisure escalation—for this tiny breach in a still very solid wall of bureaucratic antipathy.

Welcome then to the Seventies, Cheshire and your belated but accurate realisation that hotels and boarding houses don't appeal to everyone and that if our outdoor-loving visitors cannot pitch, they simply won't visit.

Enough badinage though, and unreserved congratulations, Cheshire County Council, for at last providing a base-camp for tenters on the perimeter of a precious piece of protected England, the Wirral Country Park. Congratulations which I'm sure will be echoed by all enthusiasts who read this magazine.

Development of the site was planned with financial assistance from the English Tourist Board, yet another body to whom we who camp owe a sincere thanks. The result is the provision of a touring site for tents only, with facilities that compare favourably with many to be found already in Europe.

There is room for 40 tents, toilets

● *Anyone who has backpacked the length of the South-west peninsula paths will know it's a sport and one which deserves the support of the NSC, if only moral*

that include hot showers, a coin-operated launderette and—a nice imaginative touch this—a covered cooking area complete with work-tops and hot water supplies to sinks.

Meantime, if you fancy camping adjacent to the Park, which boasts a Visitor Centre, plus some excellent walking and fishing potential in the Park, here's how to get there.

The site is adjacent to the Thurstaston Visitor Centre and is approached via Thurstaston Village from the A540 Heswall/West Kirby main road. Site is

open all year, yet another highly commendable feature, for short stays of up to three nights. First come first served, no advance bookings. Charges 30p per person, 20p for each child.

From local to national matters and yet another small step by the powers-that-be in the right direction. I refer to the recent news of the £2¼ million boost to the funds of the National Sports Council.

A pittance maybe, but at least it is an acknowledgement by Government of the importance of active outdoor leisure. As I understand it, the subsidy will be divided up to support some 80 grant schemes covering every conceivable kind of outdoor pursuit, from sub-aqua to golf.

Which brings me to our own game, Backpacking. If shooting and golf are to enjoy benefits, then surely so should backpacking, which is every bit as much of a sport as those quoted. Certainly it would be encouraging in the extreme if we were to be found eligible for a modest grant in due course.

After all, backpacking is only a short step away from mountaineering and as such warrants a training syllabus in the interests of efficiency and safety. Meantime there is a crying need for a network of long-distance footpath staging posts.

Places where the self-contained walker can pitch his lightweight tent for the night without fear of incurring the wrath of the Law. This scheme, financially self-supporting, would cost the Sports Council nothing at all, other than moral support for our cause.

There are many farmers for example, only too willing to open their gates to individuals or small parties of light-weight campers, provided they are not breaking the law in so doing. Currently, the legal situation is very hazy and despite the 28-day ruling, many farmers are reluctant to co-operate in case they antagonise their local councils.

What we need more than anything else right now is recognition by an organisation like the Sports Council (after due study of our aims and aspirations of course).

Staging posts then would make possible continuous progress over long-distance footpaths a reality instead of a dream for the self-sufficient walker. The present, almost total, dearth of legal lightweight tenting pitches along or alongside our established footpaths, is a serious omission that must be rectified in the interests of a growing population of backpackers. With the blessing of the Sports Council, it is a discrepancy we could rapidly correct. 17

The content and style of the articles we published in the Practical Camper *magazine came from writers having a more than close involvement with what was happening in the outdoor world and where they worked on assignments. Mike Marriott had a long contact list of people in the know and was always ready to speak up for camping and for outdoor activities. He handled emerging political matters as well as being on the ball with product trends.* This page is one of the series in *Practical Camper* where Mike Marriott alerted readers to the way things were changing for backpacking.

looked through piles of back issues and soon realised *Practical Camper* was written for families, for newcomers to the outdoors and the people who used their tents and stuff in warm weather. I'd been told the Spring and through Summer issues sold up to 40,000 copies, filled out to 90 pages or so with a 60-30 split in favour of the paid for pages: ie, the ones carrying advertisements. Clearly there was some editorial space, yet across the colder end of the year there were never more than 32 pages or so for the writing team to fill with reader-inspiring features! The summer month magazines could well make 90 pages or so, so hunt the editorial! Winter magazines were always a pretty lean sized 36 or 40 pages all up because at this time of the year advertisers were well and truly in hibernation rather than in spending mode. For me to take control and sort the task a nice sweetener was offered, my new boss John Houselander told me there'd be a big hike in salary for taking on heightened responsibility, and I'd be getting my very own Fiat company car: a no-brainer of a job choice!

It didn't take so very long to clear my desk at a weekly b2b and move along the corridor to a monthly consumer magazine. I moved from under the wing of Colin Parnell, the super-thinking editor at *Gardener's Chronicle,* and said hello to a bright lad of an editor's assistant Fred Dawkins. Our offices in Foubert's Place were quite close to the Palladium playhouse at the edge of Soho entertainment offers and for me a whole new show was about to open. I'd now be treading the Haymarket boards, successfully playing in front of all-year camping backdrops with large tents and little ones, trailer tents, motorhomes and then caravans. It'd be a game of tent pitching around Europe, Scandinavia and all of the UK, in time not only as editor at *Practical Camper* but after a while I was brought in to partner Eric Fowler as his Group Editor at *Practical Caravan* magazine. Trailer tents from Raclet, Conway and Combi-Camp I had already made friends with for both towing and camping site use, now I quickly realised just how accommodating is a tin tent as the mobile office. A home for most occasions it's always a place to store kit and when coming off the hill or a bike ride then I could easily rest in my own bed.

The first 'van was a Mini-Glen T-Line model from Thomsons, I paid £740 for it then after a year the Godfrey Davis outlet in Epping bought it from me for £700. The brand was of exceptional pedigree, great at using wood for making things the Scottish operation had previously produced coffins and in their move up the scale with touring caravans they were well ahead of their time in using wind tunnel testing to produce tourers that would tow well. Mine was 9ft long, had a front end kitchen and a small toilet and washroom. A little small? The Thomson was replaced with a Cotswold Windrush 11ft long palace built at Immingham by Jim Pearman's people. They'd been bemused when I specified a single gas lantern in addition to

LIGHTWEIGHT SCENE by Derrick Booth

THE EASY COOKERS

Convenient food for backpacking can be found on most supermarket shelves

54

● *On a cold morning like this there is nothing to beat a hot cup of tea. When it is misty and the dawn air very cold petrol stoves will be found to work better than butane*

No matter how much you tinker with your gear the packweight cannot be reduced below the load of the food to be carried. A rough guide is 1½lbs a day - so for a week away that's 10lbs to shoulder up at the start.

True enough, the more you eat the less you carry. But the initial load is there at the outset. So many newcomers to backpacking despair about food - ordinary household foods - and rush out to buy expensive rations done up in foil packets which are supposed to be made specially for the man with a pack on his back.

In the United States backpack food is big industry with a range of goodies from tuna salads to 'ice cream' - all you do is open the pack and add water, simmer and eat. The ice cream needs no preparation, merely a reaction with the saliva in your mouth to give the impression of a cold, sweet confection.

I've eaten a lot of this American stuff, and I admit that some of it is pretty fine. It can be pretty foul too. I well remember some scrambled egg and ham chunks we had for one very cold breakfast deep in a canyon. It had the consistency of soggy cotton wool and tasted like trenchfoot. I went hungry that day, with a rising nausea at every stride.

These packet foods are coming to Britain to supplement the limited range of trail foods made by British manufacturers, so we can soon expect to pay much more for our rations if we buy without thinking about the problem.

For instance, most of the British and some of the American trail foods consist of rice, or pasta products, with soya additives for protein, some accelerated freeze dried meat of unknown origin, AFD vegetables and seasoning. Their utility is the one pan, one pack, one man presentation. Merely add the right quantity of water, soak well for maximum flavour and minimum cooking, toss into a single pan, cook for a few minutes and eat.

There's none of that Mrs Beeton flair of a dash of this and a dash of that about trail foods. The manufacturers have done it all for us. And when you work out the cost of the ingredients you will find that is what we pay for too!

The main considerations one must make about backpacking foods originate from a different point. Remember that most British backpacking trips last only three days. Nutritionally we are told that we need so much carbohydrate, protein and fat to stay healthy.

But for a three day trip the emphasis on protein intake to repair flogged out tissue is not so important. No sir, what we need is energy. And this can come from carbohydrates and fats - particularly fats. What protein we need can come from nuts instead of meat, and then we can concentrate on calories.

A hard winter trip can demand as much as 5,000 calories a day if the going is hard. Early autumn and late spring might suggest only 3,500 calories a day.

Calories can be found in all cereals - which are naturally dehydrated - sugars, which pack easily, and a combination of the two. However, carbohydrates soon burn out in the first few miles of hiking, so we need another, slower burning source of energy - fat.

It is possible to make up a mixture of wheat germ, ground almond, butter, oats and salt and produce an ideal ration which can be eaten morning, noon and night to sustain us in proper protein, carbohydrate and fat needs. It doesn't taste half bad either. But it deteriorates and gets boring after the first day.

You will notice I have said nothing about meat and eggs, cheese and fish. In fact, I seem to be leading up to a vegetarian diet.

Yes, I am in a way. Not that I am a vegetarian, but keeping perishable foods safe in my pack is not easy. Therefore I have turned to other sources.

Mike Marriott, one of the country's leading backpackers, is a vegetarian and swears by his diet as a healthy way of

I shared a lot of backpacking time on trips with Derrick Booth, he was writing for another camping magazine until I poached him away from Link House. After that we didn't have to hide from each other the gear we were testing. What else for an easier life, usual though in the days when we gained access to pre-production samples so any suggested tweaks could be effected at the factory where they were made! The Lightweight Scene column here in *Practical Camper* is from Derrick Booth, he also was regularly covering other topics for our market leading magazine such as beingThere in America and visiting suppliers out there to put us ahead of others.

the 12 volt electric lighting, the standard for 1970 caravans. I explained that with a gas lantern you could generate a little heat before turning in of a chilly evening, and more importantly it worked one hundred percent as a midge or gnat killer! Without there being mains electric hook up fitted the small leisure battery wouldn't last, so let there be gas! The Cotswold Windrush cost what I thought was a fortune at the time, and at £1,470 it meant I had to double my investment to get this dual purpose home and hostelry for my wandering and travels. Ten years later I swapped it for my first ever Compass, Mike Kinsell at Catterick Caravans did me a trade-in deal where he priced my favourite friendly Windrush at £1,400. Sold to the man who would then supply me with other tourer caravans made in County Durham, and all through Catterick where just about the very best accessory boutique in all of Britain is there to make your outdoor life so much better. The latest 'van they delivered came with an *"exclusively made for"* advertising strapline for them on the back panel which people have seen in many European countries north of Lake Garda. It took a while to realise this wasn't the regular livery! In 2017 we used this Compass Concerto for a trip around Britain, ninety days checking out how others do hike, bike, travel and tourism in their own beingThere lives. The trip last year showed how weather can change the ambience of any site, not that weather should ever be allowed to get in the way of sharing campgrounds when researching the market to see just what people are finding out as they travel around in the outdoor world. You meet all sorts and you learn something new every day.

It was quite like that once I settled into the editor's chair at *Practical Camper,* working on having a lot of fun creating auditorium pleasing Haymarket magazine productions with a close up engagement of the very best supporting cast in outdoor equipment, the accessories, apparel and the people selling and using it. All this was played out on stages set out in the best of UK countryside and around Europe and Scandinavia, getting there without going through an airport departure lounge. This was mountains, moor, sea, sand and sun being all in tune with the orchestra pit, and in other words the job being to inspire people to go try the travel idea and show them how to fit camping and tourism into the games they'd be playing in the countryside. It really all has to be experience first-hand, of course! Checking it out wasn't always a bed of roses - but what the hell, it beats being a desk jockey in a nine till five job which so many of the magazine people around me in London were enduring! The beingThere way of life was panning out to bring hike, bike, travel and tourism activities based mainly on campgrounds, all of it more than a long way from the bustle of our magazine offices at the heart of London's West End. Certainly no bad way to earn your living! Haymarket gave me the space to do it, King Juan Carlos1 of Spain liked what I wrote about his country and I received a letter from

It is March 1974, along with Ken Ward, Dennis Noble and wee Boots we're on Montrose beach to start a backpacking trip across Scotland to Fort William. On the way Ken worked on designing a new boot dry-warmer system. Patent applied for!

A trip with Ken Ward on the banks of the River Blackwater just round the corner from St Cedd's Chapel of St Peter's on the Wall.

On a day of snow Matt McKinley and Cameron McNeish plot the next bit of our walk towards a mound of frozen water under a tap at Corrour Station. We had started out from near the summit of Cairngorm and fought off herds of hungry staggies near Loch Ericht, skirted Ben Alder and wondered how long before we could catch a train from just about the most remote rail station ever.

Media and makers together - Bill O'Connor (centre) with James Boylon and Eddie Craig. The other picture shows Practical Camper's *Tony Anthony (l) with his chum Len Durrent from the Reliance business in Canada.*

Buckingham Palace to tell *"HM The Queen is Graciously Pleased . ."* I've worn the Medal for Services to Tourism with pride, ever since the sun came up twice that morning. It's continued to shine ever since, because even rainy days can't alter things when you are having fun, and you find lots of that on camping sites.

There was plenty of work to be done when having fun of course, there was a big audience in summer time and at school holidays but no year-round audience, especially from Autumn October and through to March. But remember *"that's the job"* John Houselander had told me. He'd asked I'd devise ways to end the pattern of sparse advertisement content in the magazine during the darker months, bringing fiscal rays of sunshine year round to satisfy revenue requirements was a big task. I'd also have to develop some new reader-interest topics to stem the winter-time dip in circulation, too, and unlike come the noughties and since, where sun seeking people travel to campground holiday sites in southern Europe, for us in the early 70s that wasn't so much of that available. I knew hill-walkers and mountaineers were doing their thing with little tents all through the year so I ventured to management that this was a potential readership we could persuade to buy into our family-style camping magazine. I thought that if the content was tweaked for the hillwalking fraternity then we would gain circulation. Nah! was the frosty, first reaction from my bosses and that could well have been the end of backpacking before we even got backpacking, but remembering how cycle-touring with a little tent had brought me happy rewards there is the clue explaining my persistence to argue the toss with bosses. I'd already seen the 1968 book by Colin Fletcher, writing about hiking the length of the Colorado River, his wearing heavyweight Italian made boots and using gear that included a Svea stove which, as for me, was already a real friend.

But how do you portray that sort of life when you don't have access to the Grand Canyon and the typical weather that prevails there? Nearest things could possibly be *on the beach*, which was how Mike Marriott put it. As our *Practical Camper* retained correspondent he toured the country to check on camping sites, often camping wild in farmer's fields as he surveyed the regions for us. He really thought backpacking had potential: *"we can go hike the coastline, put up a tarp and light a fire of driftwood"*. He'd done lots of that already, and as the author of *Desert Taxi*, for sure Mike knew all about sand from the Saharan adventure he'd embarked on with a standard London Black Cab. Reading his book I could see exactly what he was talking about, yes the beach could give promise, but as there aren't too many beaches on a hillwalker's trail in Britain then perhaps we'd need to re-think the plan. *That's a great idea, but could we just try with using a tent not a tarp"* was a quick suggestion. The reasoning was that with tents and camping gear as part of the exercise surely Tony Anthony could attract advertising revenue for the *Practical*

Camper winter time issues. So there we had it, an entirely new way for our readers to go camping, and between us we had the new word to play with - backpacking. What came next was that this new word in the British vocabulary would broaden the understanding of outdoors living. It wasn't so easy and it took a lot of hard work for us two people, but the records show that since Mike Marriott and Peter Lumley founded Backpackers Club in 1972 there has been a lot of action where the Trade discovered it worked for them with the result backpacking has never failed to ring tills. It's the best way to enjoy countryside recreation and the outdoors environment in a fully sustainable manner, the Club they formed is passionate about leaving only footprints and encourages the desire and ambition to follow these footsteps into open countryside. Today the Club is very much functioning as it began, very active in the UK and with overseas members coming to our shores to engage a year round backpacking habit. One little fable grew from the *Practical Camper* way of backpacking which has left our inner circle always amused when other people and media correspondents talk of backpacking as being just a winter activity writing as *"it is too warm to be carrying a rucksack in the summer."* That was, of course exactly how we had first presented it to our readers come autumn each year, leaving them quite unknowing of the real reason, in spring and summer *Practical Camper* would be driving the expectation to have a great holiday season on the beach and in the summertime countryside. We knew that once they retired the holiday scene later as kids went back to school, then out and along the backpacking path we'd take them, introducing people to a happy lifestyle. It was this editorial approach which helped sustain the magazine circulation and kept advertisement revenues coming in through what had previously been the magazine's slow and quiet months. The backpacking habit became a new lifestyle in 1972, it is still drawing the crowds. Forgive me for one thought though: it never fails to irk that as a word *backpacker* has been mis-appropriated, stolen, hijacked: all to suit those travel trade dimwits and numbskulls who violated the word which above all means freedom with intent . . . and in tenting ways. The sloppy thinking of people who seeing luggage carried in a rucksack then thought hey, that's a backpacker, all that has demonstrated a blind ignorance which perpetrated an intrusion into the lifestyle heritage of Backpackers Club. No kidding, I really hate to see such a horrible mis-appropriation of our word. And then along came then *"backpacker hostel"* of all things . . . I thought YHA had got there first, and a long time before? It was 1930 for England and Wales, SYHA came in '31 with Hostelling International catering for people from 1932. When I was checking Google for regional YHA Groups - *hey ho!* on a panel that popped up on the screen I saw Premier Inn listed . . *hhmmm. . .*

In those early days as Backpackers Club started out, no template existed for how we could guide and lead the backpacking movement. Of some stepping stones I do remember Tom Waghorn being quite un-impressed with the idea, there already was a Rucksack Club since 1902 of which he was a member; the offroad cycle touring fraternity had founded The Rough Stuff Fellowship in 1955 and the Association of Cycle Campers which Thomas Hiram Holding had founded in 1901 was in modern days a special interest group of the Camping & Caravanning Club. But as Tom Waghorn remarked at the time *"every magazine needs to have an editorial gimmick, Pete."* Tom was the *Manchester Evening News* guy who helped Walt Unsworth with *Climber & Rambler,* it appealed to Tom that this new word for the outdoors pastime may not be recognised amongst people in the habit of beingThere hillwalking with a home in their rucksack. I won't say his editor friend Walt dismissed the idea though, asking if I'd join as one of his magazine advisors and I'd have my name on the masthead as their backpacking contributor: it stood there in black and white for some years although he never ran any of the stories I devised. Then came another opportunity for *Practical Camper* and Haymarket Publishing to highlight backpacking, it was a telephone call by the publisher at of Teach Yourself Books offering me the chance to revise their *Teach Yourself Camping* title. This book was already selling in the stores but they thought it was now in need of an editorial update, and could I do that; I persuaded them that perhaps I'd be better employed writing the first specific book for tramping around with a tent, and they should call it *Teach Yourself Backpacking.* Published for 1974 and reprinted a year later the book sold around 60,000 copies.

As for the *Practical Camper* job, yes in the *Gardeners Chronicle* office I had told Jimmy Hopes that *"I had done some"* but it wasn't exactly much more than cycle touring with a ridge tent or spending time with an Army-surplus bell-tent in the garden which pre-dated our summer holiday months keeping children happy on a static camping site by the shores of the River Blackwater. We'd done our best to wear out a tent purchased mail order - an old bit of terminology that! from an Army Surplus Store called Headquarters & General Supplies in Surbiton. I could also recall how twenty years earlier I'd cycle-toured around Suffolk, Norfolk and Cambridgeshire with Tony Crickmore, using little tents and keeping ourselves fed and watered without needing a lotta money. Now in the early 70s I reckoned that using a rucksack rather than bike panniers fitted to carry camping gear would bring in a few changes to the go-camping ethic. The tourism bit to share becomes merely a matter of scale and place, just as is the time it takes to get up the road, towards the horizon or into the hills. A tip is that you stroll along a canal if when you are looking for a nice level trail through the countryside without having to puff up hills. Little persuasion was needed to get backing from our bosses of Haymarket and so it

On top of Whernside, Karrimor reveal their new wedge shape single skin tent designed for mountain marathons. That night most of them would get flooded in a water surge across the pitch in Dentdale! Amongst our party the photographer John Cleare stayed snug and dry and I sat it out on a hump of ground just above the rising torrent. Others? . . don't ask!

THE SHAPE OF THINGS TO COME?

Dennis Noble has been using a Karrimor Marathon for the past six months. Here are his impressions

Magazine readers were treated to how-to and what-with articles to help them select gear for camping and holidays. This is one of the "practical" demonstration of how to go about using the new Karrimor tent. Well it was new in the 1970s! Printed here with thanks to *Practical Camper*

Dennis Noble was very keen on his Marathon MkII tent, and probably got more use from his early model than the rest of us put together. Mine in the foreground here is pitched beside the sea-wall at Althorne, wee dog Boots sits guard - or more likely was just waiting for a serving of Digestives, the biscuits I carried so that both could happily have a treat to eat.

was soon Backpackers Club could develop into being recognised as a viable part of the British camping scene. The company invested around £2,000 in that first 1972 year, at today that would be worth £18,450, they followed that the next year with a similar sponsorship before Backpackers Club was left to stand on its own feet as an independent organisation. To this day the Club shuns commercial involvement, being sustained by membership dues and their own fundraising. It is fair to say that in general, today the organisation is pretty tetchy about things which point towards it towards being thought of as a Club of un-clubbables, a descriptive phrase that'd been put around in the early days.

The backpacking idea itself was initially trialled by a group of us from *Practical Camper,* a team with four of us going off to produce something for the magazine to tell a new story that was a bit different. We had the opportunity to enjoy the final days of wild camping being allowed in the New Forest, in Hampshire and already at Paddy Moloney's Camping Trade Exhibition held in London's Alexandra Palace I'd met Robert Saunders, the man behind the tent maker brand. He had taken British materials and using innovation and design expertise built and brought to the market from Chigwell in Essex one of the biggest advances seen in the lightweight camping scene since Victorian times: it was the tent called Saunders Lite Hike. Each of us he kitted out with that under 3lbs tent for our New Forest backpacking wander, that Robert Saunders had broken the mould to come up with the goods meant his tent brand got top billing in the emerging backpacking community. The magazine contributor Mike Marriott, who researched and wrote the *Practical Camper* Site Searcher features about all-around-Britain camping, organised this four day hike and camp trip with the blessing of Den Small and the Forestry Commission people who look after the New Forest with the Verderers. It was dark at night when the four of us arrived at near Lyndhurst to seek out a pitch for our first night as backpackers - we would be wild camping for the next four days. That is something you can no longer do as our 1971 backpacking trip officially signalled the end of an era in the Hampshire forest. Fred Dawkins, assistant editor on the magazine, Mike Marriott and his son-in-law George Raven from the Practical Camper shop in Sandwich, and myself all slept tight, happy and excited at the prospects of being at the dawn of a new age. I do remember thinking that a Karrimat would be more comfortable if there were armfuls of plucked bracken under the groundsheet: it made a real featherbed occasion but I vowed next time I'd use gloves to pluck at the growth as the blood stains were there for all to see come morning! Nowadays I also remember that New Forest trip as a time of experimenting with what we had already got in the locker, no rucksack with a carry supporting hip belt had yet emerged on the UK market and the choice of burning butane in a Grasshopper or brewing up with a Meta stove was how we cooked. The Camping Gaz burner was not considered an option on the basis this system operated by piercing the canister, yes it worked ok except when you wanted to separate the base from the burner to pack it into a rucksack - which you couldn't do of course. We did some cooking on the embers of a wood fire and turned in early as the wee torches we had were barely bright enough to even call in the moths. The fluttering long life styrene candle was a favourite for use in the tent but it needed close watching for safety reasons and you also needed scissors to keep the wick to the right length, The dawn of backpacking was much less a technological break-through, more the case of our make-do and enjoy way of experimenting and learning not what to do! We collected water from little runnels away from where the New Forest ponies would be drinking at wider water, we collected deadwood to turn to cold ash before we moved on next morning, and took care the night before that any sparks from a blazing log didn't scatter on to the taut nylon flysheets of our Saunders tents. We tried as best we could to avoid moving along tarmac that threads the Forest, although roads did lead to pubs or a little shop: this was not wilderness backpacking, we were linking the walk with a tent to also using countryside facilities and also putting something back into the local economy.

Pictures and our report from the New Forest trip started the ball rolling, at New Year the launch package which Haymarket contributed for Backpackers Club included quality printed promotional leaflets to explain what it was all about. Membership cards, letterheads, the very noticeable square Club badge and other trappings all helped the Club's first secretary and organiser Dennis Noble present the Club as a professional body. The badge designed by a Haymarket art-room guy was created by working from the photo of George Raven striding across the Lawns in a New Forest setting, he carries a tent bag under the top flap of a Browne Best rucksack. The badge has been changed a little over time and the *"sponsored by Practical Camper"* strap no longer is there, so those red and white badges you may see around have got a bit of history. The very first ones were square, later they were reproduced in a round shape and those all colour versions came much later. Of the first National Secretary, it had been Dennis Noble's mistake to ring us and ask what we knew about the Dartmoor Ten Tors event - *"come over and let's discuss it"* was the offer. An hour of chat, an outline of where we wanted a Backpackers Club to go and Dennis left the *Practical Camper* Foubert's Place office in London's West End full of enthusiasm, and all we had been serving was afternoon tea! Things were rolling and Dennis got to working on plans and ideas that would appeal to people who'd want to be part of the outdoor trekking world and join us in the Club. It was at COLEX, the annual early year camping exhibition at Olympia in West London where we launched the Club, it was a year when the Labour Party was in Opposi-

*a weekend on The Ridgeway gave Backpackers Club members
the opportunity to hear more about nature by the mile than
could be gleaned from any ordinary channel. Club president
John Hillaby encouraged them to count molehills, listen to
birdsong and turn over cowpats to check for residents. A story
he wrote of the experiences with members, the shimmering
night time lights on the plain below, shooting stars and jet
planes darting in the sky, it appered in* The Times.

in Derbysire it is fashion to shoot grouse
and the like. On this occasion it was felt
that soddin' hikers would be a better target
so they lined 'em up, took aim and blow me
down, look at them now. *c.1970s archives*

tion and Leader Harold Wilson would cut the Show ribbon to let in eager hordes. He was snapped on the magazine stand in a picture with Club co-founder Mike Marriott explaining why he should join the Club! Later on Harold Wilson would receive a Backpackers Club nominated gift of a Karrimor Tatra rucksack, in red of course, something to use when he was ambling around the Isles of Scilly where he spent some of his outdoor leisure time.

Across the road from the Show we'd had something of a Friday night party, especially appropriate seeing you don't launch a backpacking movement without first sitting down to a meal and having a beer or two. We chose the Hunza, the Indian restaurant where six of us around a table talking gear and the treks and trips ideas we'd organise to attract a following so that backpacking would grow along the environmentally friendly pathways which figure so much in the writings of the first Club president. The book *"Journey through Britain"* is a John Hillaby classic book describing striding from Lands End to John O'Groats, the absolute ideal lead in from a President to those people who'd be inspired by his trek and then become members of the Club. So many would happily take on similar pilgrimages and as I write this over 45 years of the Club activity has been rolled out, the people who have been there on a trail will tell you there is nothing quite like living with a little tent companion to a backpacking trip. It brings a feeling of being independent and self-reliant and putting so little impact on the environment. With Backpackers Club about to enter the wide public domain other characters joined our drive to make backpacking the number one outdoor activity - the London based professional journalist Derrick Booth made his Friday evening visit to the Press Office at COLEX before he'd catch a train to home close to Martlesham Heath in Suffolk. He was an instant supporter of the magazine's initiative, having just returned from a trip to America he was able to bring us up to speed about his contacts and friends at the Phoenix based Camp Trails company. They made rucksacks like never had been seen on sale in Britain, and of all the icons that have marked the progress of the backpacking movement in this country, the Ponderosa rucksack on a 515 Astral Cruiser frame takes top marks and rivals the adaptability and capacity of anything that the 21st century yet offers. From 1972 it soon became *THE* bit of kit which identified the Club, Derrick had his, I quickly was carrying one and on the day when John Hillaby led a gaggle of backpackers on a two day dawdle along The Ridgeway he also had his gear inside a CampTrails Ponderosa. The articles he wrote about the trip for magazines and *The Times* drew in membership enquiries so when he crossed to America for his *Journey through Love* book on this trek he packed his gear into that same CampTrails set up. In the kit he carried was a spirit fuelled Trangia storm stove and when we were talking about equipment before he left to cross The Pond he told me that should he run out of liquid fuel then he could always heat his brews by running the stove on moose turds! On the Ridgeway walk one recruit to the fold turned up carrying just the 515 frame with his tent, stuffsacks and other bits strapped to it. This was Robin Adshead beginning his contribution to help build awareness of backpacking through a humorous mix of written gems and his photography, then his books. Of that pioneering rucksack from Camp Trails it was the fine workmanship of the rucksack, stitched together in Mexico for the American company, along with the advanced metallurgy of the crafted frame that was a space-age ahead of what was currently offered from European makers which was quickly noticed. Karrimor's Mike Parsons told me they were astounded by the stitch count and the fabric, the overall build quality and the excellence of the light aircraft quality alloy frame. It was reckoned that operator Åke Nordin at Fjallraven was very impressed with the product so took on distributor rights for Scandinavia. The brand's potential against other designs and products was immense, giving backpackers what became an icon in load carrying and which game-changed the manufacturer sector. They changed the product so it became a sweaty-back, something you could avoid by simply picking up the rucksack as CampTrails provided with their 515 Astral Cruiser frame. The Camp Trails rucksack weighed 1.8kg all up it would be no hardship to stuff an elephant into it! Those originals we all carried were produced in Phoenix, later a manufacturing subsidiary and marketing operation was set up in Waterford, Ireland, where Jim Hayes headed up the operation with Bernie Flanagan. My first visit to see the factory in Ireland was set up in the London offices of the Irish Export Board where my contact was Alan Rushton, it was during our meeting we shared that common interest we had in cycling. Remember The Kelloggs' City Centre Cycle Race series that graced tv? Same Alan, same interest with things cycling, which shows the strands of life are sometimes so closely, happily, woven.

At Haymarket, with two years of the Backpackers Club now lived between us we set about putting into place what bosses had requested, so the Club began to fully manage their own affairs and it was in Essex where we heard Dennis Noble explain he needed to change his lifestyle a bit, so was moving away from Islington where the Club's first secretarial address had been receiving so much Royal Mail traffic. Backpackers had turned the Chelmer Canal towpath into an approach trek to Danbury for a busy two day stop-over and local trekking as members began their discussions of plans for going forward with a Club programme. Derrick Booth and Mike Marriott met up for the first time, Tony Lack of Pindisport was there, Robin Adshead shot rolls of 35mm on his camera, and amongst us dozens of new people showed up ready to pay membership dues. In a week or so the beginning of Eric Gurney's stewardship of Backpackers Club affairs began, the peaks and the troughs

Pitching in Wensleydale in the first caravan I'd own, the Thomson Mini-Glen here at Bainbridge Ings. For an outdoors writer the caravan makes both an office and a home, but don't anticipate the Royal Mail will know at which address to find you this week - after all they do call them tourer caravans!

In recent years Compass have built my touring homes, this one has a sort of beacon affair fitted which helps ensure wi-fi, the music and all the e-mail stuff streamis in where-ever I am. It's great, having this technolology although tricky when passing under some bridges.

of membership activities over time brought changes and the near crunch-time when another contingent would step in to carry the flag. The lead rakes near Tideswell were a regular meeting place, the Scottish Borders along the old drove road that is Clennell Street attracted numbers, coast to coast routes were devised, Scarborough to Morecambe Bay, Montrose to Fort William, the fingers of backpacking have prodded into dales and glens and crossed cols with members in groups or on solo travels of days into weeks.

This was the UK countryside opening up for Backpackers Club and a 70's member was to coin the phrase Footpath Touring to demonstrate to us that Britain held the hand of those who wanted to explore places on foot. Ken Ward knew all about the Kungsleden, Sweden's longest trail, he took trek parties to Everest Base Camp but his fondness for the green byways, the local footpath circuit and LDFPs put people on pathways they'd may never have otherwise discovered. His was the first illustrated guide to the South West Peninsula Path, a diagrammatic word-aided introduction to the lie of the pathway along the edge of the sea on one side and a land full of history and drama and vistas and forgotten tin mines on the other. Ken and Margaret Ward became UK countryside ambassadors, going abroad on official Visit Britain presentations for tv, radio and Press conferences. The messages they carried would introduce Britain's footpath network that gilded the greenery and the heather all around the UK and having that close attachment to outdoor Britain was a bonus for Backpackers Club. The couple produced smart illustrated leaflets and the Club's own house magazine, they put marketing muscle into the Club and in Ken Ward's book *Six Feet to Lands End* the tale describes an adventure played out across the folds of land in the South West where so much backpacking takes place. This story starts out from the Cotswolds, just a short distance from where Robin Adshead opened his Wilderness Ways retail shop in about 1975, sharing retailing experiences just as with his hike and bike trips, all related to readers in words and pictures on the pages of books and in magazines.

Both these dear friends had, separately, been at the front line of wars - Ken being a Red Beret jumping into Germany and Robin as a helicopter pilot fighting against communist factions in the Far East. They have both been great trail mates and we've shared many a brew sitting beside a little tent in the back end of places wherever, happy with listening as dusk turned to night sounds and sleep came. I remember backpacking with Ken Ward, remembering his putting a lighted candle inside yesterdays still wet boots on a Scottish trek, and other times when we'd be ambling along a leafy trail and at the instant snap of *SPG* being mouthed by him, we'd dive off the trail, laughing at the silliness and the happiness and the life we were enjoying. He always reckoned Boots was made for walking, that little dog who trotted from Montrose and all the way to Fort William, yet finally was told there was no room in the inn at the south end of town for him so he was not allowed to rest in a pub bar: the three of us departed without paying for the sipped beer they'd placed on an over polished bar. But we didn't slink out!

Once the initial launch ideas were settling into shape and we recognised that backpacking would definitely catch the imagination of *Practical Camper* readers we plotted to attract wider media coverage, Derrick Booth through Peter Warwick with his Link House *Camping* magazine joined our journey, them devising that first *Travelling Light* column to follow themes from the pages of the Robert Hale hardback *The Backpackers Handbook*, the book was already at page proof stage more or less as the Club was founded. Spending quite a bit of time backpacking together, Derrick and I often travelled out of London on Friday evening through to Monday morning, leaving our city clothes draped in an office wardrobe. Soon both of us were finding it was silly for both of us to ask the other not to look at a particular bit of kit we were using and reviewing for our separate magazines. We found the solution by going into a darkened room, our discussion on prospects for the solution was fittingly taking place at BBC studios whilst we watched a preview of an upcoming John Hillaby's film. Before the final credits rolled I had poached Derrick from Peter Warwick's team, then he joined *Practical Camper* and quickly produced a backpacking column for us, his moving gave an opening at Link House

Among some of the files, letters and the documents which have come my way as an outdoor magazine editor this one is a real smart bit of nonsense, quite nasty with it in places and distinctly anti-tent camping. They reckoned this could bring a "rapid spread of infectious disease" to the countryside!

A place that's been my home for days, weekends, even weeks, is the farm site at Bainbridge Ings in Hawes. Here that bank of trees behind the pitch of caravans arrived as a little bunch of brown sticks Tommy Raw planted along his boundary wall so that Natonal Park people wouldn't call campers an eyesore. I first went there in 1972, using it as base for walking on the Pennine Way before buying chunks of Wensleydale cheese to take back to my family and friends. This dale is one of the best places to stay when touring, slap bang in the middle of some of the country's top destinations for hike and bike holiday breaks.

Visiting Northumberland I'd get just about a last pitch at the Caravan Club site before the basin of countryside here is lapped by a rising Kielder Water. (right) An official "site closed" notice near Keld fails after protestors including Practical Camper object to the National Park planners. Indication of their mindset I met in the '70s at the tourist TIC in Aysgarth Falls, surveying "where could families stay locally" led us to publish a "We don't want campers in the Dales" report of their retort in ourmagazine. Time and again in that period Wensleydale officialdom seemed to treat the dale as a fiefdom. High horse people!

where Robin Adshead took on the *Travelling Light* column in his inimitable style: without any hassle at all we were all keeping it in the family! Time then came when a different life in another job took Derrick Booth on new travels, but it happened I'd spotted a feature in the Scottish YHA magazine written by one of their guys who was Warden at the Aberdeen SYHA. Through them I met Cameron McNeish and he began writing the *Practical Camper* column with backpacking ideas all from the heart and about his homeland, of the Highlands and the places he'd then introduce me to: without his arm around my shoulder I would have struggled to see glens and granite places, or find Scotland is the place at its best for hike and bike times.

That friendship goes wider by far than beingThere trips, as with a warm one when with my long standing chum we shared a Danish Trio made Gore-Tex panelled tent on very up and down Robert Louis Stevenson country trail. Heavy on the French accent it's one that Rob Neillands engineered for us as a modern day version of *Travels with a Donkey* in the Cévennes, one of Robert Louis Stevenson's earliest published works in 1879, considered to be a pioneering classic of outdoor literature. Things were a lot colder when Cameron, Matt McKinley and I stood chipping at a glacier of ice formed below a slow dripping tap at the ruined looking Corrour Station on the Crianlarich to Fort William and Mallaig branch of the West Highland Line in dead of winter. It was probably because we were thirsty but the work of swinging an axe was also warming us. We huddled inside a waiting room that had lost glass from the windows and there was no fire in the grate and you don't get much warmth off a Trangia as it wets out slivers of ice in the billy. It was close to -15c and we'd been living in little tents since leaving the top of Cairngorm where hoar frost had streaked solid and white my wool balaclava. We often were doing things together in snowbound country, as with the time of my marriage to Kate with Cameron and Gina's kilted sons as pageboys and Diana a quite blue of nose bridesmaid for her mother that day. Our wedding was at the Swan's Chapel beside a frozen Loch Insch with temperatures no-one should endure when wrapped airily below the waist in plaid and with much draught around the knees. My cycling chum John Potter did the kilt thing as best man and Tony Oliver turned up on his Anglesey made bicycle with the heaviest set of panniers you could imagine. Inside those bags? He would have been able to warm the atmosphere with his mini brazing kit, joining a length of chain to a solid round chunk of metal, but with the victim not playing ball . . .

This sort of togetherness Backpackers Club people put into building the friendships and awareness and interest in the outdoor movement, our magazine work in the mid-70s had reported the efforts of supporters putting in much, our *Practical Camper* people were helping a whole raft of family and share wide skies

The walking companion that is Boots in these pictures is a short legged dog who did long trips, here he is on the South West Coast Path having walkies with Ken Ward and I. We did other places together, walked coast to coast across Scotland and in the pictures below faced the wind and the hills of Derbyshire. Michael and Steven loved it too!

and a camping pitch where it did all sorts of weather and build the experiences we could talk about, and some we couldn't! I recall my tent pitched amongst big Beech trees on the Tideswell lead rakes, half waking to feel the earth below the tent groundsheet move up, down and sideways as if it was the chest of a giant who'd ran a mile uphill: I laid there hoping there wouldn't be a sneeze which snapped the tree roots, thinking maybe I'd get up and move the tent, or is my sleeping bag about to serve as a coffin, and what if a branch snapped and speared through the tent flysheet! The big question as I laying there at the edges of a fitful slumberland was what will I have for breakfast, or maybe I'll strike the tent, pack and move on? Questions like that would be on the mind of any camping family, listening to a blow crackling tent fabric, twinging at guylines, sleepers wriggling on an airbed and wondering if the other sleeper was dreaming about being a trampoline star. There was daily chatter on the camping sites when we reported for *Practical Camper*, there was such a variety in topics, gear to check and prototypes to sort, ideas to discuss. This was a 70's thing for sure, perhaps closing into the 80's time and by then I was already up the road a bit as I'd moved on, back into b2b and books and magazines and guides, things connected to helping people find answers on everything cycling, everything camping, a lot of travel with caravans and networking at Trade events and public Shows where it all came together.

For a bit of r&r, some time away from road fumes, hot or noisy crowded places I'd hard boil eggs, butter some slices of malt loaf, check through a partly packed rucksack and slip away into the solitude of almost secret little places where the loudest noise was water flowing close to the tent pitch. It may seem noisy there, at first the quiet is pierced more by thoughts than intrusive sounds, then the urban tensions relax and you hear new sounds. Hey, was that a vixen, perhaps an owl at dusk telling their neighbour they were hunting. This is backpacking lifestyle, it happens wherever you put yourself, all you need is to practice the beingThere and as I remember Derrick Booth's writing about it was always tempered by his explanation that every trip happens when you step through the home gate and get on your way. For those who've tried both, backpacking is a bit like living in a touring caravan - even vice versa: it's making things work for you, it puts a roof over your head at the end of a day, lets you make up your mind where tomorrow will be happen for you. On my first lightweight travelling with a bike sometime after 1951 I had tried a home-made bivvy, a waterproof ex-Army sleeping bag around me, a stretch of what I recall as oilcloth and probably a tablecloth bought from a hardware store, little wooden stakes I'd have used with rabbit snares were handy to fasten the cover draped over the bicycle top tube in modern tarp style. Draughty, uncomfortable beneath me and barely habitable, this was an early bikepacking try out and I am so glad Robert Saunders gave us a far better product to use when we really got going with our outdoor ideas. Yes, I come back to those words . . *"it ain't what you've got that matters, it's what you do with it that counts.."*

Danbury in Essex was a place Backpackers Club gathered to plan their way forward and here Mike Marriott on the left is chatting with Derryck Booth, tent is an Ultimate Tunnel single skin.

Mottagit av
för räkning ONE WAY SJÖF - U-SITAS.

Kronor ETTETTHUNDRAKRONOR Kr. 1100:-

som härmed kvitteras. Beloppet inkluderar mervärdeskatt med Kr

FISKFLYG AB, den 5,8 1986

It was a two year plan which already had unhinged more than the once, a trip with Tony Oliver to do our own thing for five weeks or so North of the Arctic Circle. We'd reached a place where we'd intended to turn left and wander towards Narvik, but things that were not there got in our way. The ferry to cross a wide lake was missing! Acid rain had wiped out the fish that swam in the lake where Saami once had a village on the far shore. No fish, so no village, no place to reach by ferry, so no ferry. We again changed plans and to save the day, or a longer ride by too far if we'd gone by road, we hired a Cesna to airlift us from one lake to another in this heaven of a land where it is no hardship to marvel at the scenery. The Fiskflyg trip worked out at just about £1 a mile for a flight we really did come to fancy, and it gave us the sight of the majesty of this land from a quite different aspect than you could get when pedalling or hiking across this part of Lapland. Memorable!

16 not the last chapter

Eventually I came to realising London wasn't where I actually wanted to be, rambles aside Essex mud flanked salt creeks failed to bring solace, living in the leafy suburbs of Chigwell was a different lifestyle to what had got me to here since Lime Street and 1936 and things were also about to change for the magazine titles I worked with at Haymarket Publishing. The company relocation from Regent House offices out to Teddington scheduled for 1978 was a spur to making decisions, I didn't know too much about Surrey other than I'd occasionally go that way to visit Wisley when working on *Gardener's Chronicle* assignments. I knew that shortly The North Downs Way National Trail long-distance path would officially open, which could get you to walking to a full 804ft near the Kent border, not at all like the terrain where I could go lose myself in with a little tent and Boots, us sharing the Pennine Way trail across the Northumberland wilderness to the Cheviot. That hill comes three times or so higher at 2,676ft than the south of London path along the North Downs Way, beck water is more potable up north, essential for a backpacking overnight, so that was just another counter towards suggesting it was time to move.

Looking for inspiration and countryside to write about I would often head north to Derbyshire, park my Windrush at a favourite farm camping site just outside Tideswell then take a short walk from the Lead Rakes to a pub. That'd help restart my engine so when back in the 'van I'd unzip the Olivetti Lettera 32 typewriter from its leather style carry case and set about working on a piece about people, places, product and stuff, which shows how important it is to occasionally quaff in the company of people totally unaware of the world you have just escaped. As to drinking, I'd discovered a red bottle of Calor gas would take ten or twelve days to empty when fuelling the cooker or the gas heater and as this site didn't have ehu, for electricity I'd link an extension lead to the grey plug on the car, but no longer than for two evenings. The small bottle of gas was a good pointer to time as well and nine or ten days with a weekend in the middle was as long as I could viably slide away from the London office during a magazine production month. But then few of my work colleagues could get anywhere like that, telling bosses they needed to be away from the desk for purely research reasons. Publication schedules ruled both my time and that of Eric Fowler, who took *Practical Caravan* readers into a new world by showing how to fit just about any gizmo on the market into his 25 feet of caravan parked on his Epsom driveway. He never toured much with that one, didn't need to as there was always a test model from a UK caravan manufacturer that he and his wife Mimi could use. Eric once confided that even with his heavily engined Jaguar, there was not the punch for towing the 'van happily over the hump of a railway bridge. Eric and I would do some touring trips together but then in Spain he died: certainly that was the impression when I awoke on a morning near Tarragona. It looked to be a corpse laying there by me in the twin bedded camping chalet, no sounds, no movement, just a body flat on its back covered from head to foot by a single white cotton sheet. And how would you react? My sharp exclamation of surprise, fear even, brought a near gibbering Eric to sit bolt upright volubly cursing the disturbed lone circling bluebottle fly that had made all of his night a total misery. There's a lot to be said for packing your own mosquito netting folks! To escape office telephones and piles of Royal Mail post I'd often fly around too, away from London with a rucksack and the company of Derrick Booth showing me attractions of Derbyshire, which took that local guy back to hideaway places he'd tramped as a kid. I explored canal networks and British Waterway paths, but you needed to buy a license to tread there. One good trip was to go by train to Bristol then take a few days walking east alongside the 90 or so miles of the Kennet and Avon canal, flat as a pancake!

As to higher places it was Mike Parsons who guided my first strides in the Lake District, probably to Borrowdale. As we headed straight uphill for an overnight pitch he asked why I was carrying a litre of water, *"for drinking of course!"* was Burnham boy's reply. It turned out there'd be more of that stuff than we needed or wanted, both being almost drowned in an hours-long deluge where the beck beside my pitch thundered with trundling rocks as I'd never experienced, nor could have imagined before. Mike evacuated his borrowed Ultimate Tunnel tent a long time before the grey dawn and we shared the groundsheet tray of my single person, modified Saunders' Like Hike tent. It now had a lower flysheet and a longer vestibule, the forerunner of the Mk1 version of Backpacker 1; a final model would see a deeper groundsheet tray, resulting from how Mike and I had squashed the inner tent walls to the ground so that trickles of water swamped our sleeping bags, and the sodden box of matches failed in the job of lighting our Trangia. No hot coffee, no cooked breakfast, but muddy slip-slide down to the valley floor. Not bad for my first time camping in The Lakes! We met Kerry Noble in the valley, updating an annual survey on walkers, campers and the like. When he asked what sort of trip we'd had I lied about having found a superb pitch for the tents and how much I was enjoying The Lakes.

I'd not needed much persuasion to make Wensleydale and the Bainbridge Ings campsite especially, something of a second home. When I now visit Hawes I can reflect on how a tall row of Poplar Robusta reminds me I've been here many times before. I'd been talking with site owners and had heard how Tommy Raw and his wife Doreen were facing the wrath of the Yorkshire Dales National Park planning fellows' objections: *"the caravans and tents can be seen from the road so new restrictions will have to be applied"* was their unbridled threat. I suggested to them some trees would be the answer and helped by a *Gardeners' Chronicle* contact, on my next trip north I brought Tommy a handful of foot long brown twigs for planting against the east side drystone boundary wall. Poplars can grow six feet in a year, and have, so it now works as an effective screening and wind break! In a working week at other times I'd take an evening drive from the London office to crash out at Ken Ward's place in Northamptonshire, we'd then make the next morrow or two the very best reason for carrying a rucksack and sleeping in a wee tent. Together we did stretches of the South West Peninsula Path or would head out of Hawes and up Great Shunner Fell so we could sup at the Tan Hill Inn. Shame how on our first visit there all the beer was off as indoors was a bit fire-wrecked, doors and windows were bolted shut: no welcoming host then! It wasn't like that the next time though, and if this highest pub in all of Britain could speak then we could be listening all the way into the next millennium about how it has welcomed people inside for over the last three centuries or so. I often go back and it pays to pick the right time because this is a part of the Dales which now gets very popular.

Caravan touring, backpacking and with cycling trips thrown in this all became very important to me during the period following my Dad's passing, and before he properly had made even 61 years old. I had my marriage in tatters, life wasn't making too much sense and for me world had gone wrong. The strong thread I managed to retain in my life was writing and photography with the monthly magazine deadlines bringing some order and discipline. Above all I needed to find quiet places or perhaps head for new places and from a little either side of being half-hearted about it I began packing a large rucksack with the things I reckoned were my immediate essentials to begin a new life. I fancied New Zealand countryside near where the 1953 hero Ed Hillary had grown up, there or on the ranges near where WWII solider Charles Upham VC and Bar had worked as a sheep farmer. He was the only combat soldier to be twice awarded the VC during the Second World War, of both these guys I had read the books and felt able to identify with how they found a good life being out there in hilly or open country. I'd a penchant for hearing Curlews call, see Oyster Catchers in shrill flight and especially when their fledglings began to believe that a bit more sound would increase their speed,

I first went shopping at Condor Cycles in 1952, a little time after the Monty Young business opened. I've a bike he built and just this last week I was with his son Grant *(right)* chatting about cycling and what it means to us at the Bespoke Handbuilt Show being held in Bristol.

Herbert Kropf from the Puch operation *(left)* with John N. Moore who built a strong trade in product from the Austrian company at his Moore Large & Co Ltd operation in Watford. In 1974 ML was established to market Puch, a year later bicycle accessories were added to their range and in 1976 ML became the first bicycle wholesaler in the bicycle trade to go fully national across Britain.

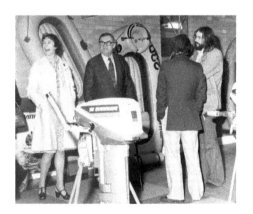

I'm a Burnham boy now based in the North East of England, but then why not seeing the ancient pile of Lumley Castle is at Chester le Street, a few miles from my home. The North East Camping Caravan and Boat Show run by Ziggy Kurek *(centre in the picture above)* was the annual event which brought me opportunity and earnings when Kate Spencer's company took on the press and promotional work for the Show. This was the year when an Everest The Hard Way series of appearances and tableau presentations highlighted Doug Scott *(seen right)* and Dougal Haston's scaling to the summit of the mountain, he was there as Official Guest to open the Newcastle Racecourse event.

10th NORTH EAST CAMPING CARAVAN AND BOAT SHOW

Newcastle Racecourse, Gosforth Park.

so they piped louder and louder as they jinked in flight. Perhaps that sounding off was showing they were enjoying a new found freedom, or simply being joyous. The Skylarks is like that, birds I'd admired since first hearing them on Burnham Marshes and now would hear them over Yorkshire moors and County Durham hay meadows up in Weardale, each and every one of them singing their little hearts out, to then plummet from high like a stone to hit knee high grass in a meadow speckled with the colour of flower heads. I have always thought the Skylark actually thrusts itself aloft and heavenwards merely on the power of song, when they drop to ground from the sky it's then a ground level, sideways move to head for their nest. It's a place I have found only twice over all my many years in the countryside. Bird song and the outdoor habit helps dispel life's pressures, although I do reckon it takes mostly to the third morning of backpacking to become totally oblivious to stuff left back in urban land and the office, before you properly hear the countryside talking back. In those times the mobile phone was only a very heavy device we associated with soldiers in a battle zone so we relied on map and compass to keep us on track and if you really *needed* to contact the home or office then you checked the OS map to find a red Telephone Box and do a reversed charges call. On the hill and being in the countryside for days meant that by now your small change was stashed away somewhere deep in the rucksack and contacting the phone service operator to be put through was saving you more than the time needed to find hidden dosh. Come the day, other thing happened in my life so I'd not head for New Zealand after all, despite how strong the call had seemed.

I'd first crossed Hadrian's Wall in the mid 1960s when I rode my scooter in the Esso Scoot to Scotland trial which was the introduction to Ae, then Ayr and lots of other places where it needed a few more letters to make up the place name. Mind you, with Tony Oliver twenty or so years later I'd find that Å is a village at the foot of the Lofoten, and you don't get less letters in a name than that! For backpacking my first trips to the Highlands were with Cameron McNeish who showed me his Scotland, and so many has been the time when we'd pitch a tent in jewelled places where rock meets water, meets sky and meets every wish you'd ask. Cameron had joined us as regular backpacking correspondent for *Practical Camper* and from the pages he introduced people to the beauty of wilderness living. It was the beingThere in such places which helped refresh enough spirit for me to want more of it, and that cemented the realisation that working from London no longer was attractive.

It came as something of a struggle at first but I'd manage to disentangle myself from the responsibilities for other Haymarket magazines and let other editors get on with their own pages. The ability to absence myself from regular editorial management meetings was the strategy I followed, so as a meeting date loomed

I'd have to excuse myself for another "appointment" telling management I was on a mission which would help "sell advertising space." It was often hastily organised, a ruse which eventually wore so thin that bosses upstairs decided to relegate me to responsibilities for just two magazines instead of six or so in the b2b and consumer grouping. Internal memos at Haymarket circulated in large brown envelopes with holes punched in them so they resembled a colander and you could see there were contents. I found the yellow Memo slip inside the envelope they'd attached by Sellotape to my desk typewriter was pretty to the point: ".. You are relieved of all duties other than *Practical Camper* and *Practical Caravan*. Your salary has not changed." Job done and no regrets, gone was the headache of overseeing those other magazines and now I could get to doing more things along with Eric Fowler, on the caravan magazine. Mutually we agreed to watch out for the office politics which may pop up when either was away on assignment, appropriate seeing Eric wasn't then aware that an outside agent was suggesting to our up-line management that Haymarket should rid themselves of him. In his defence I argued that his engineering expertise and dedicated input to *Practical Caravan* was so far ahead of the stuff in any rival monthly that Link House could offer, then for that reason I intended to keep him working with us. He stayed, but not so very far apart in time both of us would leave Haymarket, Eric first moved to being Information Officer for the Camping Club of GB & Ireland, as it was then known, then later being appointed launch editor for Warners' new *Caravan Life* magazine. Old dogs, they always know the best and real tricks and also when to make a run for it!

It was a lot of fun producing the two *Practical* titles, although I'd always needed to persevere with the uncomfortable downside of having to be whistling away and happily engaged somewhere out there in the countryside, I'd go stay on camping sites, busily try out new goodies coming to market or explore places you reached by simply getting out of town and upcountry or jumping a ferry on a Gold Pass to the continent provided courtesy of Townsend-Thoresen Ferries. That special facility offered free passage for car, caravan, driver and passenger more or less at will, so is it any wonder I'd often be heading through Dover or Felixstowe to check out the weather on the other side of the water and bring back bottled stuff the French assured us was much stronger. Just as when loaned a pre-launch model of a family caravan I towed to sites in the *Île*-de-France to find out how long a French bread stick lasted before getting dry enough to feed to ducks who could soften it up in their swimming pool. On one trip, back from the local market and sorting the internal storage space and shelving it was to discover no room in a kitchen locker for a full length stick of French bread, nor was there one with enough height inside to pack away the box of Kelloggs' cornflakes I had brought from England. Don't ask who built this model of caravan with such elementary failings, not that it's so unusual or different today, seeing some launch models at the 2017 nec Caravan Show. For years my touring mate and I have always wondered why it is caravan designers don't think as do the wives and mothers who know the way to arrange the home. Today you regularly find the caravan micro-wave cooker sits well above eye level, even for a tall person: enough said? You can take it that mentioning this gives a clue to confirm an editorial stance should never be to clone catalogue and brochure words or repeat syrupy marketing speak as being gospel: checking it all out rather that just glancing at the product is what all your readers deserve, and nothing less. There will be the objectors of course, but the writer with practical experience and having gained the knowledge that counts in these things, they will find reasonably minded people always accept the considered opinion does better for the brand and product awareness than will parrot fashion reporting. I found the set up at the Haymarket Publishing magazines gave plenty of room for us to do our editorial jobs with a high degree of personal confidence, management sometimes suggested we cut down on being so frequently away from the office but they'd always agree it produced the right style of editorial accountability to the people who matter most: the reader who pays for the magazine. After that, and yes time to take a note: what good editorial content does or damn well ought to, is attract marketing people to allocate their promotional budgets towards sustaining quality reporting and proper involvement in the subject rather than tummy-tickle the parrots who squawk sales speak to editorial types. I guess that is how, and why, our magazine teams in the Haymarket line-up hit top marks in both the circulation count and the level of repeat advertising attracted to the periodicals. It's well reembered what I learned there.

Teamwork at periodicals doesn't just arrive on the desks but comes through trusting others in the partnership, something recalled when in Manchester some years after leaving Haymarket we were having a KSA dinner during SOLTEX. With us at table with my wife Kate was George Gingolf from the ski accessories trade along with the very best deputy editor I have ever known. It could have been as though working in London had been only yesterday even though for all of us there had been considerable water under the bridge since. That evening Wendy Hilder had her own tales and take on those last couple of years when we had worked together on *Practical Camper* and the *Caravan* title. Here was someone with an all-action approach to a topic, one time packing a shopping trolley to go backpacking *"well, why carry a rucksack when you can wheel it!"* she explained. The Lady could also helm a racing dinghy better than quite well and we recalled the occasion of an important sailing championship, both laughing about how coincidental it was that she'd happened to head there whilst on an assignment for our magazine which we had decided to theme *"a sailing and camping trip."* That was when Wendy Hilder and Cathy Foster brought home the 1975 European Women's Sailing Championship trophy. Before setting off from the office I had warned her that an expenses claim for the trip would only be signed off if they won! True to form how super that the Winner's Cup sat proudly on her *Practical Camper* desk so Haymarket colleagues could call by to congratulate her for that European Championship win. This was a happy office partnership enjoyed with Wendy and went far beyond what I had appreciated at the time, at dinner in Manchester Wendy chuckled, which I always remember was her way in conversations, telling Kate *"he was a true maverick and the bosses didn't quite know how to fathom him, it was quite good fun watching them try though and I guess he hasn't changed so much by the look of it."* What I hadn't known at the time was how well she had covered for both Eric and me when we missed getting back to the office for a management meeting, a mark of the loyal spirit which prevailed with Haymarket people. A great deal of our being that way helped us to thrive because at boss level it was appreciated just how well people performed when they were given responsibility for their own patch. My Haymarket days were a learning curve on how to develop and fulfil your way of working, and that made it very easy to build magazines which gave our readers insight material gained only because of our beingThere and never have the worry of oh! God it's Monday again, nor passing the days of a week and thinking only of the escape on Friday.

It was exciting, it was a privilege which rewarded me well, working amongst people who made the running at a publishing company Michael Heseltine had founded the business in 1957, and it would become the UK's largest independently owned publishing company. When he relinquished his role as executive chairman in January 2010 he'd spent more than fifty years at the helm of the business. Along the corridors there were some very talented people who'd help and guide you through problems, even of your own making, and if there was an idea to float then come on, let's hear about it! In the role I had across the magazines I do not mind people knowing that after supplements and special editions were published, such as *What Tent*, *What Greenhouse*, and then an offer declined to take on a *What Motorcycle* publication it was my words suggesting that the title *What Car* simply was a no-go. Well it was 1977 time, in my defence I'd been told by Haymarket bosses that my idea to publish a cycling periodical wasn't going to work, but anyway there were consumer titles in the leisure group to keep me busy enough.

I've based a lot of my working practices on how things were done at these Haymarket titles, it's never been too hard to make things work and certainly it's never been boring. At KSA we have always encouraged people to be hands on and get stuck in, that helps people realise their potential as the writers we've worked with over the year can tell. I'd liken that ethic to finding a backpacking pitch on a high hill so when the dawn breaks it brings spectacular vistas, perhaps glorified by temperature inversion which hides the working world down in the greyness: so who wouldn't want to work outdoors, closer to a subject, and get away from the office! Bringing back the pictures and writing down what you have seen and felt, that's done for readers in the same way as developing a sixth sense for finding somewhere to park a caravan, or which fork in the road to follow. Choosing those places where you decide to stop over, then it has to be the best choice or why did you head to where you are in the first place, I lived in Chigwell for a time, it was both town and countryside and very handy for the London Central Line tube train from the village or Redbridge or Newbury Park. Returning after office work one evening in the late 70s I came across Delia Smith, well not the actual lady but herself in the guise of an *Evening Standard* recipe, and the easiest fall back snack you could prepare on a camping stove. Heat a tin of Heinz 57 baked beans, add diced luncheon meat or Spam, then in another Billy heat Green Giant sweet corn to pile that on the mass: in true camper style it's eaten without a plate! I like it, a lot of family and friends don't, and perhaps Delia the Chef quickly forgot it. Travelling and testing gear for the *Practical Camper* and *Practical Caravan* desks had kept me fully amused, an expanded freelance output keeping me busy although a great deal of that commissioned material was derived from reports I'd be writing anyway. Amongst that magazine work I covered the UK outdoor scene for *Sport & Spel*, working with the two Lady owners for the Dutch magazine, one in which I could never really understand a word of my stuff printed in Dutch text! They paid good money, it came in Sterling, it gave brilliant connect to the companies working the outdoor and bicycle trade as manufacturers, mainly, the distributors and plenty of retailers I got to know.

When I started out to write this book the opening lines told that WWII would be kicking off before I got to toddling far from my Burnham home, as 1978 approached I was living on the far side of Essex from there and close to landmarks from the Battle of Britain air struggle I had known about when younger. Up the road was Debden, down the road was Hornchurch and on the edge of the chalk weald country that is north Essex, a bomber base was built by an US Engineering Air Battalion in 1942: it's now known as Stansted. These are just some of the airfields constructed in Britain under the orders of the Air Ministry Directorate General of Works Construction, all being a contribution to the war effort and reckoned to be the largest constructional programme in all of British history: eat your heart out Emperor Hadrian, your Wall needed to be a lot, lot longer to even reach the bottom rung in the airfield build listings. Sorry. According to one 1950s writer the creation of so many temporary air strips transformed Britain into a giant aircraft carrier anchored off the north-west coast of Europe. Adolph wasn't so happy about that, although in later generations many factory farming companies saw the now unused expanse of these vacant airfields the ideal place to site poultry units. In East Anglia especially the companies have often taken up complete runway circuits which now generate tons and tons of farm fertilisers *aka* chicken dung: and all from millions of birds, none of which can fly of course. In building the wartime airfields it's said that a labour force of 60,000 men was employed exclusively on the civil engineering task for the RAF. Some would also have a FIDO system installed for foggy weather and night time landings - and these used enormous amounts of petrol, with something like 90,000 gallons burned every hour. The Americans had around 3,500 aircraft available at any one time in the UK and with the RAF these two forces flying over Europe took off from some 125 airfields. If I did a quick count today then that is about the same number of top camping sites I'll regularly land at for one of my own sorties.

I'd leave Haymarket and the whole big group of friends and colleagues there who there were doing things plus a bit to put words and pictures on pages, it ended an era of working in London for a big operation and gaining big rewards as well as learning more about how to develop my trade. Working in that publisher environment brought the realisation that a future was there to take ideas forward with others, each of us could be headed up by our own steam but we'd all get to do things better because of linking into partnerships. The organiser of the North East Camping, Caravan & Boat Show, Ziggy Kurek was quite persuasive with ideas about going independent, I had also seen John Prior do things with the Raclet brand despite others unsuccessfully trying to thwart him and brand boss Guy Raclet. The company's operation near Paris I had visited with John Prior, on the factory roof I was shown new nylon fabric tents in a *"them & us"* check which had failed the test of time under sunlight and atmospheric pollution: some models becoming mere horizontal flaps of fabric, as though a knife had been slashed against them and it confirmed what was being said about UV degradation and brands who used unsuitable fabrics. Yes, the effects of air pollution and solar intensity was already being noticed, although few wanted to talk about it nor let in the public on problems they'd probably be having later with their gear.

In the fabrics world the American company of Bill Gore had received its initial order for Gore-Tex material in 1976, Newcastle operation Berghaus then used it for their rainwear and two of us wore these on a trip in the Cairngorms but discovered the garments didn't live up to expectations. Tony Sharp at the clothing brand probably recognised what wasn't quite right with things, and that precipitated dialogue which engaged Bill Gore himself and others in a Swan Hotel meeting room during a Harrogate COLA. Explanations and problem solving were going nowhere until his American colleague Joe Tanner, who'd sat quietly listening for an hour or so, put forward his reasoning for our getting very wet and nearly dead in Scotland. Joe Tanner contended that there was a hundred years of knowledge in the observed law stating that the rate at which one substance diffuses through another is directly proportional to the concentration gradient of the diffusing substance. *Yes.* This was probably one of the first instances when I fully realised there would always be people wanting you to accept their answers. Robert Saunders showed us that you didn't need to rely on science like that or a vast factory, nor have a pile of pr people and a huge budget to produce stuff that people would find kept them dry and safe in bad weather conditions. He designed the top brand in tents then led from the front as others tried and hoped they could catch up or match his functional designs.

Banton's Point Five and Mountain Equipment sparred in the sleeping bag market, as did Polywarm in Scotland, alongside them the Vango brand was launched on Clydeside. Their Essex arm was the Andrew Mitchell operation in Harold Wood where Jim Murray was a main contact point, I was soon pitching their Vango tents which had a lot of Hamish Hamilton design expertise put into them. For tents and a lot more I learned things from the American Bill Wilkins who founded and built the Ultimate business to being top league in clothing and tents. Bill urged me to strive, helped me thrive and 40 years on he's still both the person and the communicator with a real appreciation of how things can tick and not stick. John Jackson, the boss at Blacks of Greenock put their marketing man Phil Rose to encouraging the Trade to support Backpackers Club initiatives and at their Ruxley Corner office we sat around a table with Keith Rugg sorting out plans that'd see a big contingent of their shop managers coming with us for a trek along a tough bit of the Pennine Way. Some routes work out right, others you just by-pass and ignore if it sours, I'd wound my way from the *Gardeners' Chronicle* post through to camping and caravanning desks, working in a Haymarket Publishing operation which gave me time to think and react and communicate what was believed in, much of it the exchanged views and counsel from those who wanted things to be right, and would work to make product do what it said on the tin.

Time flies, it's now forty years since I decided to get out of London and that was an easy task seeing I based my activities around a Cotswold Windrush and I could always tow it to where I'd need for a spell of beingThere. From amongst the people who talked the sort of messages I understood made sense an invitation came to work with the business founded by a gentleman and his daughter, I was now a freelance and if that equates to freedom then you've got it! The KSA business

For crossing glaciers, rocky ground and a lot of rivers which were a bit cool despite running fast, Tony Oliver built special bikes which were very light and with extremely low gearing. We overloaded them because crossing the Padjelanta Wilderness in Lapland isn't an ordinary bike tour with shops and cafes along the way. Reindeer crossed our path, eagles soared and the mozzies were in droves. We had to push the bikes quite often, it rained but the route was quite distinctly marked with a big red T blazed onto rocks. Someone renews the markers and we were told these were people you'd easily recognise as wearing one large rubber glove and in their other hand a large can of the red stuff. They don't normally travel by bike!

Uphill is one thing to tackle. Uphill when you are unfit is harder. Add two weeks rations, clothing and gear for a trip like ours and the going gets quite difficult!

James Robinson had set up with his daughter Kathleen was to market and distribute books, annuals, maps and guides, something allied to Kate Spencer's own writing career in the sphere of family travel and camping. It was her understanding of camping weekends with children and holidays that helped the KSA business expand with partnerships alongside Tourist Board affiliates in Britain and abroad. Working with Clubs and Associations the output built to innovative guidebook publishing, a series of annuals and then consumer and b2b periodicals. I was invited to join KSA as a Partner after the passing of James Robinson and if you reckon there could be a book about KSA, then probably it's being written right now. Without giving away too much of the plot you'll find that the central character is a person instrumental in founding Outdoor Writers Guild. That idea came from Spur Books publisher Rob Neillands when the three of us were chatting on his booth at COLA, the idea was then developed with discussions through to the next Harrogate where Kate Spencer would arrange a session with seven like-mindeds attending who elected Derryck Draper to be their first chairman and together they bonded the writing community.

Kate would serve the Guild as secretary, officer and a committee member for over seventeen years, with a philosophy always to share opportunities across the growing membership and work to encourage better understanding between both the trade suppliers and brands with the journalists and communicators who were, mainly, attending trade functions such as Harrogate COLA, the ski trade show in Manchester and the fairs and events in Cologne, Milan and Munich. Now a Life Member of the Guild, Kate Spencer had a day job that that fully spilled over into her being quite a hike, bike, travel and tourism person, engaged with the caravan scene on campsite pitches across Britain, Europe and Scandinavia. These have often been her base for following up on her KSA trade connections at Shows in Britain and across Europe for the thick edge of forty years, she treats these occasions like a family affair, along with the backing of The Reliables at *tradeandindustry* b2b operating in a style which hasn't gone un-noticed across the business community. Of her beingThere she will tell you that she does love France but mostly ends up on caravan trips to the other side of the Rhine, so Altenahr is a favourite place on the journey southwards. In Britain the first choice for a weekend would be to Town Yetholm and the Kirkfield site where she has pitched for over 35 years, then after that looking to be . . *"amongst people who are enjoying having their own time to do their thing and be happy with it."* That is simply the good life really, and the mix of bike, hike, travel and tourism is how things should be for you, trick is to not just read about it!

Always travel safe and enjoy your beingThere. That's the call.

This is quite rare footage from the annals of the backpacking movement in the UK from late 1971, a Practical Camper *team embarked on what was the last allowed wild camping trip in the New Forest. In a short while the shutdown would be implemented by Forestry Commmission who managed these former hunting grounds where King Rufus got one in the eye for beingThere in 1100 AD. There is thought that the younger son of William the Conqueror may well have been assassinated, but one thing is certain, for Royalty it was an 'arrowing time. The four page, two-colour leaflet was part of the Haymarket Publishing help to promote the new Club at the 1972 COLEX Show.*

Join a new club

Be an independent camper, try your hand at

BACKPACKING

For long an established pursuit in North America and Canada, backpacking is now beginning to boom in Britain. And with good reason, for here is an exciting way of exploring the wilder areas of our country, offering a real escape from cars, crowds and concrete. Backpacking is a combination of hiking and lightweight camping with a measure of orienteering and self-reliance thrown in to add the spice of adventure. It is a sport that can be happily pursued by almost every age group and both sexes. In essence, backpacking is the art of being totally self-contained for periods ranging from short week-ends to full annual holidays. For ardent enthusiasts there is no close-season and intrepid purists would submit that the least attractive backpacking season is high summer. For those who find it absolutely essential to be 'fully stretched' physically from time to time, to offset the soft life we live normally, it is the

● Left: About to abandon their vehicles for four days of total independence are (left to right) Lumley, Dawkins, Raven and Marriott. Right: With winter backpacking you have to contend with 15 hours of darkness, a cheery campfire is essential.

I first met Ken Ledward on the Wirral with his wife Elizabeth and son Phillip. Just back from Loketok as the fastest person up and down Kilimanjaro on foot - but a bit out of breath? In Niarobi he married a hockey boot sole to the upper part of a walking boot so it was hey presto! he'd designed an innovative piece of KLETS footwear bringing secure walking when on the varied terrain you can meet when beingThere. I've always valued the stuff that Ken taught me, a real masterclass of safe and sure-footed outdoor living.

bike . hike . travel . tourism

www.beingthereguru.com   www.tradeandindustry.net